APPLIED FORTRAN IV PROGRAMMING

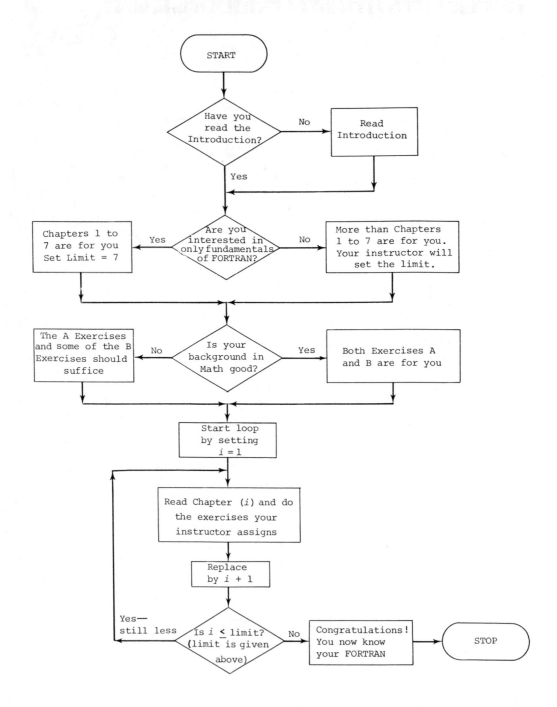

APPLIED FORTRAN IV PROGRAMMING

John R. Sturgul
Michael J. Merchant

The University of Arizona

Wadsworth Publishing Company, Inc.
Belmont, California

Cover design by Russell K. Leong

ISBN 0-534-00128-9

L.C. Cat. Card No. 77-183574

Printed in the United Stated of America

  2 3 4 5 6 7 8 9 10---76 75 74 73

To keep the price of this book as low as possible, we have used an economical means of typesetting. We welcome your comments.

PREFACE

The use of electronic computers has become so common that a basic knowledge of programming has become virtually essential in most branches of science and engineering. Programming courses are required early in the engineering and science curricula of most universities today, and the subject is being taught in many high schools to third and fourth year students.

A common and widely applicable language used for programming is FORTRAN. This is the language with which many students normally become first acquainted, and for many students (those in the sciences in particular) it is the only programming language which they will ever use to any extent.

The object of this book is to present a self-contained, thorough treatment of FORTRAN which presupposes no prior knowledge of computers on the part of the student and which will show him not only how to write programs in FORTRAN, but how to set up and solve problems using FORTRAN programming.

The book would probably find its optimum application as a text for a one-semester first course in FORTRAN programming. However, it is not restricted to such a course. For example, the first seven chapters, which make up Part One, Introduction to FORTRAN, would be quite suitable in themselves for use in a short course of the type that is often presented by computing facilities to acquaint users with FORTRAN. Also, the entire book contains sufficient material to be used for a two-semester course, especially at the high school or junior college level. Chapters 8 through 13 constitute Part Two, Additional FORTRAN. The material contained in these chapters can be used for such a course.

The authors firmly believe in the value of demonstrating each aspect of the material covered by applying it to typical examples, and this method has been followed throughout the book. Most of these examples presuppose nothing more than a basic knowledge of high school algebra, and great care has been taken, particularly in the first six chapters, to present examples which are simple and relevant, yet interesting and typical of the sort of problems which one encounters in programming. However, for students interested in slightly more sophisticated applications of FORTRAN programming, there are examples in later chapters of how FORTRAN can be used to solve problems involving calculus, advanced algebra, and matrix algebra. Even these, however, do not really require of the student any previous knowledge of the subject.

There are several shortcomings in existing books on FORTRAN which this book attempts to overcome. Many books present the subject without motivating it, without emphasizing the basic logical nature of computer programming, and without clearly showing how to solve problems on the computer using FORTRAN. In this book, the student is immediately introduced to the idea of the flowchart as a method of graphically describing a program. In Chapter 1, he learns what a computer can and cannot do, and he learns how to write a flowchart for a program. The examples illustrate basic techniques of programming such as decision statements and iterative procedures, and the emphasis is on how to solve simple problems by making a flowchart to represent a method of solution which could be performed by a computer.

The authors feel that the use of flowcharts for setting up solutions to problems is a valuable instructive aid, and this method has been used throughout the text.

Another problem with many existing texts is the sequence in which the material is presented. For example, double-precision and complex variables are of rather little importance to a beginning student, and to include a discussion of these topics in an early chapter (for example, along with fixed and floating-point variables) would either confuse the student or necessitate an unduly cursory treatment. This has been handled by treating this topic separately in a later chapter.

Similarly, there are some statements in FORTRAN (such as the PAUSE and assigned GO TO) which are primarily of use only to an advanced student or professional programmer, and these topics have been deferred to Chapter 13 rather than included in the early chapters.

The philosophy throughout has been to get the student writing flowcharts and programs as soon as possible so that he will understand what FORTRAN programming is about before getting into details which may obscure an overview of the subject. For this reason, input and output statements are introduced in Chapter 4—after the student is already writing programs of his own. This chapter is kept as simple as possible, since at this point the main problem facing the student is in writing and successfully running a complete program. Later, in Chapter 7, more detailed features of Input-Output operations are discussed. This arrangement allows the student to run his programs at an early stage without having to first master the complexities of the different types of FORMAT statements.

The exercises at the end of the chapters have been chosen not only to provide the student with a review of the subject matter just covered, but to give samples of the types of problems he should now be able to solve. The first chapters in the book contain more exercises than those near the end of the book. As the student learns FORTRAN, he needs less review-type problems but more actual problems requiring complete programs to solve. For the first eight chapters, the exercises are in two parts, A and B. The A exercises are rather straightforward and require no special training or background. The B exercises differ from these in that they may require either more background or originality to solve.

Another feature of this book is a detailed treatment of magnetic tape and disk operations. This subject is of great importance to anyone who works with a medium- or large-scale computer today, and basic techniques such as sorting a tape are discussed here.

Logical variables and conditional statements are treated in Chapter 9 and alphanumeric data are treated in Chapter 10. A knowledge of this material is essential for anyone who is interested in acquiring a real proficiency in programming. The material in Chapters 11, 12, and 13 is more advanced, but was considered worthy of more consideration that it is generally given in introductory texts.

There is another reason for this particular organization of the material: many small computers (such as the IBM 1130) do not allow the use of logical or complex variables or magnetic tape operations in their versions of FORTRAN. For use with such a computer, Chapters 1 through 8 plus 10 would be a complete treatment of the subject. Chapters 9, 11, 12, and 14 complete the student's introduction to FORTRAN. Beyond this, it is expected that a student will be able to read the reference manuals supplied for each particular computer system for descriptions of other permissible statements.

Finally, a few words about the FORTRAN used in this book. We have tried to present a general introduction to the language in Part One, being general enough so that it can be used on nearly any computer that handles FORTRAN, but not oriented toward any one specific machine. Part Two is strictly FORTRAN IV. Several main differences are covered in the Preface to Part Two; others remain as separate chapters. In general, we have tried to present the FORTRAN in Part Two based on what is given as standard FORTRAN IV by the American National Standards Institute (ANSI). This also includes flowcharts, symbols, and computer terminology. Several deviations have been made and have been either noted or indicated by a footnote. In one particular case, we choose to use the terminology "statement number" instead of the ANSI's "statement label," since the former seems to be much more widely accepted.

We are deeply grateful for the assistance furnished by the University of Arizona Computer Center in providing us with their computer facilities. Professor Loren P. Meissner, University of California at Berkeley, and Professor John D. Stevens, Iowa State University, reviewed portions of the manuscript and did an excellent job of showing us what a complex subject a computer language really is. Responsibility with the final choice of subject matter lies solely with us.

The manuscript was typed and retyped numerous times by Alison Odell. Finally, special thanks for their patience to our wives, Nancy and Alison.

J. R. S.
M. J. M.

CONTENTS

FORTRAN STATEMENTS

FIELD SPECIFICATIONS

OPERATIONS

PART ONE

Introduction to FORTRAN

Chapter 1

PROGRAMS AND FLOWCHARTS

The design of electronic computers has advanced to a level
of complexity and sophistication where it is a rare individual
indeed who is familiar with all the details of the construction
of any particular computer. Furthermore, advances in this field
have been so rapid that it is quite probable that the computers
of today will seem slow and almost obsolete in ten or fifteen
years. Fortunately for us, however, it is not necessary to know
about the design of computers in order to program them, any more
than it is necessary to know about the design of a television
set in order to operate one. What concerns us is not how a computer operates as an electronic device, but rather how it behaves
as a logical device.

A computer is a mechanism capable of manipulating numbers
and symbols according to a well-defined program. For example,

        Input a number
        Input another number
        Add them
        Output the result

is the sort of program a computer can perform. Obviously, a
computer would not be particularly useful if this were the only
kind of thing it could do; a computer is useful because it can be
programmed to do many different jobs.

Roughly speaking, a program is a process described in terms
of instructions which a computer can understand. Computers, of
course, do not really *understand* anything; they can only perform
certain basic operations (such as addition). So a program is
really a sequence of instructions, each instruction describing
one basic operation. Since each instruction tells the computer
to do something, the order in which the instructions are performed is important, and must also be specified by the program.

Specifically, a program is a sequence of instructions and a
set of rules for performing them such that

(1) only one instruction at a time is performed;
(2) after performing any given instruction, it must be
    clear which instruction is to be performed next.

3

INSTRUCTIONS

A program consists of instructions. Not all instructions, however, are meaningful to a computer. The familiar instruction "Wipe your feet," for example, is simply not the sort of thing a computer can do. Actually, there are only four basic types of operations that a computer can perform:

(1) input-output,
(2) storing,
(3) computation,
(4) simple decisions.

Input-Output. The input and output of data is obviously necessary. To add 3 and 5 on an adding machine, we must first "input" the 3 by pushing one of the buttons on the keyboard. This keyboard entry corresponds to an input operation. The answer must subsequently be displayed in some legible form.

On a computer we shall be able to handle large amounts of data; to input and output this data, more efficient means than pushing buttons have been developed. But whether punched cards, high-speed printers, magnetic tapes, or other devices are used, the purpose is the same—to read in or write out data.

Storing. Every item of data that is read into the computer has to be stored somewhere, and we have to have some way of getting at it again. This is the purpose of the memory of the computer. The memory is a sort of electronic filing cabinet in which thousands of numbers can be stored and referenced. This enables us to work with many numbers in a job and to keep intermediate results internally.

The computer refers to each location in its memory by an address. Thus, the memory may be thought of as many mailboxes; the address specifies a particular mailbox to the computer, and the contents of the mailbox is the number itself.

In FORTRAN programming, we do not actually use the internal address itself; for convenience, we use a name that has some meaning in the problem at hand. The machine will associate each name we use with the address of some empty mailbox; each time we want to refer to the contents of that mailbox we use the same name. For example, to read in a number and store it at a location which we shall refer to by the name *A*, we could have an instruction like: INPUT *A*. Then the instruction OUTPUT *A*, would refer to that same location, whatever it happens to be.

Computation. Arithmetical computation is performed electronically in a computer, but it is programmed in a very

4

straightforward way. Once a computation is performed, the result must be stored somewhere. For example, we cannot just say, "Add A and B." We must say, "Add A and B and store the result at C." We write this: C = A + B. This does not mean the same thing in a program as it does in algebra. In algebra it is an equation; in a program it is an instruction specifying that the computation on the right of the equals sign be performed and the result stored in the location whose name is C. Consider the instruction X = X + 1. In algebra it is false; as an instruction, however, it means to take the number at address X, add one to it, and put the result back at address X.

Simple Decisions. A computer can make decisions only in a very elementary way. Given two numbers, it can compare them to determine whether the first is less than, equal to, or greater than the second. Then, it can transfer control to another statement, which simply means that the next instruction to be executed is determined by the outcome of the comparison. For example, we might have the following procedure to print the larger of two numbers, A and B:

        If A < B, output B.
        If A ≥ B, output A.

The ability of the computer to perform this type of operation, though elementary, is one of the most important tools of programming.

These four types of operations—input-output, storing, computation, and simple decisions—form the basis of programming. Basically, these are the only things a computer can do. The job of the programmer, then, is to formulate his problem in terms of these instructions.

LANGUAGES

In order to tell a computer what to do, we must write our instructions in a language that the machine understands. Each computer has its own language, called machine language. This language is difficult to use because it consists solely of numeric codes. Furthermore, a program written in machine language for one computer would not run on a different model computer. To make it easier for the average person to use computers, several standardized languages have been developed. FORTRAN is such a language. When a program written in one of the standardized languages is input to the computer, a translator program (called a *compiler*) converts the instructions in the standardized language to instructions in the machine's own particular language. The computer then executes the program, using the machine-language instructions.

FORTRAN (from FORmula TRANslation) is widely used because it is logical and is similar to familiar algebraic symbols. It is particularly useful in coding problems of engineering and mathematics, although it is also often used for business applications. But before we examine FORTRAN itself, we should learn the basic method used to represent a program by a flowchart.

FLOWCHARTS

A flowchart is simply a way to diagram a program. The idea is to represent what is going on in a form that is easy to read and to work with. It is often most helpful to flowchart a problem before trying to write a FORTRAN program to solve it. This procedure is almost indispensable for programs that are lengthy or complex.

Various shapes are used to represent different types of operations. For example, an input operation is represented by a parallelogram. To read in values for *A* and *B*, we would use the following diagram:

The same-shaped box is also used for output operations. This is not as confusing as it may seem, since a programmer always writes either Input or Output at the top of the box to indicate which is meant. Thus, our output operations will be represented by the following box:

The next most important box is where we do our actual work. This is represented by a rectangle, and the instructions for what is to be done are written inside it.

6

In order to show in what order the operations are performed, the boxes are connected with arrows indicating the direction of flow. For example, to read in two numbers, add them, and write out the result, we could use the following flowchart:

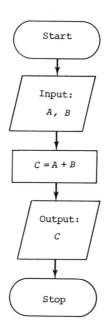

The Start and Stop terminals are an essential part of every flowchart. The Start terminal indicates the first instruction to be performed, and the Stop terminal indicates that no more instructions should be processed after reaching it.

A decision statement is represented by a diamond-shaped box. For the present, we shall write every decision in the form of a question; later we shall introduce notations to simplify this procedure.

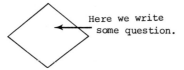

We shall now construct a few problems (two of which would not normally be solved by a computer) that illustrate the applications of flowcharts.

Problem 1

Suppose that you are the president of company *X*. Two of your employees, *A* and *B*, come into your office. You look at them and simply decide to give the better-appearing one a pay raise. Then they leave.

Solution. We must, of course, use a Start box. This might correspond to your arrival at the office in the morning. The next part of the flowchart is the Input box, representing when the two employees entered your office. The Decision box comes next. This is where you make the decision: "Is employee *B* better appearing than employee *A*?" You then do the actual "arithmetic"—this is when you give *A* or *B* the raise. The next step is the output, when the employees leave your office. Your flowchart would be as follows:

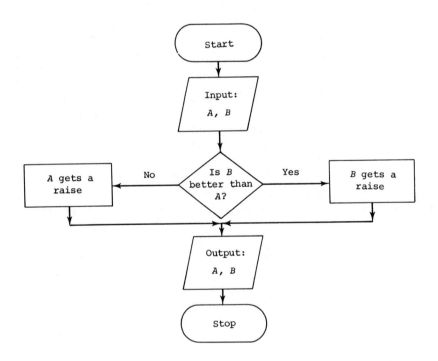

Problem 2

This is the same as Problem 1, except now you must apply the process to many pairs of employees.

Solution. We can use the flowchart for Problem 1, but this time we must add a Decision box after the Output box, and we must test to see if we are done. For now, let us just ask the question: "Are we done?" If so, we shall terminate. If not, we shall want to input two more employees; so we draw a line of flow back to the Input box to indicate that this is the next instruction.

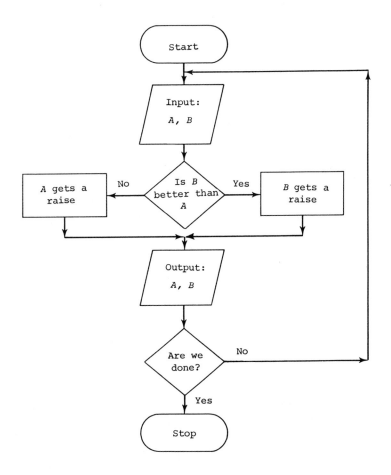

Note that every employee in this flowchart is called *A* or *B*. This is all right because we have the Output box in our loop that allows the old pair to leave. If, by chance, we had put this box *after* the last Decision box, we would effectively be allowing the office to continuously fill up with people!

9

Problem 3

Input three numbers and output the largest one.

Solution. Since we can compare only two numbers at a time, we shall need three Decision boxes, comparing A to B, B to C, and A to C. The flowchart would be:

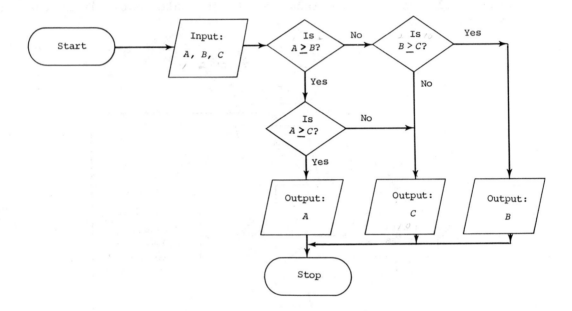

The student should convince himself of the validity of this solution by assigning values to A, B, and C, and tracing these through the flowchart.

We have been placing a question in each Decision box, and different branches coming out of them, depending on whether the answer was yes or no. Actually, there are several ways to make a Decision box. We could write $A:B$ in the box, meaning "compare A to B," and then put a greater than ($>$), less than ($<$), or equal to ($=$) sign on the branches coming out of the box.

For example, the Decision box shown in the following diagram means to take the left branch if $A < B$, the right branch if $A > B$, or the lower branch if $A = B$.

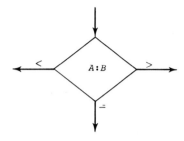

If we wanted to go to the same place when $A = B$ as we do when $A > B$, we could combine the two branches and put

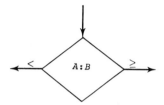

Another way to do this is to use a question form, as we have been doing.

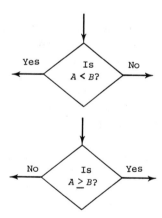

Either one represents exactly the same thing; it is just a matter of personal preference as to which one is used. The important fact is that for any particular result derived from making the comparison, there is exactly one branch out of the box. Hence,

11

we could *not* have

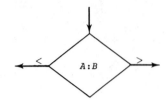

because if *A* were equal to *B*, there would be no place to go.
Even if we knew that in a particular program *A* would never be
equal to *B*, we would have to construct something like

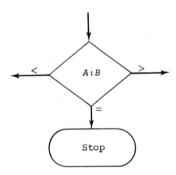

By now it should be clear how a flowchart represents an
actual program: the boxes are the instructions, and the lines
of flow specify the order in which the instructions are to be
processed. Furthermore, flowcharts visually illustrate the
principle that after one instruction is performed it must be
clear which instruction is to be performed next, and that only
one instruction at a time can be performed.

The flowchart should be a flexible and useful tool. In a
completed flowchart, the differently shaped boxes help to
quickly identify different types of instructions, and the lines
of flow are easy to follow to determine what actually happens
in the process that the flowchart defines.

There are a few conventions involved in writing flowcharts
that should be mentioned. Usually, lines of flow are drawn
either vertically or horizontally. It is often convenient to
have the main line of flow proceed vertically from the top of
the page to the bottom. The only purpose of these restrictions
is to improve legibility, however.

When a program loop is represented (that is, when a group of instructions is performed more than once), the line of flow can return to the box representing the first instruction in the loop, as shown in Figure 1-1.

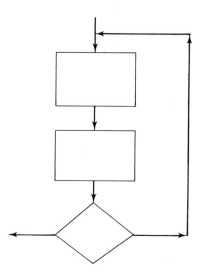

FIGURE 1-1. *Method of showing a program loop*

In some situations it is inconvenient to draw a line of flow to an instruction, so a connector can be used. This is a small circle with some identifier unit indicating that the next instruction to be performed is identified by a similar connector rather than by a line of flow. Figure 1-2 gives an example of a situation that can occur where the use of a connector is called for. If a flowchart requires more than one page, the same connector can be used to indicate that the next instruction is on a different page.

The purpose of the flowchart is to help the programmer. In the end, clarity and convenience should be the governing factors. Flowcharts also help us construct the program as we go along. Usually, a flowchart is not drawn from start to finish; the main instructions are done first and then the rest filled in. Even an experienced programmer may have to make several tries before getting a flowchart that suits him. A little practice will give you a pretty good feeling for the method.

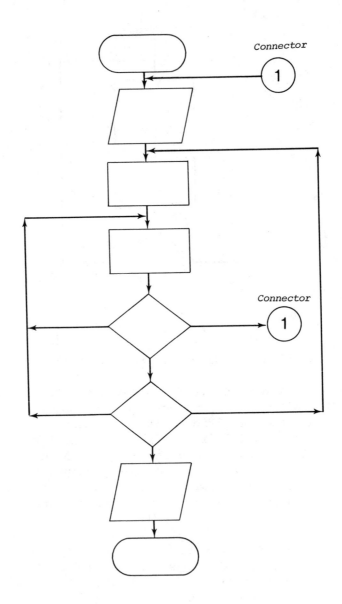

FIGURE 1-2. Use of a connector

14

Example 1

Suppose we want to compute the sum of the integers from 1 to N [and suppose we do not remember the formula $S = N/2(N + 1)!$]. We shall use the method, not uncommon in programming, of taking a partial sum; that is, at some step we have a location, called SUM, which contains $1 + 2 + \cdots + (I - 1)$. To the contents of this location, we shall add I. So the main instruction is:[1]

```
SUM =
  SUM + I
```

After that, we must test to see if we are finished; so we compare I to N. If I is equal to N, we output the answer SUM. If not, we add one to I and go back to the computation. So far, our flowchart, which represents the essential part of the program, looks like this:

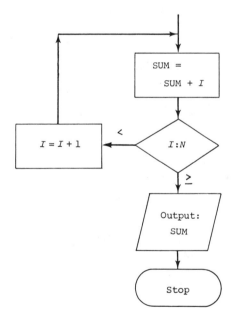

---

[1] Notice the equals sign in the instruction SUM = SUM + I. This obviously cannot have the normal arithmetic meaning. Instead, it has the computer meaning "is replaced by." We can read the statement as follows: "replace the value of the variable SUM by the old value plus I." Some authors use the symbol ←to indicate replacement.

15

But the flowchart is incomplete—the quantities SUM and *I* need to be initialized (that is, they must be given a starting value). For this purpose, we use the instructions SUM = 0 and *I* = 1. Finally, we shall want an Input box to read in a value for *N* so that we can use the same procedure for any value of *N*. The completed flowchart is now:

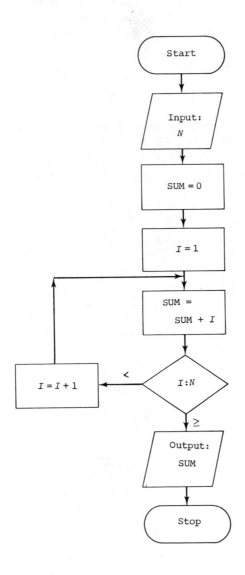

AVERAGING NUMBERS

Let us now consider a simple problem of a practical nature.

Example 2

Suppose we have a sequence of items and we want to read them in one at a time, sum them, and find their average. To do this, we shall need to know how many numbers there are, and we shall need to find their sum. One way to handle this is to read in the number of items, N, and then follow a procedure similar to that of Example 1. In this case, we would input N, and then input the items and find their sum by performing some loop N times. After this is done, we would compute the average and then output this average. The exact procedure is given by the following flowchart, where each number in turn is called X.

In this example, notice that one work box has been used to represent the two instructions SUM = 0 and $I = 0$. This is occasionally done to conserve space when the two (or more) instructions are not separated by a Decision or other box affecting the flow. Note that if we wish to specify N before reading them in, it is necessary to actually count the number of items to be averaged. This might be inconvenient if there were many items. Actually, we can modify the program so that the machine will do the counting for us. To do this, we first choose some value that we know will not occur among the items to be averaged and we read this in as an extra item.

Example 3

Suppose we are averaging a student's semester grades. Each grade is one of the numbers 4, 3, 2, 1, or 0. For the last item to be read in, let us put the value 999. Then, in the program we begin by reading in a grade X. We then test to see if we have read in 999. If not, we add one to N and add X to SUM. Then we begin again by reading another grade. If we have read 999, however, we compute the average, AV = SUM/N, and output this result.

We might go one step further in this example by writing a program to find the averages of several sets of items. For example, we might want to find the average of the semester grades of each student in a school. After the last set of grades, we would put the value 9999. So, if John has grades 1, 2, 3, 4, and 4, and Fred has grades 4, 4, 3, and 4, we could find both averages by running the program once with the data 1, 2, 3, 4, 4, 999, 4, 4, 3, 4, 999, and 9999.

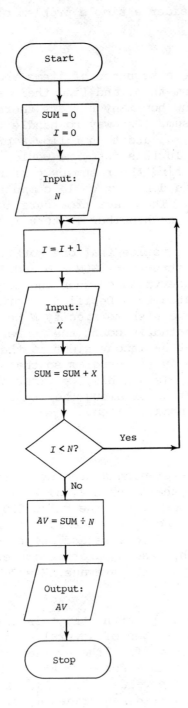

To construct a flowchart for this problem, let us begin with the Decision boxes. We shall first test the value of X to see if $X = 999$. If not, we want to see if $X = 9999$, and if it does, we stop. So we have the flowchart:

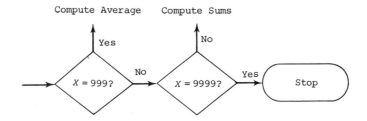

Now, if the value of X is neither 999 nor 9999, we add X to SUM, add 1 to N, again input X, and test. A partial flowchart showing this would be:

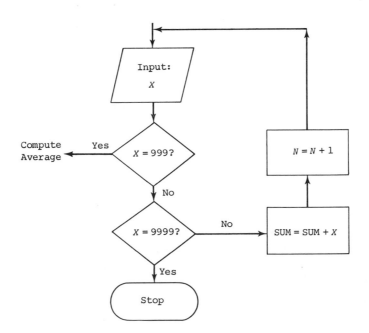

If, on the first test, $X = 999$, we compute the average and output it. Then we initialize the quantities N and SUM and begin again. Finally, we must remember to include a Start terminal and to initialize N and SUM before the first time through. The completed flowchart is:

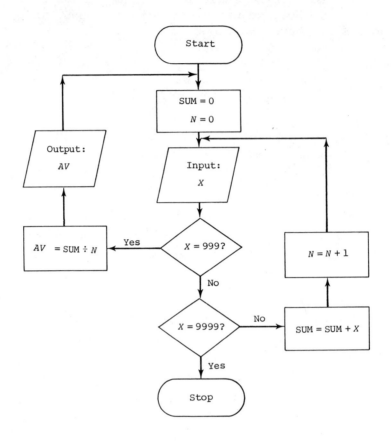

A frequently encountered problem is that of sorting data into an ascending (or descending) sequence.

Example 4

Assume that you are given a set of N storage locations named X_1, X_2, $\cdots$, X_n. One problem is to rearrange them so that the location named X_1 contains the smallest numerical value, X_2 the next smallest, etc., until the numbers are all in the desired order. We shall present one of several ways this can be done. The method presented here, though not the fastest, is one of the simplest to understand.

Start with the first location named X_1, and compare its value with that of X_2. If $X_1 \leq X_2$, do nothing, but if $X_1 > X_2$, interchange the values of X_1 and X_2. Next, compare the number in the

X_1 position with that in the X_3 position and do the same as before. After finishing with all N numbers, we shall have succeeded in placing the smallest number in the first position. Next, compare the number in the second position, X_2, with X_3 and either leave them alone or interchange them. Continuing as before, we eventually have the second smallest number in the X_2 position. Next, go to the X_3 position and continue as before. When we reach the $N - 1$ position, we are through. The following flowchart shows these steps (it assumes that the X_n values are already stored in the computer).

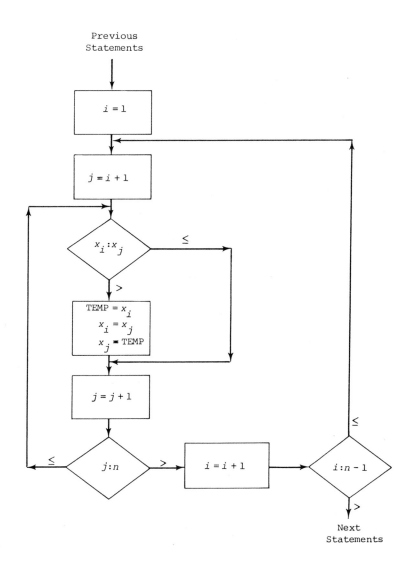

Notice that a new variable, called TEMP, has been introduced. This is necessary because if we had just the operation $X_i = X_j$ followed by $X_j = X_i$, we would not accomplish what we need to do. The first operation *replaces* X_i by X_j instead of *interchanging* them. By introducing the variable TEMP, we accomplish the interchange.

A EXERCISES

1. According to the following flowchart, what is the final value of Y if I is 1? What happens if I is 2? How would you guard against this possibility?

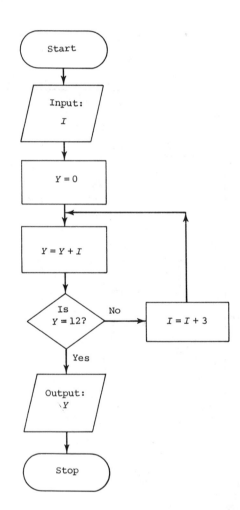

Construct a flowchart to illustrate a solution to each of the
following problems.

2. Read in the radius R of a circle and output the diameter D,
    the circumference C, and the area A.

3. Read in two numbers P and Q and output the quotient $X = P/Q$.
    Include a test to stop if $Q = 0$.

4. Input an integer N and output the sum of all even integers
    less than N.

5. Input X and output the absolute value ABS of X (i.e., $ABS = X$
    if $X \geq 0$; $ABS = -X$ if $X < 0$).

6. Input A and B. Set $C = 1$ if A and B are equal to 1. Set
    $C = 2$ if A or B, but not both, equals 1. Set $C = 3$ if neither
    A nor B equals 1. Output C.

7. Compute $y = x^2 + 5x - 3$ for values of $x = 0.0$, 0.1, 0.2, ...,
    5.0. Output x and y for each value of x.

8. Input three numbers I, J, and K. If they are all different,
    set $N = 1$. If any two of them (but not all three) are the
    same, set $N = 2$. If all three are the same, set $N = 3$.

9. Input an integer N between 1 and 20 and determine whether
    it is even or odd by subtracting 2 repeatedly until either
    zero or a negative number is reached. If N is even, set
    $M = 0$; if N is odd, set $M = 1$.

10. The accompanying flowchart is supposed to count the number
    of elements of a doubly-subscripted variable that are equal
    to zero. There is an error in the flowchart. Correct the
    error and trace through the flowchart with the following
    data:

    $n = 4$ $m = 2$

    $a_{11} = 2.0$ $a_{12} = 3.1$ $a_{13} = 2.0$ $a_{14} = 0.0$

    $a_{21} = 0.0$ $a_{22} = 5.0$ $a_{23} = 0.0$ $a_{24} = 6.1$

23

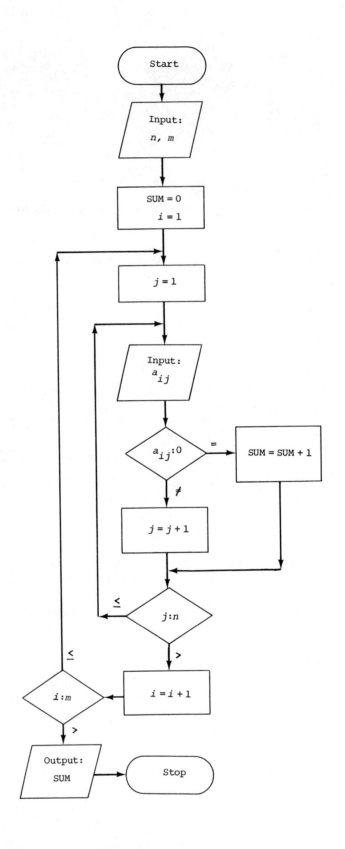

1. The general quadratic equation has the form $ax^2 + bx + c = 0$. It has two solutions, x_1 and x_2, given by

$$x_1 = \frac{-b + \sqrt{b^2 - 4ac}}{2a} \qquad\qquad x_2 = \frac{-b - \sqrt{b^2 - 4ac}}{2a}$$

Write a flowchart to read in three values a, b, and c and output x_1 and x_2. Since we cannot take the square root of a negative number, include a test to make the program stop if $b^2 - 4ac < 0$.

2. Write a flowchart to input a positive integer N and output $X = 2^N$.

3. Write a flowchart to input a positive integer N and output $Z = 1 + 1/2 + 1/3 + \cdots + 1/N$.

4. If M is any positive integer, the number M *factorial* (written $M!$) is defined to be the product $1 \times 2 \times \cdots \times M$. Write a flowchart to read in M and output $M!$. Include a test to stop if $M < 1$.

5. The *binomial coefficient* C_{nk} is defined by

$$C_{nk} = \frac{n!}{k!(n - k)!}$$

(where $n!$ means n factorial—see Problem 4). Write a flowchart to read n and k and output C_{nk}. What would happen in your flowchart if the number read in for k is greater than the number read in for n? Include a test to stop if this happens.

6. What does the accompanying flowchart do? Find the value of Z which is output if the values read in are

 a. $X = 0$; $N = 1$
 b. $X = 1$; $N = 2$
 c. $X = 1$; $N = -2$
 d. $X = -2$; $N = 3$

 Can the final value of Z ever be zero? Can it ever be less than zero?

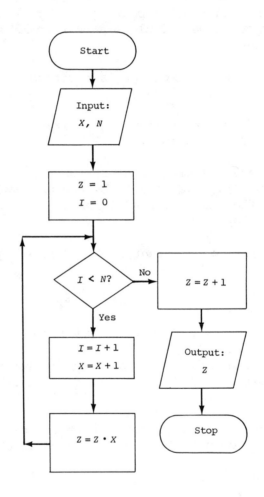

26

7. Given a set T_1, T_2, $\cdots$, T_N of test scores, write a flowchart to read them in and determine:

	equals number of scores from
NA	90 to 100
NB	80 to 89
NC	70 to 79
ND	60 to 69
NF	0 to 59

8. In solving differential equations, it is sometimes necessary to compute with what are called the *Legendre polynomials*. The first six of these are given by

$$P_0(x) = 1 \quad \text{(for all } x\text{)}$$

$$P_1(x) = x$$

$$P_2(x) = 1/2(3x^2 - 1)$$

$$P_3(x) = 1/2(5x^3 - 3)$$

$$P_4(x) = 1/8(35x^4 - 30x + 3)$$

$$P_5(x) = 1/8(63x^5 - 70x^3 + 15x)$$

Write a flowchart to read a number x and an integer $0 \le N \le 5$ and output $P = P_N(x)$.

Chapter 2

CONSTANTS, VARIABLES, AND ARITHMETIC EXPRESSIONS

In an algebraic expression we are familiar with seeing numbers and variables used together. The numbers are referred to as *constants*. In general, any quantity that does not change in value is called a constant. A quantity that can (or might) change in value is called a *variable* and is written in the form of a symbol. Quite commonly, the symbol used is a letter, but sometimes it may even be a name, depending on what we happen to choose. For example, the formula for the area of a circle is often stated as

$$A = \pi r^2$$

Here the constant is π. The variables are A (area) and r (radius). Alternately, we could have written the formula as

$$\text{Area} = \pi(\text{Radius})^2$$

or, for that matter, in any form, as long as we know what the variables represent and we understand what arithmetic operations are implied.

A computer has the property of being able to evaluate a formula for certain values and then, at a later time, to evaluate the same formula for different values. This is done, in part, because as in algebra, we can use both constants and variables in our computer programs. We shall now learn what restrictions are imposed when writing the variables and constants in our computer language, FORTRAN. We have only a few, but since a computer requires absolutely precise information, they must be followed exactly.

CONSTANTS

In FORTRAN, a constant is represented simply by a decimal number (i.e., a string of decimal digits, possibly having a decimal point and a sign). This means that constants must be composed from the digits 0, 1, 2, 3, 4, 5, 6, 7, 8, and 9. Thus, a constant such as π, $\sqrt{2}$, or e, must be represented by a decimal equivalent. Although it is often impossible to write the *exact* decimal equivalent of a desired constant, we can normally express it correctly to at least seven significant decimal places.

There are two different types of FORTRAN constants. Remember that the same is also true for ordinary numbers. For example, in an arithmetic examination each problem is given a sequence number, and then various real numbers are used in the problems. The computer, unfortunately, does not possess our common sense; we must be very careful to distinguish between the different types of constants. If we want to indicate a number that is to be used in a calculation to give us the correct arithmetic result, we simply write the number with a decimal point. This is called a *floating-point constant*. Some floating-point constants are listed in Table 1.

TABLE 1

Normal Arithmetic Constant	FORTRAN Constant
1	1.0 or 1. or 1.00, etc.
26	26.
1,000.2	1000.2
-16	-16.0 or -0016.0, etc.
1,000,000	1000000.
+2	+2. or +2.0 or 2.

The following rules are illustrated in Table 1 and *must be observed*:

Rule 1: Commas are not permitted in FORTRAN constants. Thus, the numbers in Table 1 that we normally write with commas must be written without them.

Rule 2: As in algebra, if a number has no sign, it is taken to be positive. Negative numbers *must* be written with the minus sign.

Rule 3: Zeros in front of a number are not counted. One may thus place them there for convenience.

Rule 4: The size of a constant depends on the computer used. In general, one can assume that a computer can handle up to and including seven digits, not counting the sign or the decimal point.

We shall use numbers to keep track of what we are doing in the program. These numbers are "counting numbers," that is, they count the number of times operations are being done, refer to various parts of the program, and so on. Such a number is called a *fixed-point constant*,[1] or simply an integer, and is distinguished from a floating-point constant in that it has no decimal point. This means that no decimals or fractions are used as fixed-point constants. Thus, some programmers refer to them as integers. It may have a minus sign, however, and later we shall learn under what circumstances we would want to use it this way. Table 2 gives a few examples of fixed-point constants.

TABLE 2

Arithmetic Number	FORTRAN Fixed-Point Constant
31.3	31 or 313 (number must somehow be written with no decimal)
-6.2	-6 or -62 (number must somehow be written with no decimal)
1,000	1000 (no comma)
25	25 (number was already in fixed-point form)

The size of the fixed-point constant is more severely restricted than that of a floating-point constant. In some early computers it was as low as 32767. In modern computers, the size can be 4294967295 or even larger,[2] and in many systems up to eleven significant digits are acceptable.

There is a method of representing floating-point constants, analogous to "scientific notation." Often numbers arise that are either very large or very small, but that have only a few significant digits. For example, numbers such as those shown in Table 3 are frequently encountered in physics and engineering problems.

---

[1]Alternate terminology is *real* for "floating point" and *integer* for "fixed point." Some authors prefer to use "real" and "integer," especially since there are corresponding FORTRAN statements (see Chapter 13). Unfortunately, the words "real" and "integer" have other meanings. For example, "a complex number is said to have a *real* and an *imaginary* part." To avoid any possible ambiguity, we prefer the terms "floating" and "fixed" point.

[2]The numbers 32767 and 4294967295 may seem to be strange limits. However, they are actually obtained by powers of 2, namely $2^{15} - 1$ and $2^{31} - 1$. Digital computers work on the binary number system and so they are indeed logical maximum sizes.

TABLE 3

Arithmetic Number	Scientific Notation
.0000000666	$6.66 \cdot 10^{-8}$
.000000375	$37.5 \cdot 10^{-8}$
8,000,000	$8.0 \cdot 10^{6}$
.000086	$.86 \cdot 10^{-4}$
50000000000000	$5.0 \cdot 10^{13}$

The method we use to represent these numbers as FORTRAN floating-point constants is known as the "E-form" (or exponential form). If we want to write 62,000 in E-form, we write:

$$\underset{\text{(a)}}{6.2} \quad \underset{\text{(b)}}{E} \; \underset{\text{(c)}}{+} \; \underset{\text{(d)}}{04}$$

Let us examine what we have done here:

(a) First, we wrote a floating-point constant. This, we recall is a number with a decimal point. This *must* be a floating-point constant.

(b) Next, we put the letter E.

(c) Here we placed a plus sign to signify that the exponent is positive. If we had, instead, .00062, we could have written 6.2 E - 04. If no sign appears here, the computer assumes that it is positive.

(d) This portion consists of the exponent, or power, of 10. This *must* be a fixed-point constant. In fact, this illustrates one application of fixed-point constants. As mentioned before, they are used to count the operations being done. In scientific notation, say 7.4×10^{5}, the number 5 counts the number of places the decimal is to be moved to the right and thus determines the number of zeros to be added to the number when converting back to an arithmetic representation. The zero before the 4 is not necessary but has been added to illustrate the point that, in general, leading zeros are not counted in FORTRAN. Table 4 provides further examples of the E-form.

31

TABLE 4

Arithmetic Number	E-Form
20,000	2.0E4 or 2.E4 or 2.E + 4 or 2.E + 04
-2	-2.0E + 0 or -.2E1 or -.002E03, etc.
.00001	.1E - 4 or 1.E - 5 or 1.00E - 05
160000000000000	16.0E13

The limits on the sizes of such numbers vary with the computer. For some computers, the sizes may be between 10^{-77} and 10^{77}; other computers will accept even larger numbers. Most of the time, these limits will not concern us, as our numbers will be well within these ranges. However, if it is desired to use very large numbers in a program, one should consult the reference manual for the particular computer to be used to determine what the actual limits are.

VARIABLES

There are several different types of variables which are used in FORTRAN. These types correspond to the different types of numbers used in a program. In this chapter we shall confine our attention to the two most commonly used types of variables: fixed-point and floating-point. The student may wonder why it is necessary to make a distinction between these. The reason is that the different types of numbers are stored differently in the computer and used differently in the program. For example, we shall see in a later chapter that a variable used to represent a subscript must be a fixed-point variable. We shall now see how these different types of variables are formed.

Fixed-Point Variables. A fixed-point variable is represented by a name consisting of from one to six characters.[3] Each character must be a letter (A-Z) or a numeric digit (0-9). The first character *must* be one of the letters I, J, K, L, M, or N. This is how FORTRAN distinguishes fixed-point variable names from floating-point variable names.

As long as we comply with the above rules, we can give a fixed-point variable any name we choose. Usually, we choose variable names to help us to remember what the variables represent. For example, if a certain variable is going to

---

[3]Most large computers will handle variables with seven-character names. For the sake of uniformity, we shall use names with six or fewer characters.

represent the sum of a group of numbers, we might call the variable SUM. However, this is *not* a legal name for a fixed-point variable, since it does not begin with a letter I through N. To comply with the rule, we could call the variable NSUM.

The examples below show correct fixed-point variables:

```
I
JUMP
MASS
K1234
NNNNNN
L
LENGTH
```

Here are a few examples of incorrect fixed-point variables:

Variable	*Reason for Error*
I + J	Illegal symbol (+)
K1234567	Too many characters
HELLO	Does not start with a letter I-N
4HG	Does not start with a letter
NAME$	Illegal symbol ($)

Floating-Point Variables. The rules for naming floating-point variables are the same as for fixed-point variables—with one exception: *the name of a floating-point variable must begin with some letter other than I, J, K, L, M, or N.* Thus, we can determine the type of variable name by looking at the first letter. If it is I through N, the variable is fixed-point. A variable beginning with any other letter is floating-point. Below are some examples of valid floating-point variable names.

```
A
X
X1234
FØRCE
ACCEL
ØHM
ETC
```

Some examples of errors in floating-point variables are shown below:

Variable	*Reason for Error*
X + Y	Symbol used (+)
JUMP	Starts with J

Variable	Reason for Error
1XY	Starts with number
X$Y	Symbol used ($)
GØTØFØUR	Too many characters
DØ3J = 1	Symbol used (=)

ARITHMETIC

Just as in algebra, in FORTRAN we must learn how to form *expressions*. To do this, we introduce the arithmetic operations which are done in FORTRAN and the symbols used to perform each.

The following are the basic arithmetic operations done in FORTRAN and the corresponding symbols.

Operation	FORTRAN Operator Symbol
Addition	+
Subtraction	-
Multiplication	*
Division	/
Exponentiation	**

FORTRAN constants or variables are combined in an operation to form an *expression*. Normally, the modes of all variables and constants in an expression will be the same. If two or more different types of data appear in the same expression, the expression is said to be of "mixed mode." Special rules apply to such expressions, and they may not be allowed in some versions of FORTRAN. Also, care must be taken so that no two FORTRAN arithmetic operators are placed next to each other. Some FORTRAN expressions are shown below together with their possible algebraic equivalents.

FORTRAN	Algebra
X*Y	xy
A + (B - C)	$a + (b - c)$
DELP1 - DELP2	$\Delta P_1 - \Delta P_2$
3.14159*R**2	πr^2
.5*B*H	$\frac{1}{2}bh$

ORDER OF OPERATIONS IN FORTRAN

In more complicated expressions it is important to know which of the operations should be performed first. The order in which the operations in an expression are evaluated is given by the following set of rules:

34

(a) First, any part of the expression enclosed in parentheses is evaluated completely before proceeding to evaluate any part of the expression outside the parentheses. This rule applies to each set of parentheses. Thus, in the expression

$$6. * ((A + B) + C) - D ** 2/E * F$$

A + B would be evaluated first; C is added to this sum. The operations are then performed as follows.

(b) First, each exponentiation is performed. This means that for the above expression, the term D ** 2 is evaluated.

(c) Next, multiplication and/or division is performed from *left to right*. This means that the expression D ** 2/E * F has the algebraic equivalent of

$$\frac{d^2}{e} f$$

(d) Finally, addition and/or subtraction is performed from *left to right*.

Example

Let us consider the FORTRAN expression

$$E/A ** 2 + B ** 3/(C + 6. * D ** 2)$$

First, the computer will calculate what is in the parentheses, (C + 6. * D ** 2). There is an exponentiation here and so the computer next calculates the value of D ** 2. The sequence of steps performed by the computer is shown below. (We have mixed together FORTRAN and algebra only to illustrate the above rules.)

Original expression $E/A ** 2 + B ** 3/(C + 6. * D ** 2)$
After 1st operation $E/A ** 2 + B ** 3/(C + 6. * d^2)$
After 2nd operation $E/A ** 2 + B ** 3/(C + 6d^2)$
After 3rd operation $E/A ** 2 + B ** 3/\{c + 6d^2\}$
After 4th operation $E/a^2 + b^3/(c + 6d^2)$
After 5th operation $\dfrac{e}{a^2} + \dfrac{b^3}{c + 6d^2}$

Finally, the addition is performed. It should be clear from the rules that

A/B * C means $\dfrac{a}{b} \cdot c$ and *not* $\dfrac{a}{bc}$

35

If $\dfrac{a}{bc}$ is meant, be careful to insert parentheses, i.e., A/(B * C).

The following table gives examples of the FORTRAN equivalent of algebraic expressions. Notice how every constant is written with a decimal point to keep the modes the same (except in the case of exponentiation):

Algebraic Expression	FORTRAN Equivalent
$x^2 - y^2$	X ** 2 - Y ** 2
$\sqrt{b^2 - 4ac}$	(B ** 2 - 4. * A * C) ** .5
$v_0 t - \dfrac{1}{2} g t^2$	V0 * T - 0.5 * G * T ** 2
$c q_1 q_2 / r^2$	C * Q1 * Q2/R ** 2
$\dfrac{\Delta g}{p^2 A + \dfrac{\Delta g}{AX}}$	DELG/(P ** 2 * A + DELG/(A * X))

These are all floating-point expressions. Every FORTRAN variable or constant has been written in the floating-point mode in order to observe the rule of not mixing modes. In the case of exponentiation, the modes may be mixed if a floating-point variable (constant) is raised to a fixed-point power. In fact, *this is a more desirable programming practice as it saves computer execution time.* The following are examples of this:

Algebra	FORTRAN
x^3	X ** 3
$\sqrt{x^2 + y^2}$	(X ** 2 + Y ** 2) ** (0.5)
$a^4 b^3 / (a^2 + b^2)$	A ** 4 * B ** 3/(A ** 2 + B ** 2)
z^R	Z ** R
I^J	I ** J

Thus, I ** J is all right, but I ** A would be incorrect. Each of the following FORTRAN expressions has at least one error in it:

Expression	Error
A + I	Mixed modes
C + -D	Two operations next to each other
A + (B - D/E * F * A((B))	Parentheses do not match

Expression	Error
FORCE * MASS	Mixed modes
DELX/P(E + D)	Operation missing
R1 ** Z/16 - A	Mixed modes

FIXED-POINT ARITHMETIC

Most computer programs that involve arithmetic calculations are naturally done in the floating-point mode. This is so because the size of the numbers that are allowed is larger than in fixed-point arithmetic, and also because decimals are used. There are occasions, however, when a programmer will find it convenient to use the properties associated with fixed-point arithmetic.

The same operations are allowed in fixed-point expressions (i.e., +, -, *, /, and **) as in floating-point expressions. The difference in this arithmetic lies in the fact that no decimals are permitted. As a computer evaluates a fixed-point expression, it will truncate all characters which would normally follow after the decimal. This means that the expression

$$4/3$$

would be evaluated as 1, the remaining .33333 having been truncated. Similarly,

$$50 * (49/50)$$

is zero and not 49.

THE EQUALS SIGN IN FORTRAN

Remember that every time we compute an arithmetic expression, we have to store the result somewhere. This storing operation is denoted by an equals sign in FORTRAN. For instance, the FORTRAN statement

$$AREA = 3.1416 * (DIAM/2.0) ** 2$$

tells the machine to evaluate the expression on the right of the equals sign and to store the result at the location named AREA.

Two rules govern the use of the equals sign in FORTRAN.

Rule 1: The quantity on the left of the equals sign must be a variable, not a constant or an expression.

Rule 2: The value of the expression on the right will be converted to the mode of the variable on the left before storing.

The first rule means that it is not allowable to have a statement like

    A + 1.0 = B

It is always the expression on the *right* that is evaluated. The variable on the left simply tells where the result is to be stored. Thus, it would be all right to have the statement

    B = A + 1.0

This tells the machine to add 1 to the value of A and to store the result in B. For that matter, it would be all right to have the statement

    A = A + 1.0

This, of course, would be nonsense in algebra, but in FORTRAN it means to add 1 to the value of A and to store the result back in A.

The second rule may be illustrated by the following examples. In the statement

    N = 7.0

the expression on the right is a floating-point constant (with a decimal point). The variable on the left is a fixed-point variable and as such must not have a decimal point. Rule 2 means simply that the floating-point constant 7.0 will be converted to the fixed-point number 7 before it is stored in N. If we had the statement

    N = 7.3

then the same process would occur. This time, since a fixed-point constant cannot have a decimal point, the .3 would be truncated, and N would have the value 7.

If the expression on the right is a floating-point arithmetic expression and the variable on the left is a fixed-point variable, we would have the same sort of situation. For example, suppose that the variable ABC has the value 4.0. Then the statement

    I2 = (ABC + 1.9)/2.0

would result in the following:

First, 1.9 is added to 4.0, giving 5.9.

This is divided by 2.0, giving 2.95.

Finally, this result is converted to a fixed-point number—so the decimal part is truncated, and we have I2 set equal to 2.

Similarly, if the expression on the right is a fixed-point expression and the variable on the left is a floating-point variable, a conversion from fixed-point to floating-point will occur before storing the result. For instance, if J has the value 5, then the statement

$$X = (J - 1) ** 2$$

will cause the expression on the right to be evaluated (in this case the answer would be 16), and then a decimal point would be inserted so that X becomes 16.0.

This form, with an arithmetic expression on the right of the equals sign and a variable on the left, is called an arithmetic *assignment statement*. We say that the value of the expression is *assigned* to the variable when it is stored in the cell named by the variable.

Let us consider some examples involving the computation of some familiar formulas.

Example 1

Given the variables A, B, and C, write statements to compute the solutions X1 and X2 to the equation $Ax^2 + B + C = 0$.

There are two solutions to this equation, given by

$$\frac{-B \pm \sqrt{B^2 - 4AC}}{2A}$$

Now, if $B^2 - 4AC$ is less than or equal to zero, we run into trouble, since then there will not be two real solutions. For this example, we shall assume that $B^2 - 4AC$ is greater than zero.

One way to write the program is by using the statements

```
X1 = (-B + (B ** 2 - 4.0 * A * C) ** .5)/(2.0 * A)
X2 = (-B - (B ** 2 - 4.0 * A * C) ** .5)/(2.0 * A)
```

Note that in this method, however, we are duplicating much of the work. For instance, $B^2 - 4AC$ is computed twice, although, of course, the result will be the same both times. We want a more economical way to accomplish the same thing. Consider the statements

```
    D = ((B ** 2 - 4.0 * A * C) ** .5)/(2.0 * A)
    E = -B/(2.0 * A)
   X1 = E + D
   X2 = E - D
```

Here we have broken up the computation into parts. We have more statements, but less work is actually done since $B - 4AC$ is evaluated only once. This means that the computer could compute X1 and X2 faster by the second method than by the first. While in this case the difference would be negligible, if we were to perform the computation for thousands of different values of A, B, and C in some program, the difference might be considerable.

Example 2

Given the variables A, B, C, D, E, and F, find X and Y, which satisfy

$$AX + BY = C$$
$$DX + EY = F$$

The solutions are given by

$$X = \frac{CE - BF}{AE - BD} \qquad Y = \frac{AF - CD}{AE - BD}$$

The real first step in solving this problem would be to see if $AE - BD$ is zero; if it were, we would not want to divide by it. This could be handled by a decision statement, which we shall learn how to program in the next chapter. So for now, we ignore this possibility and write

```
    X = (C * E - B * F)/(A * E - B * D)
    Y = (A * F - C * D)/(A * E - B * D)
```

As before, we see that we would make the computation more efficient if we did not have to compute $AE - BD$ twice, so let us introduce the variable DENOM and rewrite the computation as

```
   DENOM = A * E - B * D
       X = (C * E - B * F)/DENOM
       Y = (A * F - C * D)/DENOM
```

Example 3

Consider the polynomial

$$Y = Ax^4 + Bx^3 + Cx^2 + Dx + E$$

One way to evaluate this would be to use the single statement

$$Y = A * X ** 4 + B * X ** 3 + C * X ** 2 + D * X + E$$

Following the rules on page 35, let us see what actually happens when this expression is evaluated by the machine. First, the exponentiations are performed: X is multiplied by itself four times to give X ** 4, then multiplied by itself again three times to give X ** 3, and so on. X is multiplied by itself nine times in all. Then the terms are multiplied by the coefficients, requiring four more multiplications, and finally they are added to give Y. A total of ten multiplications and four additions is required for this computation.

Now, suppose we compute Y by the following method. We use the formula

$$Y = (((A * X + B) * X + C) * X + D) * X + E$$

The nested parentheses may make this formula seem unnecessarily complicated, but notice two things about this method. First, we are really computing the same formula as before. That is, the above formula amounts to the same thing as the polynomial, but the terms are grouped differently. This time, however, only four multiplications instead of ten are required. Thus, the above computation is quite a bit more efficient that the first method. Furthermore, we can avoid the parentheses if we divide the formula into several statements:

```
Y = A * X + B
Y = Y * X + C
Y = Y * X + D
Y = Y * X + E
```

The first of these statements sets Y equal to the expression in the innermost pair of parentheses of the former statement. The second statement multiplies the Y calculated in the first statement by X, adds C, and stores the new result back in Y. After the fourth statement is performed, Y will have the desired value of the original polynomial.

MIXED-MODE ARITHMETIC

We said before that it is incorrect to use fixed-point and floating-point expressions in the same statement. While this is quite true on some compilers, other versions of FORTRAN will allow mixed modes to appear in the same expression. You should consult the reference manual for your system to find out if mixed-mode arithmetic is allowed.

In its most general use, mixed-mode arithmetic provides a whole hierarchy of rules for mixing various types of numbers in the same expression. We shall see in later chapters how this applies to arithmetic using complex or double-precision numbers. For our purposes now, the function of mixed-mode arithmetic can be summarized in the following

> *Rule:* If an arithmetic operation involves both a fixed-point and a floating-point number, the result will be a floating-point number.

This means, for example, that it would be allowable to have the statement

$$Y = X + 2$$

X is a floating-point variable and 2 is a fixed-point constant, so this is a mixed-mode expression. The rule means that the result of the addition will be a floating-point number, just as though the statement were

$$Y = X + 2.0$$

As another example, suppose we want to add the variables X and K together to give W. One way to do this would be

$$Y = K$$
$$W = X + Y$$

Here we have used the statement Y = K to convert K from fixed-point to the floating-point variable Y. Using mixed-mode arithmetic, we could do this in one statement by writing simply

$$W = X + K$$

As another example, the rule for mixed-mode arithmetic means that the statement

$$SQ2 = 2 ** 0.5$$

would set SQ2 equal to the square root of 2 (i.e., 1.41424 approximately) just as though the whole statement were written in floating-point form as

$$SQ2 = 2.0 ** 0.5$$

Note that although the above two expressions give the same result, they are not identical in terms of what the computer does. In the first case, one more operation must be performed: that of converting the fixed-point constant 2 to its floating-point equivalent 2.0. Thus, it is slightly more efficient to avoid mixed-mode expression where possible.

PUNCHED CARDS

The FORTRAN statements that we have just learned make up a portion of a complete program. Later, we shall learn other statements, and finally we shall learn what constitutes a complete program.

We need a means by which we can transmit our FORTRAN program to a computer. Several are available, but we shall consider only the most common one—punched cards. The standard punched card has 80 columns, numbered 1-80, into which a character can be punched. The color and printing on the cards are for identification purposes only; all that the computer senses are the holes punched in the card. (The card is punched by means of a *key punch machine*.)

The only characters allowed in forming statements are:

Alphabetic:	A, B, C, D, ···, X, Y, Z
Numeric:	0, 1, 2, ···, 8, 9
Special:	+ Plus sign
	− Minus sign
	* Asterisk
	/ Slash
	. Period
	, Comma
	(Left parenthesis
	) Right parenthesis
	= Equals sign
	b Blank space that can be considered as a special character
	$ Dollar sign
	' Apostrophe

A FORTRAN statement must be punched only in columns 7 through 72. It need not start in column 7 but generally does. The first six columns are used, but not for the actual FORTRAN statement. The last eight columns (73-80) are not used for the FORTRAN statement; they may be used for whatever the programmer wishes—for example, to number the cards so that they may be kept in order.

Figure 2-1 illustrates these characters as they appear on a typical card. The punched code for numbers and letters is the same for all computer systems. However, the code for some of the other characters may vary.

43

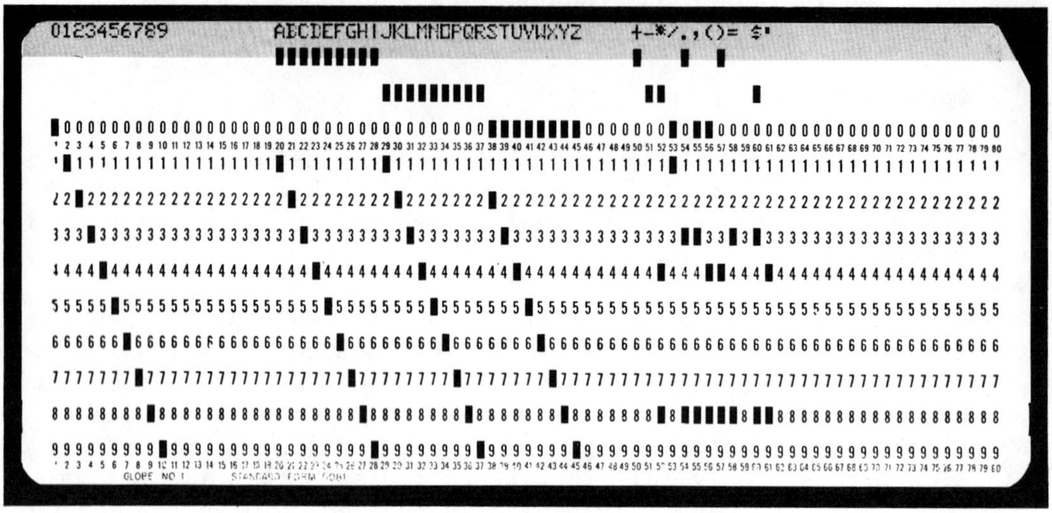

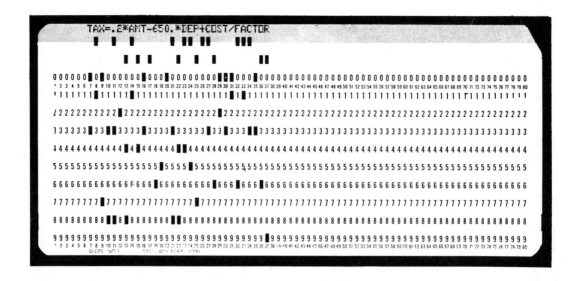

FIGURE 2-1. FORTRAN character code for punched cards

Figure 2-2 illustrates how the arithmetic statement

TAX = .2 * AMT - 650. * DEP + COST/FACTOR

looks after it has been punched on a card. In this case, the statement begins in column seven, but it could just as well have started in any column after seven and up to and including 42 and still be interpreted in the same manner.

FIGURE 2-2

CONTINUATION CARDS

A FORTRAN statement can occupy more columns than the 66 alloted per card by using cards with a number other than zero punched in column six. The cards are called *continuation cards* and serve only to continue the FORTRAN statement from one card to another. Any of the digits 1 through 9 may be used to continue the statement. (Some computer systems allow other FORTRAN symbols as well.) The number of allowable continuation cards for each statement varies with computers from 9 to 19. In practice, only a few such cards are ever needed; exceptionally long statements can be broken into two or more smaller statements.

Example

From now on, when we write the FORTRAN statement

$$Y = A + B + C/D +$$
$$1E - F$$

it means that two cards are to pe punched, the second with a 1 in column six. Thus, the punched cards could be as shown in Figure 2.3.

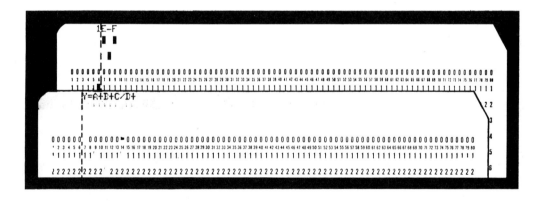

FIGURE 2-3. Example of a continuation card

Of course, the statement could just as well have been written

$$Y = A + B + C/D + E - F$$

and then punched on one card.

Example

The FORTRAN statement written

           TEST = GRADE * SCORE

       2   - 4. * OLD
       2   + CASE
       2   + TEACH
       1   - CLASS

means that the *one* statement is to occupy five punched cards.
The first card has nothing punched in column six, the second
a 2 in column six, the same for the third and fourth cards, and
the fifth card a 1 in column six. The computer will interpret
the statement the same as if it had been punched on the card:

      TEST = GRADE * SCORE - 4 * OLD + CASE + TEACH - CLASS

.

A EXERCISES

Write each of the following numbers in E-form.

1. 6.2
2. .0017
3. 43.6×10^{-6}
4. one million
5. 10^{-10}

6. 12345
7. $.002 \times 10^{5}$
8. $.002 \times 10^{-5}$
9. 300,000,000
10. 1/1000

Write each of the following numbers in decimal form with no
exponent.

11. .1 E-1
12. .1 E10
13. 100.0 E-2
14. 314.16 E-2
15. 0.0101 E5

16. 14.14 E-1
17. 10.0 E-4
18. 111.1 E-4
19. 10,000 E2
20. .077 E-3

State whether or not each of the following is a valid FORTRAN
variable name. If it is, is it a fixed- or floating-point variable? If it is not, what is wrong with it?

21. I12
22. FICA
23. 7AB
24. YES
25. TWENTYFIVE
26. Q
27. ANS

28. K2K3
29. KK.KK
30. XXXXX
31. ABC-1
32. 2UM
33. UM2
34. TANGO

35. NUMB
36. LETTER
37. P
38. MIKE
39. D/D
40. PLUS

For each of the following FORTRAN expressions, write the algebraic expression which it represents.

41. A ** B/C
42. A/B/C
43. A * B/C
44. A/B * C
45. A + B/C

46. ((A + B)/C) + D
47. A ** B * C
48. A * B ** C
49. (2.0 ** (2.0 * X))/X ** 2.0
50. 4.0 * 3.1416 * R ** 2 * 3.0 ** -1

For each of the following algebraic formulas, write a single FORTRAN statement to evaluate it, renaming variables where necessary to comply with the rules for naming floating-point variables in FORTRAN.

51. $A = R^2$

52. $W = (X_2 - X_1)y^2$

53. $R = \dfrac{1}{1/R_1 + 1/R_2 + 1/R_3}$

54. $A = \frac{1}{3}Bh$, where $B = \dfrac{d}{4}$

55. $v = \sqrt{x^2 + y^2}$

56. $Area = \sqrt{S(S-A)(S-B)(S-C)}$

57. $Inner\ product = x_1y_1 + x_2y_2 + x_3y_3$

58. $Middle = minimum + \frac{1}{2}delta$

59. $g = \dfrac{d}{b + \dfrac{c}{(d + e/f)}}$

60. $p = A(1 + r)^{-n}$

Check each of the following FORTRAN statements to see whether or not it is correct. If it is not, state why it is wrong (keep in mind the rules for naming variables and the rules for mixing fixed- and floating-point numbers in an expression).

61. A = A
62. .A = I
63. 2 = M
64. Z = 123
65. K = -1.06 E2
66. 2ZX = A + 10.0 ** .04
67. Z1234 = A ** R + FIN - Z1234
68. A = B/C ** D * E
69. SMALLEST = LEAST * 2 * K
70. BHAT = (B1 - B2)/2

71. X1 = (Y + Z12 + C.X - W1 + 4.0) ** I
72. Y = (X ** 2 + 2 * X + 2)
73. J = H/I
74. Y = Z * -X
75. Y = -X * Z
76. Y = A * B/-C
77. X = X + 1
78. X + 1 = X
79. ABS = (X * X) ** .5
80. REMAINDER = N - (N/M) * M

If A = 3.0, B = 6.0, and C = 2.0, find the value of D computed by each of the following statements according to the rules for floating-point arithmetic.

81. D = (A - B) + C
82. D = A - (B + C)
83. D = -A ** 2 + C
84. D = A/B/C
85. D = A/B/(B/A)

86. D = (A.B)/B/A
87. D = A * B + C
88. D = A + B/B + A
89. D = A * A/A * A
90. D = A/A * A/A

47

If I = 1, J = 2, and K = 3, find the value of N computed by each of the following statements according to the rules for fixed-point arithmetic.

91. N = I/J   96. N = K/(J/J)
92. N = J/I   97. N = K ** I/J
93. N = J ** K   98. N = I ** J ** K
94. N = I * K/2   99. N = J ** I * K
95. N = K/J/J   100. N = J/J - 1

Rewrite each series of statements as a single statement. For example,

$$M = N + 1$$
$$J = J + M$$

could be written as the single statement:

$$J = J + N + 1$$

101. N = N + 1   104. E = Y ** 2 + 1.0
      N = N + 1   X = E * X
                                      X = E * X
102. M = N + 1
      M = M - 1
      N = N + M

103. Z = W1 - W2   105. K4B = K4B + 1
      Y = W3 - W4   K4B = K4B + 2
      X = 4.0 * Y - Z   K4B = K4B + 3

Try to simplify each of the following statements by rewriting it as several statements which together accomplish the same thing. There will be more than one correct way to do this, but try to make each statement quite simple. For example,

$$Y = X + X ** 2 + X ** 3$$

could be written as three statements:

$$Y = X$$
$$Y = X + Y * X$$
$$Y = X + Y * X$$

106. E = (X1 - X2) ** 3 - (X1 - X2) ** 2
107. X = (C1 * D - B * C2)/(C1 * C4 - C2 * C3)
108. E = ((A + B + C)/(B + C)) * A * B
109. C = (A + B + C)/(1.0/A + 1.0/B + 1.0/C)
110. E = A * (A + B) * (A + B + C)

B EXERCISES

Write the algebraic expression that corresponds to each of the following FORTRAN statements.

1. C = X/(X ** 2 + Y ** 2 + Z ** 2) ** .5
2. Y = X ** 3 + 4.0 * X - X * X
3. A = (B + C/(D + (E/F)))
4. Y = 2.0 * ((A1 + A2)/3.0 + A)/X ** N
5. AREA = 4.7 * ((X2 - X1)/2.0) ** 2 - 6.0 * ((X2 - X1)/2.0)

Write FORTRAN statements to evaluate the following formulas, giving suitable names to the variables to comply with the rules. You may find it helpful to break up the computation into steps, as in Problems 106-110, A Exercises.

6. $F = \left\{ \dfrac{(p_1 - p_2)^{1/3}}{1 + [R(q_1 - q_2)]} \right\} + \left\{ 10^5 + \dfrac{a}{b + c/d} \right\}$

7. $x = \dfrac{-b + \sqrt{b^2 - 4ac}}{2a}$

8. $w = \dfrac{e\left[\dfrac{(az + b)}{(cz + d)}\right] + f}{g\left[\dfrac{(az + b)}{(cz + d)}\right] + h}$

9. $G = \dfrac{4/3[(x - y)/(z - w)]e[(a - b)/(c - d)]f}{\sqrt[3]{p^2(r - s)}}$

10. $r = \dfrac{p_1 - \dfrac{p_2}{T} - 1 + \dfrac{2\pi y}{x}}{\left[v^2 a + \dfrac{x}{(A - B)}\right]^{3/2}}$

Chapter 3

CONTROL STATEMENTS

A program consists of a sequence of instructions and a set of rules specifying in what order the instructions are to be performed. So far, we have seen how FORTRAN statements are formed. Now, we shall learn how to specify in what order they are performed.

Unless otherwise specified, FORTRAN statements are performed in the order in which they are written. The statements

$$Y = 5.0 * X + 2.0$$
$$Z = X * Y + 3.0$$
$$W = X * Z + 9.0$$

do the same thing that is indicated in the flowchart boxes:

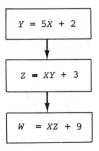

An obvious question arises: How do we change this one-after-another order? For instance, how can we go back to the beginning of a group of instructions and perform them again, and how can we represent a Decision box with a FORTRAN statement? These tasks are performed by *control statements*. This name comes from the fact that they pass "control" of the program to something besides the next statement.

The three basic control statements that we shall consider in this chapter are the STOP, GO TO, and IF statements.

50

THE STOP *STATEMENT*

The purpose of this statement is simply to terminate the operation of the program. In other words, the STOP statement is the FORTRAN equivalent of the Stop terminal in a flowchart. We mentioned in Chapter 1 that every flowchart must have one Start terminal and at least one Stop terminal. Now, there is no such thing as a START statement in FORTRAN. It is not necessary, because operation always begins with the first statement in the program. However, every complete FORTRAN program will normally have at least one STOP statement.

The following statements illustrate the use of the STOP statement:

```
X = X + 1.0
Y = 5.0 * X
STOP
```

We can use more than one STOP statement in a program if necessary, and we shall see an example of such a situation when we discuss the IF statement.

THE END *STATEMENT*

The STOP statement terminates the running of the program. It can appear at any place in a program where the programmer wishes to stop the operations. There is another statement, called the END statement, that *must* be used at the end of every FORTRAN program. This instructs the computer that the program is ended. The form is simply

END

Later, when we start writing complete programs, we shall see more of this statement.

Statement Numbers.[1] Both the GO TO and IF statements make use of statement numbers, so we shall first look briefly at what a statement number is, and then when we come to the GO TO statement, we shall see how they are used.

A statement number is just a number we put before a statement so that we can refer to the statement in another part of the

---

[1] The ANSI term for these is *statement labels*. Most programmers are more familiar with the notation "statement numbers" and so it is also used here.

51

program. It is actually more of a label than a number, in that it is used only to determine which statement we are talking about. We can give a number to any statement in a program simply by putting any number from 1 through 99999 in front of the statement. For instance, we could have the following four statements:

```
999   Y = X + 1.0
      Z = X
  3   W = 4.5 * Z - 11.6
  7   X = W - Z
```

If we were then to refer to Statement 7, we would mean the statement

$$X = W - Z$$

This does *not* mean the seventh statement in the program; it means the statement whose number is 7. Similarly, if we were referring to Statement 999, we would mean the statement whose number is 999, that is, the statement

$$Y = X + 1.0$$

We can use any numbers, in any order, for any statements we choose. The only restriction is that *any given number may be used only once*. We cannot have two different statements with the same number.

Location of Statement Numbers on Punched Cards. We mentioned earlier that the first five columns of a punched card cannot be used for a FORTRAN statement. Instead, they are reserved for the statement number. The number can be punched anywhere in these columns, although most programmers prefer to place them right justified. Thus, the three statements punched on cards as

```
                                    ⌐ column 6
                               | ↙ |
(card 1)    100|  |X = 10.0
(card 2)    100 |  |X = 10.0
(card 3) 100  |  |       X = 10.0
               |  |
```

are equivalent.

THE GO TO *STATEMENT*

The general form of this statement is

$$GO\ TO\ n$$

where *n* is some statement number. This statement causes the program to jump to the statement whose number is *n*. For example, if we had

```
10   X = X + 1.0
     Y = 5.0 * X
     Y = X * Y + 1.0
     GO TO 10
```

then, after performing the statement Y = X * Y + 1.0, the program would go back and perform the statement X = X + 1.0. This program could also be represented by the flowchart boxes below.

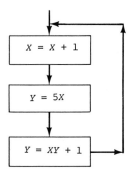

Of course, we would never use exactly this procedure in a real program because there is no way for it to stop. Usually, we would have a Decision box which would cause the program to stop after X got to a certain number.

The GO TO statement corresponds to the lines of flow in the flowchart. In the above example, the statement GO TO 10 corresponds to the line of flow returning to the first box.

THE ARITHMETIC IF STATEMENT

The arithmetic IF statement in FORTRAN corresponds to the Decision box in a flowchart. The general form of this statement is

IF (*E*) *a*, *b*, *c*

where *E* is any FORTRAN expression and *a*, *b*, and *c* are statement numbers. This statement works in this way: if *E* is less than zero, the next statement performed will be the statement whose number is *a*. Similarly, if *E* is equal to zero or greater than zero, the next statement performed is that whose number is *b* or *c*, respectively. So, depending on whether the expression in

53

parentheses is negative, zero, or positive, the IF statement acts like the statement GO TO *a*, GO TO *b*, or GO TO *c*.

If (*E*) *a*,*b*,*c*	if *E* < 0 then GO TO *a* if *E* = 0 then GO TO *b* if *E* > 0 then GO TO *c*

Example

If given the statements

```
        X = -10.0
10      X = X + 1.0
        Y = 10.0 * X
        If (X) 10, 20, 30
20      Y = 5.0
30      STOP
```

we would follow the procedure shown in the following flowchart.

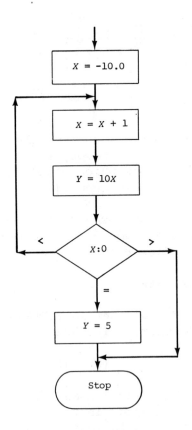

In this example, the IF statement is executed ten times, the first nine times transferring control back to Statement 10. But on the tenth time, X is zero and so control transfers to Statement 20. In this case, the IF statement never branches to Statement 30. Instead, it is executed in normal sequence.

Example

Now suppose we want to compare two numbers, A and B, and we want to go to Statement 5 if A is less than B, Statement 1 if A equals B, or Statement 900 if A is greater than B. The flowchart box would be

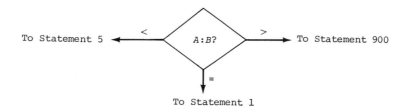

The corresponding IF statement would be

$$IF \ (A - B) \ 5, \ 1, \ 900$$

In this statement, notice that we compare the expression $A - B$ to zero. This accomplishes the same thing as comparing A to B, for

$$A - B < 0 \text{ if and only if } A < B$$
$$A - B = 0 \text{ if and only if } A = B$$
$$A - B > 0 \text{ if and only if } A > B$$

We can also make any two of the statement numbers a, b, and c the same. (Actually, we could make all three the same but, of course, that would be the same as a GO TO statement.) For example, the Decision box

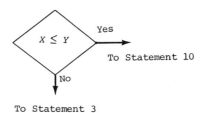

55

would be programmed as

$$IF \ (X - Y) \ 10, \ 10, \ 3$$

Similarly, the Decision box

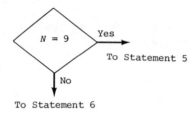

would be programmed as

$$IF \ (N - 9) \ 6, \ 5, \ 6$$

Although the quantity inside the parentheses of the IF statement is often a single variable or a difference of two variables, it can be any FORTRAN expression. If we wanted to go to Statement 10 or 20, according to whether $(5xy + 14)z$ is zero or not, we could write

$$IF \ ((5.0 * X * Y + 14.0) * Z) \ 20, \ 10, \ 20$$

To get a better idea of how control statements are used in a program, let us consider some simple examples.

Example 1

Write a program to set the value of Y equal to the absolute value of X, then stop. For this we need only one Decision box. If X is less than zero, we set Y equal to $-X$; if X is greater than or equal to zero, we set Y equal to X. This would be written in FORTRAN as

```
      IF (X) 5, 10, 10
   5  Y = -X
      STOP
  10  Y = X
      STOP
```

Notice that two STOP statements are used. If the first of these were omitted, Y would always be equal to X when STOP was reached. Why? Rather than use two STOP statements, we could use a GO TO statement if we preferred, and put

56

```
        IF (X) 5, 10, 10
    5   Y = -X
        GO TO 15
   10   Y = X
   15   STOP
```

In this case, it really does not make any difference which way
we do it.

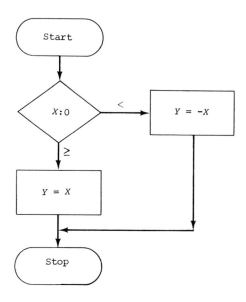

Example 2

Find the sum of the integers from 1 to *N*. For the moment,
we shall ignore input and output statements. At the beginning
of the program, let us set *N* equal to 20, and when we are done
we shall stop, rather than writing out the answer.   The flowchart will be as shown on the following page.

Since we are dealing with integers, we use the integer
variables N, I, and ISUM. We initialize these, and proceed to
add I to ISUM:

```
            N = 20
            ISUM = 0
            I = 1
            ISUM = ISUM + I
```

57

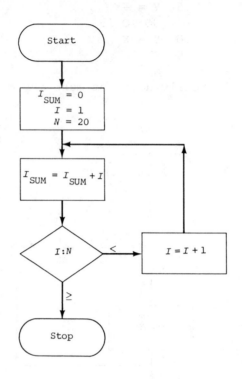

Then, we use an IF statement to compare I to N. If I is less than N, we want to add 1 to I, and the statement to do this will need a statement number, say 10. If I is equal to or greater than N, we want to stop, and we shall give a statement number 20 to a STOP statement. So far, we have added the statements

```
        IF (I - N) 10, 20, 20
   10   I = I + 1
   20   STOP
```

This does not yet specify what we want it to, however, for as written, the program will always stop immediately after performing Statement 10. Actually, after performing this statement, we want to go back to the statement

$$ISUM = ISUM + I$$

so we shall make this Statement 5, and after Statement 10 we shall use a GO TO statement to return. The completed program is as follows:

```
            N = 20
            ISUM = 0
            I = 1
      5     ISUM = ISUM + I
            IF (I - N) 10, 20, 20
     10     I = I + 1
            GO TO 5
     20     STOP
```

An alternate set of statements accomplishes the same thing as the set just discussed. These are

```
            N = 20
            ISUM = 0
            I = 1
      5     ISUM = ISUM + I
            I = I + 1
            IF (I - N) 5, 5, 10
     10     STOP
```

Notice that the GO TO 5 statement has now been eliminated. This is a more desirable way to write the statements, since it is more efficient.

Example 3

The problem is to determine whether an integer N is even or odd. This can be done using fixed-point arithmetic. Recall that if 2 does not divide N exactly, then the fixed-point $N/2$ will be truncated. For example, $9/2 = 4$. Now consider $(9/2) \times 2$. This is $4 \times 2 = 8$. Since 2 divides 10, $(10/2) \times 2$ is $5 \times 2 = 10$. In general, if $(N/2) \times 2$ is equal to N, then N must be even. If it is not equal to N, then N must be odd.

Suppose in a program, we want to set L equal to zero and go to Statement 100 if N is even, and we want to set L equal to one and go to Statement 200 if N is odd. This could be done using the procedure given in the flowchart on the following page.

This method can be programmed as in the following FORTRAN statements:

```
            IF ((N/2) * 2 - N) 5, 10, 5
      5     L = 1
            GO TO 200
     10     L = 0
            GO TO 100
```

Each IF statement corresponds to a single decision. Frequently, however, we may want to perform some instruction only

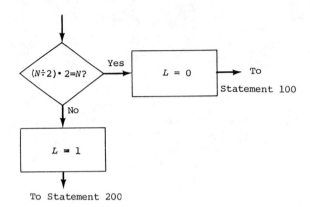

if both $A \leq B$ and $B \leq C$. This sort of situation may easily be treated by using a series of IF statements. The following example demonstrates this method.

Example 4

Given three numbers A, B, and C, we want to set D equal to 0, 1, or 2 according to the following rules:

If both $A \leq B$ and $B \leq C$, set $D = 0$.
If $A \leq B$ or $B \leq C$, but not both, set $D = 1$.
If neither $A \leq B$ nor $B \leq C$, set $D = 2$.

In order to solve this problem, we can first compare A to B. If $A \leq B$, then we compare B to C and then set D equal to 0 or 1, depending on whether $B \leq C$ or not. On the other hand, if $A > B$, we again compare B to C and set D equal to 1 or 2, depending on whether $B \leq C$ or not. This process may perhaps be seen more clearly by referring to the flowchart opposite.

The FORTRAN program for this procedure uses three IF statements, that is, one for each of the Decision boxes in the flowchart. The final program reads:

```
        IF (A - B) 10, 10, 20
    10  IF (B - C) 30, 30, 40
    20  IF (B - C) 40, 40, 50
    30  D = 0.0
        GO TO 60
    40  D = 1.0
        GO TO 60
    50  D = 2.0
    60  Next Statement
```

60

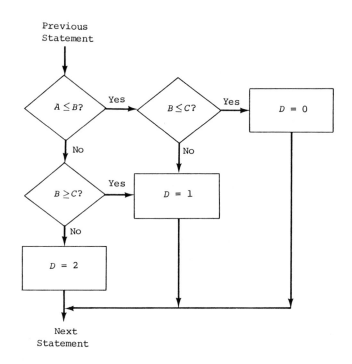

Notice how the IF statements are interrelated. Notice also that two GO TO statements are used. Could we omit these two statements? Why not?

Example 5

A parcel of land is shown in Figure 3-1. The boundaries are the x- and y-axes, and a curve whose shape is described by the equation $y = -4x^2 + 16$, where x and y are in miles. You are asked to find the point P on the boundary for which the rectangle shown in the figure will have the maximum area.

You can solve it by writing a computer program in which you take values of x starting with $x = 0$ and going up to $x = 2$ in increments of .01.

To solve this problem, we shall use a variable *AMAX* to denote the maximum area, and we shall let *PX* and *PY* be the x and y coordinates of the point P where this maximum area is attained. To find the values of *AMAX*, *PX*, and *PY*, we note that if X is any number between 0 and 2, then the value of the corresponding Y on the curve is $Y = -4X^2 + 16$, and the area of the rectangle with the point (X,Y) at the corner is $A = XY$.

61

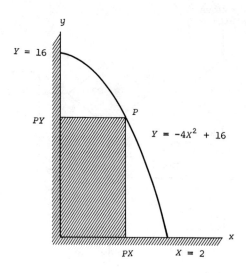

FIGURE 3-1

The central step in the program will be comparing this value *A* with the previous maximum area *AMAX*. If *A* is greater than *AMAX*, we shall replace the value of *AMAX* by the value of *A*, and also replace the values of *PX* and *PY* by the values of *X* and *Y*. If *A* is less than *AMAX*, we shall just increment *X* and continue the process until we reach *X* = 2.

The complete process is shown in the following flowchart. This procedure can be programmed in FORTRAN using two IF statements, one for each Decision box of the flowchart. The program is shown below:

```
       AMAX = 0.0
       X = .01
 10    Y = -4.0 * X * X + 16.0
       A = X * Y
       IF (A - AMAX) 20, 20, 15
 15    AMAX = A
       PX = X
       PY = Y
 20    X = X + .01
       IF (X - 2.0) 10, 10, 30
 30    Next Statement
```

62

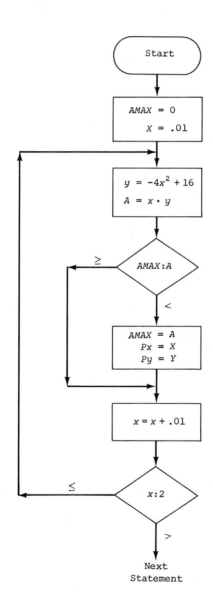

COMMENT CARDS

As our FORTRAN programs become longer, we shall need to check back over the program quickly and determine what is being done at some particular point. *Comment cards* help us to do this. These are any cards that have the letter C punched in column one together with whatever else we want to write on the cards. These cards are not processed by the FORTRAN translator but will be listed out when the whole program is printed. Thus, we could write the previous program as follows:

```
COMMENT THIS IS AN EXAMPLE OF A COMMENT CARD
C          PROGRAM TO FIND LARGEST RECTANGLE
C          THAT WILL FIT UNDER A GIVEN CURVE
C
C          AMAX WILL BE THE AREA OF THIS RECTANGLE
C          FIRST SET AMAX = 0.0
           AMAX = 0.0
C          START WITH X = .01
           X = .01
    10     Y = -4.0 * X * X + 16.0
C          A IS USED AS AREA ALSO
           IF (A - AMAX) 20, 15, 15
    15     AMAX = A
           PX = X
           PY = Y
C          INCREMENT X
    20     X = X + .01
           IF (X - 2.0) 10, 10, 30
    30     Next Statement
C
C          WE ARE NOW THROUGH
C
```

A good programmer uses many comment cards. Several reasons for their use are:

1. Comment cards can be used to give an abstract of the program. This is especially helpful if another person will be using the program.

2. A listing of the variable names and what they represent is often made at the start of the program.

3. Special directions in the use of the program can be noted using comment cards.

When writing a program, be careful that the program eventually reaches a STOP statement. We could have a program containing the statements

```
10   GO TO 20
20   GO TO 10
```

In this case, no provision has been made to terminate the program. Such a situation occurs not as infrequently as one might expect, although the error is usually not so obvious.

In the next example, we consider a numerical computation in which this problem could arise in a more subtle fashion.

Example 6. A Recursive Method of Finding a Square Root

There are several methods to find the square root of a number in FORTRAN. In this example, we shall use a recursive method. The method used is as follows:

1. To begin, take any estimate X of the square root of Y, say X = Y/2.

2. Divide Y by X to obtain the quotient Z = Y/X.

3. For a new estimate of the square root of Y, take the average of X and Z.

It can be shown that this new estimate will be closer to the true square root than the original estimate. We continue the process to get better and better estimates until we have reached the desired degree of accuracy. The method is illustrated in the table below, calculating the square root of 3.

Y = 3

Estimate X	Quotient Q = Y/X	New Estimate X' = 1/2 (X + Q)
1.5	2.0	1.75
1.75	1.7143	1.7321
1.7321	1.7319	1.7320

Actual $\sqrt{3}$ = 1.73205080756 ...

Now, consider the following FORTRAN program to set SQRTY equal to the square root of Y, using the above method.

```
        Y = 3.0
        X = Y/2.0
   10   Q = Y/X
        X = (X + Q)/2.0
        IF (X * X - Y) 10, 20, 10
   20   SQRTY = X
        Next Statement
```

The computation is straightforward. In the IF statement, we compare X^2 to Y. If they are equal, we go to Statement 20; otherwise, we repeat the process. At first glance, this seems reasonable enough. The trouble is that we are going to run into the problem mentioned earlier: the process will not necessarily terminate. The reason is this. Correct to five places, $\sqrt{3}$ = 1.73205. But $(1.73205)^2$ = 2.99999726250 which, although very close, is not exactly three. So, when we compared X^2 to Y, they would not be exactly equal, and the process would continue. Even if we have the best possible estimate of X correct to *n* places, the test may fail. Whether it actually does or not depends on how many digits the particular machine can handle.

In order to avoid this problem, we shall test to see if X^2 is close enough to Y in absolute value. We shall test to see if $\left| X^2 - Y \right|$ < .0001. If this is true, then it can easily be shown that for Y < 10,000, X will be correct to eight places. Now, $\left| X^2 - Y \right| < 10^{-4}$ means that $X^2 - Y$ is very close to zero—in fact, it is between -10^{-4} and 10^{-4}. This means that $X^2 - Y$ is greater than -10^{-4} and less than 10^{-4}.

We can use two IF statements in the program to accomplish the comparison. If both of the above conditions are met, we set SQRTY equal to X. Otherwise, we would go back and find a better estimate. The final program and flowchart for this example are shown below and on the following page, respectively.

```
        Y = 3.0
        X = Y/2.0
   10   Q = Y/X
        X = (X + Q)/2.0
        IF (X * X - Y - 1.0E - 4) 20, 10, 10
   20   IF (X * X - Y + 1.0E - 4) 10, 10, 30
   30   SQRTY = X
        Next Statement
```

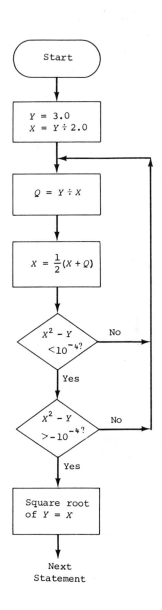

A EXERCISES

For each of the following Decision boxes, write an IF statement which will perform the test and go to the statement number indicated.

1.

2.

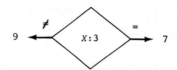

3.

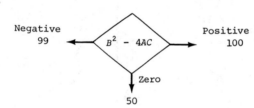

4.

5.

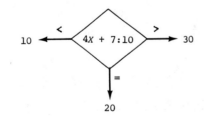

6.

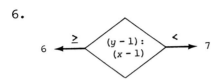

6 $\xleftarrow{\geq}$ $(y-1):(x-1)$ $\xrightarrow{<}$ 7

7.

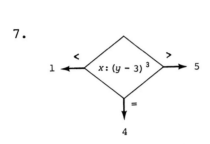

1 $\xleftarrow{<}$ $x:(y-3)^3$ $\xrightarrow{>}$ 5

$\downarrow$ =

4

8.

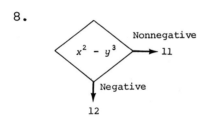

$x^2 - y^3$ $\xrightarrow{\text{Nonnegative}}$ 11

$\downarrow$ Negative

12

9.

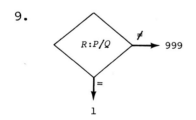

$R:P/Q$ $\xrightarrow{\neq}$ 999

$\downarrow$ =

1

10.

$$5 \xleftarrow{\ >\ } \boxed{L:M^N} \xrightarrow{\ \leq\ } 4$$

For each of the following IF statements, draw the corresponding Decision box.

11. IF (X - Y) 5, 15, 10

12. IF (N - M * N) 1, 2, 3

13. IF (J) 5, 10, 5

14. IF (R * S - 1.0) 10, 10, 20

15. IF (M + N) 5, 1, 1

16. IF (M + N - 1) 3, 1, 2

17. IF (X - Y - R) 1, 90, 1

18. IF (3.0 - R + (X - S)) 99, 100, 101

19. IF (P/Q - R) 4, 5, 5

20. IF (B - C + D - E) 2, 1, 3

For each of the following IF statements, give the values of X for which control will pass to Statements 10, 20, and 30.

21. IF (X - 9.0) 10, 20, 30

22. IF (X * X - 9.0) 10, 20, 30

23. IF (X + 6.0) 10, 20, 30

24. IF (-X + 3.0) 10, 20, 30

25. IF (6.0 - (X * 2.0 + 4.0)) 10, 20, 30

26. IF (X ** 2 - 2.0 * X + 1.0) 10, 20, 30

27. IF (X * (X - 2)) 10, 20, 30

28. IF (X - X ** 2) 10, 20, 10   29. IF (X * X) 30, 20, 10

70

For each of the following sets of Decision boxes, write sets of
IF statements to accomplish what is indicated. An example
follows:

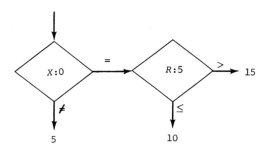

The information in the above flowchart could be written in
FORTRAN as two IF statements:

$$\text{IF (X) 5, 6, 5}$$
$$\text{6 IF (R - 5) 10, 10, 15}$$

Notice that it was necessary to make up some statement number
for the second IF statement.

30.

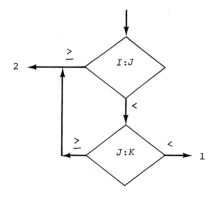

31.

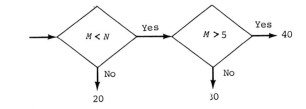

32.

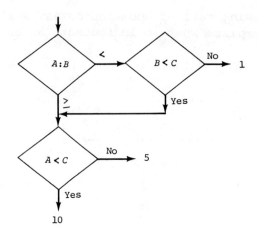

33.

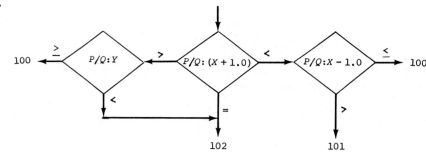

34.

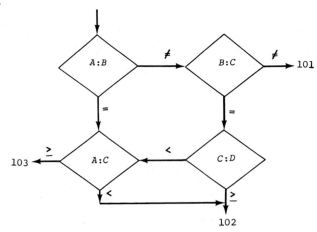

For each of the following sets of IF statements, write Decision boxes to indicate what is being done.

35.   IF (A – B) 5, 10, 5   38.   IF (A – B) 5, 15, 10
    10 IF (B – C) 5, 15, 5   5   IF (B – C) 100, 15, 15
                                        10   IF (B – C) 15, 15, 100
36.   IF (M – N) 1, 1, 2
     1 IF (L – M) 3, 2, 2   39.   IF (X – Z) 10, 99, 99
                                        10   IF (Z – W) 100, 20, 20
37.   IF (M – N – 1) 5, 10, 10   20   IF (W – X) 100, 99, 99
     5 IF (N – 1 – M)15, 10, 10

B EXERCISES

Write a flowchart and a program for each of the following problems.

1. If I is even, set $J = 0$, and if I is odd, set $J = 1$.

2. Find the sum of the positive integers which are multiples of three and less than 100.

3. If I is zero or nine, set $J = 10$. Otherwise, set $J = I$.

4. If neither I nor J is zero, set $K = 0$.
    If either I or J is zero, set $K = 1$.
    If both I and J are zero, set $K = 2$.

5. If the integer M is evenly divisible by the integer N, set $K = 0$. Otherwise, set $K = 1$.

6. The accompanying flowchart shows how to set a variable called MAX equal to the maximum value of I, J, or K. Write the corresponding FORTRAN program.

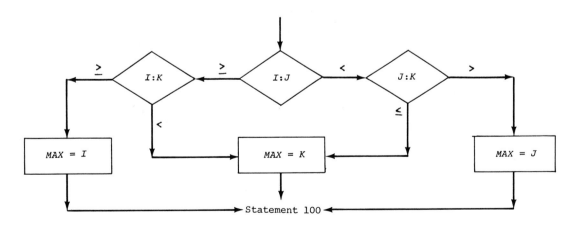

7. What is the final value of ISUM in each of the examples below? Does it matter whether I is incremented before or after it is added to ISUM?

```
      ISUM = 0                    ISUM = 0
       I = 0                       I = 0
  5   I = I + 1              5    ISUM = ISUM + I
      ISUM = ISUM + I              I = I + 1
      IF (I - 4) 5, 10, 10         IF (I - 4) 5, 10, 10
 10   STOP                   10   STOP
```

8. In a certain country, income tax is computed according to the following schedule:

Income	Tax
Less than $200.00	No tax
$201.00–$500.00	2% tax
$501.00–$1000.00	3% tax
$1001.00 and up	4% tax

Write a program to compute the tax, TAX, from a given income, XINC.

9. Referring to Problem B8, Chapter 1, write a program to compute the Legendre polynomial $P_n(x)$, where n is between zero and 5, inclusive.

10. Referring to Problem B5, Chapter 1, write a program to compute the binomial coefficient C_{nk}.

11. Write a program to average a set of numbers as in Chapter 1 (see pages 17–18).

12. The exponential function e^x is defined by

$$e^x = 1 + x + x^2/2! + x^3/3! + x^4/4! + \cdots$$

Write a program to compute EX = e^x for a given value of x. Since a computer cannot add an infinite number of terms, ignore all the terms from $x^7/7!$ on.

13. At a certain bank, the monthly service charge on checking accounts is computed as in the following table:

$.10 per check for the first five checks
.09 per check for the next five checks
.08 per check for the next five checks
.07 per check on all the rest of the checks for the month

74

13.—*continued*

The total monthly charge is the total amount of checks plus the monthly service charge. Write a program to compute the total charge for a given number of checks.

14. (The Euclidian Algorithm) The *greatest common divisor* (abbreviated GCD) of two integers M and N is defined to be the greatest number which divides both of them evenly. There is a classic method for finding this number (assume that N is greater than M):

> *Step 1:* Divide N by M and find the remainder MR.
>
> *Step 2:* If MR is zero, then M is the GCD of M and N, so output M and stop.
>
> *Step 3:* If MR is not zero, replace the value of N by the value of M, replace the value of M by the value of MR, and go back to Step 1.

It can be shown mathematically that the GCD of N and M is the same as the GCD of M and MR (unless MR equals zero). Write a program to compute the GCD of two given numbers.

15. If $y = -2.0x^2 + 4.0x - 2.0$, find the maximum and minimum values of y for $-2.0 \leq x \leq 2.0$ by trying out values of x in this range, incrementing x by .1 each time.

16. Given three floating-point numbers A, B, and C, determine whether or not there is a triangle whose sides have lengths A, B, and C. If there is, set AREA equal to the area of the triangle. If there is no such triangle, set AREA = -1.0.

17. Each of the equations

$$y = Ax + B \quad \text{and} \quad y = Cx + D$$

has a graph that is a straight line. These lines might be the same, or they might be parallel, or they might intersect in a point. You are given values for A, B, C, and D. If the lines intersect in a point, set $N = 1$ and set X and Y equal to the coordinates of the point. If the two lines are the same, set $N = 0$ and set $X = Y = 0.0$. If the lines are parallel, set $N = -1$, $X = Y = 0.0$.

18. Since a computer is not perfectly accurate, small errors will exist in all floating-point arithmetic. Normally, these are negligible, but small errors can accumulate. To see this, write a routine to find the square root of a number. Using this routine, write a program to do the following:

   a. Set Y equal to the square root of X.
   b. Set X equal to Y^2 and go back to Step a.
   c. Do this 100 times.

19. The Ninth National Bank of Timbuktu pays 5% interest compounded quarterly on savings accounts. Inflation in Timbuktu amounts to about 3% per year (which means that a dollar today will be worth only 97¢ a year from now). If Harvey Clyde puts $100.00 in a savings account, how many years will it take for his savings to grow to the equivalent (in today's money) of $1000.00?

Chapter 4

INPUT AND OUTPUT: PART I

Up to this point, we have learned how to do many manipulations in FORTRAN. However, we have tacitly assumed that the
numbers were already stored in the computer. Actually, of
course, we generally would want to read in data along with the
program, and when we have calculated the results, we would want to
present them in some manner so as to give us a permanent record.
A number of different types of devices are used for input
and output. Card readers, printers, card punches, magnetic
tapes, magnetic disk units, paper tape readers, and remote
terminals are all commonly used for this purpose. For the
beginner, though, the *card reader* and the *printer* are probably
the only machines that would be used, and so we shall confine
our attention to these two devices in this chapter. Others
will be treated in a later chapter.

The card reader is a machine that reads punched cards by
sensing the pattern of punched holes in the card. Each card
consists of 80 columns, and the pattern of holes in each column represents one character. By a character, we mean the
letters A-Z, any digit 0-9, or any other FORTRAN symbol, such
as +, -, =, ·, and * (see p. 43).

The printer is a machine that is used to output results.
The number of characters per line varies with the model of the
printer. Nearly all printers can handle at least 120 characters
per line, with some as many as 144. Each page of printed output
has 66 possible lines. Here again, we are free to determine
just what the output will look like; we may not know what values
will be printed, but we can decide how many of them will be
printed on each line, what headings will appear, and so forth.
All of this information must be specified by the FORTRAN program.

Different input-output devices are distinguished by different *unit numbers* in FORTRAN. Unit 9 might be a magnetic tape
unit and Unit 4 might be a card punch. The actual method of
determining what number corresponds to what varies among different computers. For the sake of being definite, we shall assume
that:

    Unit 1 is a card reader.
    Unit 2 is a printer.

In this chapter, we shall learn how to input data into the computer and output our results. There are many forms of the FORTRAN statements that do these operations. This chapter gives the simplest forms of input and output so that complete FORTRAN programs can be run.

THE READ *STATEMENT*

Each input operation in FORTRAN involves two statements: a READ statement and a FORMAT statement. The READ statement tells three things about the input operation:

1. It tells what device (unit) the data are to be read from (card reader, magnetic tape unit, etc.).

2. It tells what storage locations are to receive the values of the numbers read.

3. It tells what FORMAT statement is to be used to specify the arrangement of the numbers on the card. (This will be explained in more detail after the READ statement is introduced.)

The general form of the READ statement is

$$\text{READ } (u, f) \; var_1, \; var_2, \; var_3, \; \cdots, \; var_n$$

where

u is the unit number which tells which device the data are to be read from. Since we are assuming that the number 1 designates a card reader, we would put 1 for u in order to read a card.[1]

f is the statement number of the FORMAT statement to be used for reading the data.

$var_1, \; var_2, \; var_3, \; ..., \; var_n$ are the names of FORTRAN variables that are to receive the values read in.

Notice that the variables are separated by a comma but that there is no comma before the first variable.

Some examples of READ statements that illustrate this general rule are as follow.

---

[1] The unit number can also be a fixed-point variable.

READ (1, 10)X

tells the computer to read in a value of the variable X.

READ (1, 100) A, B, C

tells the computer to read in three values to be assigned to the variables A, B, and C.

READ (1, 11) I, J, K, ABC

tells the computer to read in four values to be assigned to the variables I, J, K, and ABC.

The unit number 1 in the above three READ statements means that we are reading from the card reader. The numbers 10, 100, and 11 refer to FORMAT statements, which will be covered in the following section.

THE FORMAT *STATEMENT*

We are allowed a great deal of flexibility in deciding the format of our data, but unless we used a FORMAT statement, the computer would have no way of knowing just what we had decided on. For instance, we can read in values for two variables *I* and *J* by punching two numbers right next to each other on a card. Say that we want to punch 11 for the value to be read for *I* and 22 for the value to be read for *J*. The card could look like this:

How is the computer to know that we mean that the two numbers are 11 and 22? If we had wanted the two numbers to be 112 and 2, or 1 and 122, we could have punched the same card. This is the sort of question that is answered for the machine by the FORMAT statement.

The FORMAT statement has the form

FORMAT (*desc* 1, *desc* 2, $\cdots$, *desc* N)

where each of the *desc* 1, *desc* 2, and so on, are *field descriptors* specifying the format on one data item of the card.

The FORMAT statement is a declaration, or nonexecutable statement, which means that it does not do anything in itself (that is, it causes no machine action); it is used only in conjunction with some executable statement, in this case the READ statement. The FORMAT statement can appear anywhere in the program. In fact, some programmers like to put all the FORMAT statements together at the end of the program. Others prefer to put all of them at the beginning, or to put each one immediately following the first input or output statement which uses it. This does not make any difference, since the FORMAT statement is used only to describe the arrangement of data for an input or output statement. We now see how these two statements interact.

Every time a READ statement is performed, a new card is read from the card reader. The READ statement interacts with FORMAT statement number *f* and then uses the first field descriptor (desc 1) to determine what form the first number has. This number is then interpreted according to this descriptor and assigned to the first variable in the list of the READ statement (var 1). Likewise, the second field descriptor in the FORMAT statement determines where the second number on the card is, and how this number is interpreted to become the value of the second variable in the list, and so on for all of the variables in the list. Notice that the list must consist entirely of variables. Constants and expressions are not allowed, because they cannot be assigned a value.

FIELD LENGTHS

There is a great deal of freedom in determining how data are to be punched onto a card. For instance, in writing a program to read in several numbers and find their average, we might want to punch one number per card, or to save cards, we might want to punch eight numbers on each card, right next to each other. In writing a program to do a company payroll, we might want to have one card for each employee containing his employee number, the number of hours he worked during the month, and his wage rate.

We are at liberty to set up data in almost any way we choose, but once we decide how the data are to be punched, we have to construct the FORMAT statements in a FORTRAN program to tell the machine how to read in the data correctly.

In the payroll program, suppose we have decided that an employee's card is going to have the following format:

Columns	1-4	Employee number
Columns	5-9	Wage rate
Columns	10-13	Number of hours worked
Columns	14-80	Blank

We call each group of columns containing one of these items a
field on the card. A sample card for some employee might look
like this:

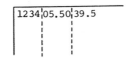

The numbers in the first field on this card (columns one-four)
indicate that the card is for employee number 1234. The numbers
in the second field (columns five-nine) show that he earns $5.50
per hour,and the numbers in the third field (columns ten-thirteen)
specify that he worked 39.5 hours. The FORTRAN program that
reads this card would have to specify that the first field consists of the first four columns, rather than the first three or
the first five, and it would have to tell the machine where to
store this number, that is, what variable receives the value
read in. We shall see how this is done in FORTRAN a little
later on in the chapter.

FIELD DESCRIPTORS

As mentioned before, the FORMAT statement consists of one
or more field descriptors. The field descriptors that we shall
be using may be one of the following types:

> I—used to read or write integer numbers.
> F—used to read or write floating-point numbers.
> E—used to read or write numbers in exponential form.
> X—used only for skipping spaces.
> H—used to print headings on a page of output.

The I Field Descriptor—Input. Used for input, the I field
descriptor means that we are reading an integer number. The
general form is

$$I n$$

where *n* is an unsigned integer constant which tells how many
characters long the field is. Thus, if an integer number is
punched in the first seven columns of a card, to read in the
number as a value for the integer variable LIMIT, we would use
the statements

          READ (1, 2) LIMIT
    2 FORMAT (I7)

The number punched in the card can be preceded by blank spaces, and these will be treated as though they were zeros. So 0065 and 65 are considered to be the same number. Although it is not essential to use zeros this way, some programmers prefer to do it since it is much easier to count characters than blanks on a card. If the number is positive, we can either punch a + in front of the number or omit it, and the number will be read as positive. If the number is negative, we must punch a minus sign in front of the number. Some examples of what would be read by the above two statements for various input are given in the table below. The b's stand for blank spaces (we wrote in the b's here to make them easier to count).

Character in Columns 1-7 of the Card	Resulting Value of the Variable LIMIT
bbb+100	+100
bbbb100	+100
0000100	+100
bb-5432	-5432
-bb5432	-5432
b-b5432	-5432
b+bbbbb	0
-bbbbbb	0
bbbbbbb	0

In general, all blanks in a field on an input data card are processed exactly as if they were zeros. While blanks to the left of a digit are not significant, blanks which follow a digit *are* significant. These also are treated as zeros, with enough zeros being inserted to fill up the field.

The table below shows what would happen for various input, using the statements

        READ (1, 97) J
    97 FORMAT (I5)

Characters in Columns 1-5 of the Card	Resulting Value of the Variable J
bb5bb	+500
5bbbb	+50000
-bb32	-32
b-11b	-110
b+11b	+110
bbbbb	0
b1b1b	+1010

82

If we want to read several integer numbers from the same card, we just use several I field descriptors, separated by commas, in the FORMAT statement. Then each of the fields will be read according to the above rules and the value will be stored in the corresponding variable in the list of the READ statement. If the first nineteen columns of a card contained the characters

```
-12b1bb229-03330011
```

(where, again, the b's indicate blank spaces), then the statements

        READ (1, 77) JIG, JACK, MOM, N1, LEM
     77 FORMAT (I3, I2, I5, I5, I4)

would result in the following values for the variables:

                    JIG = -12
                   JACK = 1
                    MOM = 229
                     N1 = -333
                    LEM = 11

The F Field Descriptor—Input. In the preceding discussion, we were talking only about integer numbers. Floating-point numbers are handled similarly, but there is the additional consideration of where to put the decimal point. In reading floating-point numbers from a card, it is quite often convenient not to have to punch the decimal point. For example, if we were reading the amounts of purchases for a billing program, all the input might be in dollars and cents, and we would know that every number read is supposed to have a decimal point in front of the last two digits. Instead of punching the decimal point in the same place for each number read, we could leave it off the card. The F field descriptor will insert the decimal point and specify it automatically when reading the number.

The form of the F field descriptor is

$$F n.m$$

where n is the number of characters in the field to be read, and m is the number of decimal places that will be assumed if there is no decimal point punched in the number being read. If there is a decimal point punched, m will be ignored and the number will be read exactly as punched. If no decimal point is desired, m is 0 (*not* blank).

The *n* serves the same purpose here as it does in the I field description; it tells how many columns wide the field is. This field width includes both the plus or minus sign, if there is one, and the decimal point, if there is one. *If the decimal point is punched, the m has no meaning, and is ignored.* It is used only if we want to omit actually punching the decimal point, but we want to insert it automatically during the reading process. In this case, the machine reads in the *n* characters which make up the field and puts a decimal point in front of the *m*th character from the right. For instance, if the characters 3333 were punched in the first four columns of a card, and if they were read in under an F4.2 format, they would be stored as the number +33.33. The 4 in the F4.2 means that four characters are to be read (that the field is four characters long), and the 2 means that a decimal point is to be placed in front of the second character from the right if there is no decimal point punched on the card. If there is a decimal point punched on the card, it overrides the assumed decimal point, and so it can be punched anywhere in the field. Thus, if .333 were read under an F4.2 format, it would be read as .333, not as 3.33. The number *m* can be zero, and in this case no decimal point is assumed if one is not punched. The characters b-456 read under an F5.0 format would be stored as -456.0.

The table below gives some examples of what the value of a floating-point variable T would be if the input shown were read with the statements

```
      READ (1, 6) T
    6 FORMAT (F8.2)
```

Characters Punched in Columns 1-8	Resulting Value of T
bb44.600	+44.6
bbb-1231	-12.31
bb-12310	-123.1
-bbbb2.2	-2.2
-bbbb222	-2.22
-2.22bbb	-2.22
-222bbbb	-22200.0
bbbbb1bb	+1.0
bbbbbb1b	+0.1
bb-b101b	-10.1
bb-1.01b	-1.01

As the table indicates, the same rules apply for leading and trailing blank spaces as did for the I field description; they are read as though they were zeros. Again, note the important rule: If a decimal point is punched in the data to be read, trailing blanks do not make any difference in the value that will be read in. Any zeros after a decimal point do not change the value of a number. In other words, 1.6 is the same number as 1.6000. If no decimal point is punched in the number read, trailing blanks will make a difference, since they are counted in determining where the assumed decimal point is to be placed. If 3bb is punched in the first three columns of a card, and it is read under an F3.1 format, the two blank spaces are assumed to be before the first character from the right. So the number would be read as +30.0.

The E Field Descriptor—Input. The E field descriptor is used to input floating-point numbers in the exponential form. Recall that a number in this form can be written as

$$iii.fff \text{ E } ee$$

and this is interpreted by FORTRAN to mean the number

$$iii.fff \times 10^{ee}$$

For example, the number -56.4E-3 means -56.4×10^{-3}, which is -0.0564.

A number in exponential form is composed of three parts: the integer part; the fraction part; and the exponent. By the integer part, we mean the part of the number before the decimal point (the *iii* number above). Similarly, the fraction part is the part of the number after the decimal point (*fff*) but not including the exponent. The exponent is the number following the E. It may be preceded by either a plus or minus sign, or no sign at all, in which case it is assumed to be positive. When punching a number in a field to be read by an E field descriptor, any of these parts may be omitted. If the integer part is omitted (i.e., if no numbers are punched to the left of the decimal point), it is assumed to be zero. If the fraction part is omitted (i.e., if no decimal point is punched), we can automatically put in an assumed decimal point with the E field descriptor just as we did with the F field descriptor. If the exponent is omitted (i.e., if the E is not punched), the number is read just as it would be read by an F field descriptor.

The general form of the E field descriptor is

$$E n.m$$

where *n* is the field length, and *m* tells how many places to the left of the nonexponent part the decimal point is to be assumed if there is no decimal point punched.

When a number is read under the specification of E$n.m$, the following takes place:

First, the n characters which comprise the field are read in.

Second, if no decimal point is punched in the number read, a decimal point is assumed m places to the left of the nonexponent part of the number.

Third, this number is multiplied by 10 raised to the exponent read in. If the exponent read is e, this has the effect of shifting the decimal point e places to the right. If the exponent read is $-e$, this has the effect of shifting the decimal point e places to the left.

For example, if we read the data

bb11.22E4

with an E9.3 specification, the number is read as 11.22E4, which is 112200.0. If we had left out the decimal point, though, and punched

bbb1122E4

then the nonexponent part of this number is 1122, and this would be read as 1.122 because of the 3 in the E9.3, which means that there is to be an assumed decimal point before the third character from the right of the nonexponent part. Then after this is done, the resulting number is multiplied by 10^4, because the exponent read was 4. In other words, the decimal point is shifted four places to the right, so that the number is finally stored as 11220.0.

As with the F and I field descriptors, any blanks in the field are considered as zeros. So the data

b477bbE1

would be read by an E8.1 description as 04770.0×10^1, which is 47700, just as though the data

047700E1

had been read. If a decimal point is punched in the data read, then leading or trailing blanks will have no effect. If no decimal point is punched in the data read, blanks may make a considerable difference in the way the number is read, just as zeros would.

The following table gives some further examples of conversion in input data by the E field descriptor.

Input Data	Field Description	Resulting Value
1111.11	E7.3	+1111.11
1111.111	E7.3	+1111.111
4.7E2b	E6.0	+470.0
1234E-1bbb	E10.4	+0.01234
1234E+1bbb	E10.4	+1.234
1234bbbE 1	E10.4	+1234.0
2E1b	E4.0	+20.0
2bE1	E4.0	+200.0
-4.98	E5.1	-4.98
-b498	E5.1	-49.8
-498b	E5.1	-498.0
.3E+5	E5.2	+30000.0
.3E-3	E5.2	+0.0003
123E2	E5.1	+1230.0
123E-2	E6.1	+0.123
9E-1bb	E6.1	+0.09

THE WRITE *STATEMENT*

Output operations in FORTRAN are accomplished with the WRITE statement. This statement is quite similar to the READ statement. The general form is

WRITE (*u*, *f*) *var* 1, *var* 2, *var* 3, ···, *var* N

where

u is a unit number that determines what device the data is to be written on.

f is the statement number of the FORMAT statement to be used.

var 1, *var* 2, *var* 3, ···, *var* N are the variables whose values are to be output.

We have assumed that the number 2 designates the printer, so to write on the printer, *u* would be 2.

When this statement is performed, the first variable in the list (*var* 1) is printed according to the first field descriptor in FORMAT statement number f, then the second variable in the list is printed according to the second field descriptor, and so forth for all the variables in the list.

The I Field Descriptor—Output. Used for output, the I field descriptor means that we are printing the value of some integer variable. The form is the same, namely, In, where n is an unsigned integer constant. In this case, the n tells how big the output field is to be. I10, for instance, means that the number will occupy 10 print positions. This includes the minus sign, if the number printed is negative. If the number to be printed is less than 10 characters long (including the minus sign, if there is one), then it will be "right justified," which means that it will occupy the right-hand part of the 10 characters allotted, with the left-hand characters blank. A positive number will not be printed with a plus sign, but a negative number will have a minus sign preceding the first digit. The table below shows what would be printed for various values of an integer variable KAT, using the statements

```
        WRITE (2, 44) KAT
   44   FORMAT (I6)
```

Value of KAT	Number Printed
123	bbb123
-123	bb-123
0	bbbbb0
23344	b23344
-7777	b-7777

We obviously cannot print a seven-digit number in six print spaces—the greatest value KAT could have would be 999999, and the largest negative value KAT could have would be -99999, since if KAT were larger in magnitude there would be no room for the minus sign. What would actually be printed if we tried to use the above statements to print a number outside these bounds would depend on the particular computer used. Some machines might print out asterisks instead of the number to indicate that the field length had been exceeded. Another machine might just truncate the number and, hopefully, the programmer can figure out what happened. In still other machines, an error message will be printed out and execution of the program will be terminated. In any case, the result would not be the one desired, and care must be taken to make certain that the fields, as described in the FORMAT statement, are large enough to handle the data that will be printed. This is usually no problem, however. By using an I12 field descriptor, virtually any integer one would normally encounter could easily be handled. If the number to be printed were actually small, the leading spaces would just be filled with blanks, and this would cause no problem. Since printers normally provide 120 columns or more, plenty of space may be allowed for wide fields.

As with input, more than one variable can be printed with a single WRITE statement by using more than one field descriptor in the associated FORMAT statement. For example, if

```
            I = 100
            J = -545
            K = 3
            L = -888
```

then the statements

```
            WRITE (2, 2) I, J, K, L
        2   FORMAT (I4, I4, I2, I5)
```

would result in the output

```
            b100-545b3b - 888
```

(where the b's again mean blank); the actual output would be 100-545 3 - 888.

It is usually desirable to make the field large enough so that there will be some blank spaces printed. If

```
            N1 = 1
            N2 = 2
            N3 = 3
            N4 = 4
```

then the statements

```
            WRITE (2, 700) N1, N2, N3, N4
        700   FORMAT (I1, I1, I1, I1)
```

would result in the output

```
            1234
```

While this is legal, it would be more readable to use something like

```
        700   FORMAT (I3, I3, I3, I3)
```

which would print

```
            1  2  3  4
```

The F Field Descriptor—Output. When used for output, the F field descriptor determines how many decimal places the number printed will have, as well as how many characters of output the number will occupy. The form is the same as for input:

Fn.m

The *n* again tells how wide (how many characters) the output field is to be. The *m* in this case tells how many decimal places of the number are to be printed. Floating-point numbers are stored with more significant digits than we normally need to print. The number of significant digits printed is controlled by the *m* in the F*n*.*m* specification. For example, suppose that we have computed a variable PI and that it has a value of 3.14159265. If we want to print this value, but we want only the first four decimal places, we can use the statements

```
        WRITE (2, 5) PI
  5 FORMAT (F9.4)
```

and this would result in the output

bbb3.1416

The field length is nine characters, including the blanks and the decimal point, and four decimal places are printed. Notice that the number is rounded rather than truncated to 3.1415-. If we had used a field description of F9.0 in the above FORMAT statement, the resulting output would have been

bbbbbbbb3

with no places to the right of the decimal point. In this case the decimal point itself is also omitted.

The table below shows what numbers would be output for various values of the variable X, using the statements

```
        WRITE (2, 31) X
 31 FORMAT (F8.3)
```

Value of X	Output
+21.3	bb21.300
5.0	bbb5.000
-2.34567	bb-2.346
-0.01	bb-0.010
-50.0	b-50.000
-1234.0	too big—results uncertain
.0005	bbb0.001 (the 5 is rounded)
-0.0005	bb-0.001 (the 5 is rounded, but minus sign remains)

The E Field Descriptor—Output. When used for output, the E field descriptor has the same form as it does for input:

E*n.m*

The *n* is again the overall field length, and the *m* is the number of decimal places to be printed. The E field is very useful for printing numbers which may be quite large or quite small, because such numbers can be represented compactly in the exponential form. The number 100,000,000,000,000, for example, can be written as .1E+15.

A number written with an E*n.m* format will always be printed as some number greater than or equal to .1 and less than 1.0, and it will have an exponent to show the scale factor. The first thing printed will be a blank if the number is positive, or a minus sign if the number is negative. Then a decimal point appears, preceded on some computers by a zero. This is followed by the first *m* significant digits of the number. Next comes the letter E, followed by a plus or minus sign, and finally the exponent, written as two digits.

For example, the number 100.0 would be written as b.10E+03 under an E8.2 format. If the field length is bigger than needed, the number is printed in the right-most positions, and the spaces on the left are printed as blanks. So, if 100.0 were printed using an E12.2 field description, the output would be bbbbb.10E+03. The number of decimal places (*m*) is the number of significant digits we want printed. Even if the number to be printed has more than *m* nonzero digits, only the first *m* of them will be printed, and the others will simply be rounded off. This means that if X = 614.753, for instance, then the statements

```
      WRITE (2, 91) X
91    FORMAT (E8.2)
```

would result in the output

b.61E+03

Since the E8.2 field specified that only two decimal places are to be printed, the rest of the number is lost. In order to get six significant digits printed, we would have to use a format of at least E12.6. This would print the number as

b.614753E+03

Notice that when using an E*n.m* field description, *n* must be equal to at least *m* + 6. This is because one position is required for the sign of the number, one for the decimal point,

m positions are required for the number itself, and four more
positions are needed for the letter E, the sign of the exponent,
and the exponent itself. Thus, a field description such as E5.2
would be too small to print any number, and the result of trying to print a number with such a format would be unpredictable
(on some machines, asterisks would be printed in the output field
to indicate that the data were too big; on others an error message is printed).

The following table gives further examples of the use of
the E*n.m* output conversion.

Value of Variable	Field Description	Data Output
-10.4	E7.1	-.1E+02
-10.4	E8.2	-.10E+02
-10.4	E12.4	bb-.1040E+02
.0102	E8.2	b.10E-01
-.0001	E12.6	-.100000E-03
-.0001	E14.6	bb-.100000E-03
50000.0	E14.6	bbb.500000E+05
5000000.0	E14.6	bbb.500000E+07
143.7	E11.4	bb.1437E+03
-14.37	E11.4	b-.1437E+02

Let us look at an example showing how input and output statements are used in actual programs.

Example 1

A certain company is taking an inventory of the floor space
in their building. They have measured the dimensions of each
room (all of which are conveniently rectangular), and a program
is required which will give the area of each room and the total
area of all the rooms.

A simple way to prepare the data for this program would be
to use one card to input the data for each room. Each card
will contain the length and the width of the room, and just to
make sure that every room is counted, it might also contain the
room number. The card for one room might then be punched in the
following format.

```
Columns  1-5   Room number
Columns  6-10  Length (in feet)
Columns 11-15  Width (in feet)
```

Since there is no room 0 in the building, we can put a blank card after the last room card in the deck to be read in. Then in the program, we test for a room number of zero, and when we find one, we will know that all the cards have been read and it is time to print out the total area.

For each room, we shall print out the room number, the length, width, and the area. The flowchart for this program is shown in Figure 4-1.

The FORTRAN program that does this is quite simple:

```
        TOTAR = 0
    2   READ (1, 5) NRM, ALEN, WID
    5   FORMAT (I5, F5.0, F5.0)
        IF (NRM) 10, 50, 10
   10   AREA = ALEN * WID
        TOTAR = TOTAR + AREA
        WRITE (2, 15) NRM, ALEN, WID, AREA
   15   FORMAT (I6, F10.1, F10.1, F12.2)
        GO TO 2
   50   WRITE (2, 55) TOTAR
   55   FORMAT (E12.6)
        STOP
        END
```

Notice that in FORMAT Statement 15,[2] an F10.1 field descriptor is used to print out the length and width. The field length of 10 assures that there will be several spaces between each number printed, so that they will be easy to read. The one decimal place is all that is needed in this case, since a tenth of a foot is accurate enough for this purpose. The area is printed with an F12.2 field descriptor because it will be larger than the length or width, and we want to have it accurate to two decimal places. The total area is printed in exponential form, just for illustrative purposes.

The X Field Descriptor. In printing two numbers side by side on a print line, we would normally want to leave some spaces between them for legibility. We already know that this can be done by making the field specification large enough so that the number will not fill up the field. For example, if we are printing two integers M and N and we know that N has a maximum size of

---

[2] In the FORMAT Statement 15, an additional space was specified for the first variable to be output. The reason for this is given on pages 97-98.

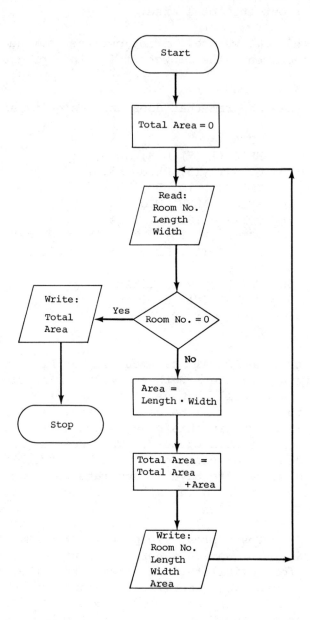

FIGURE 4-1. Flowchart for Example 1

94

six characters (including minus sign), we can write these using the FORMAT statements

                    WRITE (2, 5) M, N
          5   FORMAT (I3, I10)

Then since N will be right justified in the I10 field, there will be at least four blank spaces separating the two numbers printed.

There is an alternate way to skip spaces which is sometimes more convenient. This is the purpose of the X field descriptor. This has the form

                         nX

where n is an unsigned integer. This field simply causes n spaces to be skipped in the format. If we want to skip just one space, n can be omitted, and we can write X instead of 1X. With E or X, blanks are guaranteed.

Unlike the I, F, and E fields, the X field does *not* correspond to a variable in the list of the READ or WRITE statements. For example, the statements

                    WRITE (2, 5) M, N
          5   FORMAT (I3, 4X, I6)

would print M under an I3 format, then skip four spaces on the print line, and then print N under an I6 format.

When used for input, the X field functions in a similar way. For instance, if we want to read an integer JOE punched in columns 1-10 of a card, and then skip 60 spaces and read a floating-point number SAM which is punched in columns 71-80 of the same card, we could use the statements

                    READ (1, 1) JOE, SAM
          1   FORMAT (I10, 60X, F10.0)

The H Field Descriptor. Frequently, it is desirable to print headings along with the results from a program. This can be done using the Hollerith field descriptor (named for Herman Hollerith, inventor of punch card equipment). This field descriptor is written

                         nH

where n is an integer giving the total number of characters in the field, *including blanks*. This field descriptor means that the succeeding n characters in the FORMAT statement will be printed exactly as they are.

For example, if we were printing values of variables X and Y, each of which we wanted to print with an Fl0.3 format, we could label the numbers by using the statements

```
          WRITE (2, 12) X, Y
       12 FORMAT (10X, 3HZ=b, Fl0.3, 5X, 3HY=b, Fl0.3)
```

The first three characters following the first H are Z=b (b again means blank; blanks count in an H field just like any other character), and so these three characters would be the first things printed on the print line. Next, the value of the variable X is printed with an Fl0.3 field, then five blank spaces are printed by the 5X specification, the characters Y=b are printed by the H field, and finally the value of Y is printed in an Fl0.3 field. If the variable X had the value 20.6 and Y had the value of 100000.0, then the above statements would print out

```
          X=bbbbb20.600bbbbbY=b100000.000
```

Like the X field, the H field does not correspond to any variable in the list of the WRITE statement and is ignored in setting up that correspondence. In fact, it is not necessary to print out any data values if all that is wanted is a Hollerith field. In such a case, the list of variables in the WRITE statement is omitted altogether. For instance, to print out the message

```
          bSIC TRANSIT GLORIA
```

we could use the statements

```
          WRITE (2, 44)
       44 FORMAT (19H SIC TRANSIT GLORIA)
```

Again, the 19H means that the next 19 characters are the Hollerith field to be printed. Remember that the number of characters includes the number of blank spaces. If we had forgotten to count the three blank spaces and had put

```
       44 FORMAT (16H SIC TRANSIT GLORIA)
```

the computer would have taken 16 characters only as the H field and have tried to print

```
          bSIC TRANSIT GLO
```

Furthermore, since the computer would not know what to do with the leftover characters RIA, the results of trying to execute such a statement would be unpredictable, and we would not get the result desired.

As another example of the use of the H field, suppose that in some program MBOY and MGIRL are the numbers of boys and girls in the first six grades. These are punched on cards, with each card containing the number of boys in columns one-four and the number of girls in columns five-eight. We want to print these numbers in a column with column headings so that the output looks like this:

bbbbbbGRADEbbbBOYSbbbbGIRLS

1	423	432
2	510	540
3	411	450
4	400	380
5	396	377
6	390	400

We can do this with the statements

```
        WRITE (2, 50)
50      FORMAT (5X, 6H GRADE, 2X, 5H BOYS, 3X, 6H GIRLS)
        I = 1
80      READ (1, 60) MBOY, MGIRL
60      FORMAT (I4, I4)
        WRITE (2, 70) I, MBOY, MGIRL
70      FORMAT (I9, I8, I9)
        I = I + 1
        IF (I - 6) 80, 80, 90
90      Next Statement
```

CARRIAGE CONTROL CHARACTERS

In all the examples of the WRITE statements presented so far, we have made sure that the first character printed is a blank. This is desirable for several reasons. First, the printed output is easier to view if it does not occupy the left-most position. The other reason is very important to remember when writing FORTRAN. Most printers have a built-in feature that allows the programmer to control the spacing on printing. The way it works is that the first character printed on any line is not really printed at all, but is used to instruct the printer to single space, double space, skip to the top of the next page, or to suppress spacing. This first character is called the carriage control character, and the code used for the carriage control is the following:

Character in First Print Position	Printer Action
BLANK	Single space before printing
0 (zero)	Double space before printing
1 (one)	Skip to the beginning of the next page before printing
+ (plus)	Do not space before printing
Any other character	Single space before printing (same as blank)[3]

Normally, we would just want to leave this column blank. This could be done several ways. For example, if we are printing an integer variable KOW and we know that KOW will never be greater than 9999, we could print KOW with an I5 format (or any greater field length) so that the first column would be blank. Another way is just to make the first output field an X field. These two methods are illustrated below.

```
      WRITE (2, 44) KOW
      WRITE (2, 55) KOW
   44 FORMAT (I5)
   55 FORMAT (1X, I4) or 55  FORMAT (1H , I4)
```

Now, if we were using FORMAT statement number 44 and KOW happened to be 10000, the number printed would be 0000, and it would be printed at the top of a new page, since the 1 would be interpreted as a carriage control character (whether or not this is what we intended). Thus (1X, I4) is safer than I5.

Suppose we wanted to print out a student's numerical grade averages in mathematics, English, and history. There is one data card for each student. These grades are punched on data cards as follows:

Columns	
1-5	Student identification number
6-8	Math grade
9-11	English grade
12-14	History grade

---

[3]Some systems have additional carriage control characters. The reference manual for the system used should be consulted.

The last card in the data deck has a 99999 punched in the first five columns to assist in terminating the program. Each student is to be listed on a separate page of printer output. The FORTRAN program to do this is given as follows:

```
C       ID IS STUDENT'S IDENTIFICATION NUMBER
C       MATH IS STUDENT'S MATHEMATICS GRADE
C       IENGL IS STUDENT'S ENGLISH GRADE
C       IHIST IS STUDENT'S HISTORY GRADE

    1   WRITE (2, 100)
  100   FORMAT (1H1, 10X, 11HSTUDENT NO., 5X, 4HMATH, 3X,
        1 7HENGLISH, 3X, 7HHISTORY)
        READ (1, 101) ID, MATH, IENGL, IHIST
  101   FORMAT (I5, I3, I3, I3)
        IF (ID - 99999) 10, 20, 20
   10   WRITE (2, 102)
  102   FORMAT (13X, I5, 9X, I3, 6X, I3, 7X, I3)
        GO TO 1
   20   STOP
        END
```

A typical page of output will have the following

STUDENT NO.	MATH	ENGLISH	HISTORY
1234	75	96	100

It is essential that we keep this carriage control in mind when writing output statements. Consider the statements

```
        DO 1 I = 1, 1000
    1   WRITE (1, 10)
   10   FORMAT (1H1)
```

Their effect is to instruct the printer to skip 1000 pages, which would be a most spectacular sight if you consider the speed of some printers. Such statements obviously should be avoided. In fact, most computer centers wisely limit the amount of output to only a small number of pages.

LOCATION OF DATA CARDS IN A PROGRAM

As we have learned, every time a READ statement is performed a new data card is read. All the data cards for a particular program are referred to as the *data deck*. These cards are not located in the main program but immediately *after* the END statement is encountered. Figure 4-2 illustrates this.

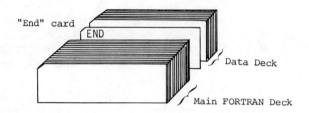

"End" card — END
Data Deck
Main FORTRAN Deck

FIGURE 4-2.   FORTRAN deck with data cards

Actually, if one were to examine a complete FORTRAN program that has just been submitted to a computer center to be run, he would notice several more cards at various places in the deck. These cards vary with the computer. Figure 4-3 illustrates where these additional cards are located.

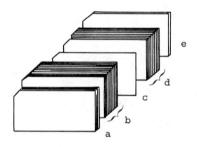

e
d
c
b
a

FIGURE 4-3

a. The first few cards generally include a billing code to charge an account for computer time used, a code to identify the program owner's special requests for when the job is to be run (large computer centers have several priorities for running programs), etc. Other cards here are needed to specify that the program is written in FORTRAN, and a separate card or cards may also be needed.

b. This is the main FORTRAN deck as shown in Figure 4-2. This is also called the *source program*. The END card is considered a part of this section.

c. One or more separator cards between the main program and the data deck.

d. Data cards, if any.

e. One or more cards to denote the end of the program. These are often specially colored or labeled for ease in spotting by the people who run the program.

100

A EXERCISES

1. Below are examples of input and output statements. If the statement is correct, mark a V next to it; otherwise, make a suitable correction to make it valid.

   a.
   ```
           READ (1, 100), A, C, D, E
       100 FORMAT (F10.2, F10.3, F10.4, F10.0)
   ```

   b.
   ```
           READ (1, 1000) X, GO TO
      1000 FORMAT (F20.19, F7.2)
   ```

   c.
   ```
           WRITE (2, 2) I, J, ZZZ
         2 FORMAT (I1, I20, I30)
   ```

   d.
   ```
           WRITE (2, 20) A, AB, ABC, ABCD, E
        20 FORMAT (F10.0, F10.8, F10.4)
   ```

   e.
   ```
           READ (1, 6) X, Y, E, Z, I, K
         6 FORMAT (F6.2, F3.1, E8.4, F30.2, I3, I10)
   ```

2. Write the FORTRAN to correspond to the flowchart on page 18, Chapter 1.

3. Write the FORTRAN to correspond to the flowchart on the following page. The flowchart solves the problem of searching a deck of cards on which are punched grades for a class. There are N of these data cards, and the variable COUNT is used to determine how many are 90 or above.

4. Write the FORTRAN to correspond to the flowchart for Problem A1, Chapter 1 (page 22).

5. Write a program to input two numbers A and B. Set C = 1 if A and B are both equal to 1. Set C = 2 if A or B but not both equal 1. Set C = 3 otherwise. Output C.

6. a. Add the necessary statements to Problem 5 so that the program will work for N sets of numbers A and B.

   b. Rather than count the sets of numbers A and B, suppose that we know that A is never larger than 1000. After the last data card add a card with a 9999 punched in the same field that A occupied. Add the necessary statements to Problem 5 to do this.

7. Write the FORTRAN to input a student's grades on three exams, T1, T2, and T3, and compute his final average as follows: T1 counts 19%; T2, 37%; and T3, 44%. Use

Hollerith specifications to have the printer display

    TEST1   TEST2   TEST3   FINAL AVG.

above the scores.

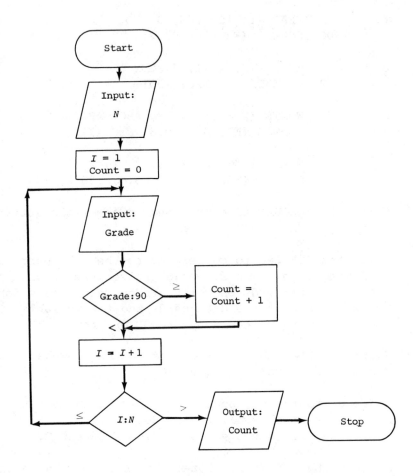

Flowchart for Problem 3

1. The equation of a circle with center at the origin is
    given by
    $$x^2 + y^2 = r^2.$$

    Write a program to input a card with three numbers punched
    on it as follows:

    Columns

    | 1-10 | X |
    | 11-20 | Y |
    | 21-30 | R |

    R represents the radius of a circle. Determine if the
    point (X, Y) is inside, on, or outside the circle. For
    your output include appropriate headings. Set up the
    program to work for any amount of data cards.

2. Write a program that will print out your initials. First,
    sketch your initials as you would like them to appear, and
    then write the program. A sample output may be as follows:

    ```
                XXXX              XXXXXXXXXX
                XXXX              XXXXXXXXXX
                XXXX              XXX
                XXXX              XXX
                XXXX              XXXXXXXXXX
                XXXX              XXXXXXXXXX
                XXXX                     XXX
         XX     XXXX                     XXX
         XXXXXXXXXX              XXXXXXXXXX
         XXXXXXXXXX              XXXXXXXXXX
    ```

    Use any other symbol if you choose.

3. Write a program to draw the following axes, properly centered
    on your printer.

    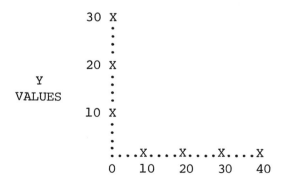

103

4. Write a program to read in a deck of cards on which are punched the results of an examination. Each student has one card punched as follows:

Columns
_____

   1-3   NAM   A three-digit student number

   4-23 MARK A number corresponding to the student's answer to the questions. These are either a 1, 2, 3, or 4 (the exam was multiple choice). The answer to Question 1 is in column 4, 2 in column 5, etc.

The very first data card contains the correct answers, punched in the first 10 columns. Since there were 20 questions, each correct one is worth five points. Have your program correct each student's results and make up an appropriate output. A sample of this might be as follows:

RESULTS OF ENGLISH TEST (20 QUESTIONS). A 0 INDICATES AN ERROR FOR QUESTION Q, A 1 IS FOR THE CORRECT ANSWER

STUDENT ID NO.	Q1	Q2	Q3	Q4	Q5	Q6	...	Q20	SCORE
121	1	1	0	1	0	1	...	0	80

5. Modify the program in Problem 4 to work for any amount of questions and the grades determined on the basis of a perfect score of 100.

6. Write a program to input a number representing an amount of money less than $100.00. The number can be read in with an F10.2 format. Then have the computer determine the amount and print out a message as follows:

    BETWEEN $ 0.00 and $20.00
    BETWEEN $20.00 and $40.00, etc.

7. Write a program to list the integers from 1 to 100. However, if an integer is divisible by 3 or contains the digit 3, an X is output. A sample output would be:

    1
    2
    X
    4
    5
    X
    etc.

Chapter 5

ARRAYS AND SUBSCRIPTED VARIABLES

FORTRAN allows us to use subscripted variables. For example, if we had a program that involved, say a hundred variables, it would be tedious just to give them each a distinct name, such as A, B, $\cdots$, SUM, or PROD, and to keep all these names straight while working with the variables. Suppose, however, that we had a hundred numbers written in a list:

```
  1.   1.3
  2.   2.0
  3.   6.1
   .
   .
   .
100.   5.9
```

If we were to talk about the third number in this list, it would be clear that we meant the number 6.1. This is the basic idea of subscripted variables. We give a name, say X, to a collection of storage locations or *array*, as it is more commonly called, and then to distinguish between the different locations in the array, we use the subscripted names:

$$X_1, \ X_2, \ X_3, \ \cdots, \ X_{100}$$

The *array name*, X, includes the whole collection of variables, and each of the names $X_1, \ \cdots, \ X_{100}$ is an individual variable referring to one of the *elements* of the array.

The chief advantage of using subscripts, however, is not just for naming variables. We can describe an operation, that is to be performed on each of the variables in turn, by including instructions in the program to manipulate the subscript itself. For instance, suppose we wanted to add up all the numbers in the above list. We certainly could do this explicitly by putting

$$Y = X_1 + X_2 + X_3 + X_4 + \cdots + X_{100}$$

if we were willing to spend the time to write out the whole expression. In algebra, however, we use the more compact notation:

$$Y = \sum_{i=1}^{100} X_i$$

105

In a similar manner, as we shall soon see, the use of subscripts in FORTRAN can greatly facilitate many procedures.

SUBSCRIPTS IN FORTRAN

In FORTRAN, a subscripted variable is denoted by enclosing the subscript in parentheses after the array name. Thus, instead of A_1, A_2, $\cdots$, A_{99}, we would write A(1), A(2), $\cdots$, A(99). The same rules apply for naming arrays as applied for naming ordinary variables. The same considerations as to type also apply. Thus, an array named ABC would be a floating-point array. This simply means that each of the variables ABC(1), ABC(2), and ABC(3) is a floating-point variable. Likewise, an array named M123 would be an integer array, so each of the variables M123(1), M123(2), M123(3), $\cdots$, would be an integer variable.

The quantity in parentheses may be an unsigned integer, as above, or it may be an integer variable, such as I, J, or NSUM. In this case, the reference is to the element of the array whose subscript is the value of the integer variable. So if we had

$$I = 6$$
$$Y = A(I)$$

then Y would be set equal to A(6). Below are some examples of correct subscripted variables.

$$ABC(94)$$
$$ABC(INT)$$
$$PRIME(1)$$
$$N123(LOC)$$

While the subscript may be either a constant or a variable, its value must always be a positive integer; zero and negative subscripts are not allowable, and neither are floating-point subscripts. Also, generally speaking, an arithmetic expression can be used as a subscript only in certain restricted cases. A subscript may be in any of the following forms:

$$con$$
$$var$$
$$var \pm con$$
$$con * var$$
$$con * var \pm con$$

where "con" is a fixed-point constant and "var" is a fixed-point variable. Thus,

$$ARRAY\ (2 * 1)$$

is correct but

$$ARRAY \ (I * 2)$$

is not. The following table shows some examples of incorrect subscripts.

Incorrect Variable	Reason for Error
ABCDEFG(1)	Too many characters in name[1]
A(0)	Zero subscript
X(-1)	Negative subscript
X(1.5)	Floating-point subscript
M(X)	Floating-point variable subscript
Y2(N + M/2)	Illegal arithmetic expression in subscript
4L(J)	Name does not begin with letter

Also, care must be taken that the value of a variable or expression used as a subscript is always positive. For instance, if we had the statements

```
        J = 5
   6    J = J - 1
        Y = ALPHA(J)
        IF(J) 7, 7, 6
   7    STOP
```

in a program, the result would be undefined since an attempt is made to set Y equal to ALPHA(0).

THE DIMENSION *STATEMENT*

Now that we have seen how subscripted variables are written in FORTRAN, let us consider briefly what a subscripted variable does in terms of the computer itself. Recall that an ordinary variable is a name that corresponds to some memory location in the computer. Each time we include the variable in the program, we are referring to the contents of that memory location. If we are using a subscripted variable ALPHA, each of the variables ALPHA(1), ALPHA(2), $\cdots$, also refers to some memory location. In order to specify how many memory locations are in the array, we must use a DIMENSION statement. The DIMENSION statement is a declarative (nonexecutable) statement and it must appear at the

---

[1] See footnote on page 32.

beginning of any program in which subscripted variables are used.

This statement has the form

DIMENSION *name1(dim1), name2(dim2), ···, namen(dim*n*)*

where *nameI* is the name of an array and *dimI* is an unsigned integer constant giving the maximum value of the subscript for that array. For example, suppose in a program that we want to use an array named CAT, and we know that we shall not need a subscript for CAT greater than 100. At the beginning of the program we would use the statement

DIMENSION CAT(100).

This statement declares the existence of the array CAT consisting of the 100 variables

CAT(1), CAT(2), ···, CAT(100).

We could refer to any of these in the program. It would be incorrect, however, to use CAT(101) in an expression.

Each array used in a program must appear in a DIMENSION statement at the beginning of the program to declare that the variable name is to be treated as a subscripted variable, and to specify the "dimension," or size, of the array, that is, the number of subscripted variables it contains. Note that it is not necessary to use a separate DIMENSION statement for every array. If we wanted to use two arrays

CAT(1), CAT(2), ···, CAT(105)
DOG(1), DOG(2), ···, DOG(9)

in a program, we could use the single statement

DIMENSION CAT(105), DOG(9)

Once we have used a DIMENSION statement to declare that a certain variable is an array name, that name should normally appear with a subscript when used in an expression. If we used the above DIMENSION statement, then it would be incorrect to have the statement

Y = CAT + 5.0

in the same program, because the variable CAT does not appear with a subscript. [But not on all computers. Some will actually treat the statement as Y = CAT(1) + 5.0.]

USE OF SUBSCRIPTED VARIABLES

Example 1

As a simple example of how subscripted variables can save a considerable amount of effort, suppose we have N numbers stored in an array X, and suppose that $N \leq 100$. To set Y equal to the sum of these numbers, we can use a procedure whereby we add $X(I)$ to Y and then increment I until it is equal to N. The complete procedure is shown in the following flowchart.

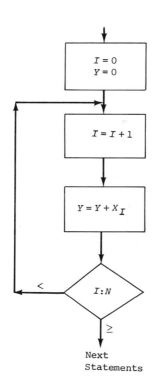

This could be written in FORTRAN as

```
      DIMENSION  X(100)
         .
         .
         .
      Y = 0.0
      I = 0
    5 I = I + 1
```

```
          Y = Y + X(I)
          IF (I - N) 5, 10, 10
      10  Next Statement
```

This program is the FORTRAN equivalent of the algebraic expression

$$Y = \sum_{i=1}^{N} X_i$$

Such procedures occur frequently in programming, and the use of the subscripted variables makes them easier to deal with. Note that the above program will work equally well for N equal to 1, 10, or 100.

Example 2

We want to tabulate values of the polynomial $Y = X^3 + 2X^2 - 3X + 1$ for values of X from -1 to 1 in increments of 0.1. We want to store the y values in an array Y.

First, note that there are 21 values in all: -1.0, -.9, $\cdots$, .9, 1.0. So we can set up the array Y with 21 variables. The program to perform this job is as follows:

```
          DIMENSION Y(21)
          I = 1
          X = -1.0
      1   Y(I) = ((X + 2.) * X - 3) * X + 1.
          IF (I - 21) 2, 3, 3
      2   I = I + 1
          X = X + 0.1
          GO TO 1
      3   Next Statement
```

In some cases, we can perform a procedure using subscripted variables or not using them. For example, the flowchart on page 58 gives a procedure for adding a list of numbers without using subscripted variables. Compare this with Example 1, where we do the same thing with subscripted variables. The difference is that in the first case, we did not store all the numbers internally (that is, not all at once). It is sometimes necessary to store a list of numbers internally, rather than to read them in and work with them one at a time. In such a case, the use of subscripts is a practical necessity.

110

Example 3

There is a quantity called the variance of a set of measurements that occurs frequently in statistics. This is defined as

$$VAR = \frac{1}{N}\sum_{i=1}^{N}(X_i - AV)^2, \quad AV \equiv \overline{X} = \frac{\sum_{i=1}^{N}X_i}{N}$$

where N is the number of measurements X_1, X_2, $\cdots$, X_N and AV is their average. One would think that we must have the average of the measurements before we can begin to compute the variance. So we have to "go through" the list of numbers twice: once to compute the average, and once again to compute the variance. But it is easy to show by algebra that $VAR = 1/N\Sigma X^2 - (\overline{X})^2$. We merely need to keep two sums as we go along.

If we have read the numbers into an array X, specified by

DIMENSION   X(100)

(so we assume that N $\leq$ 100), we can than use the following statements to find the average AV.

```
         I = 1
         SUM = 0. 0
         SSQ = 0. 0
    10   SUM = SUM + X(I)
         SSQ = SSQ + X(I) ** 2
         I = I + 1
         IF (I - N) 10, 10, 20
    20   AN = N
         AV = SUM/AN
```

After doing this, we can compute the variance, VAR, with the statement

VAR = SSQ/AN - AV ** 2

In fact, it is evident that this problem could be done without any array at all, merely adding X and X^2 to the two sums during input.

Example 4

Suppose we have N numbers $X(1)$, $X(2)$, $\cdots$, $X(N)$ and we want to set *XMAX* equal to the maximum of these numbers. To accomplish this, we begin by setting *XMAX* equal to $X(1)$. Then we compare each $X(I)$, starting with $X(2)$, to *XMAX* and, if $X(I)$ is greater, we

111

replace the value of *XMAX* by *X(I)*. The flowchart for the whole procedure is shown below.

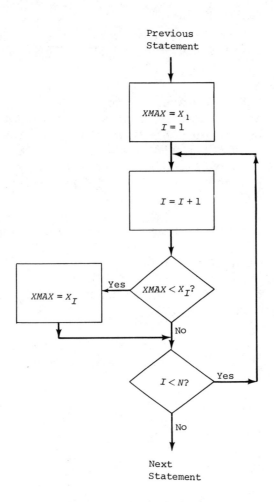

When the STOP terminal is reached, *XMAX* will be equal to the maximum of the given numbers.

This procedure could be performed with the following FORTRAN statements:

```
          DIMENSION X(100)
               .
               .
               .
          XMAX = X(1)
          I = 1
      5   I = I + 1
          IF (XMAX - X(I)) 10, 15, 15
     10   XMAX = X(I)
     15   IF (I - N) 5, 20, 20
     20   Next Statement
```

Example 5   SORT - Simple Exchange -

Let us carry the previous example one step further. Instead of just finding the maximum of $X(1)$, $X(2)$, $\cdots$, we shall rearrange these numbers in descending order, so that the greatest number is stored in $X(1)$ and the smallest in $X(N)$. There are many ways of doing this, and when many numbers are to be sorted, it is important to use a very efficient method. Some of the most efficient methods, however, are also rather complicated, and for this example we shall use a method which is really just an extension of the method used in Example 4.

First of all, we find the maximum of X(1), X(2), $\cdots$, X(N) just as we did above. Suppose it is X(J). We then interchange X(1) and X(J). That is, the value of X(J) is stored in X(1), and the value of X(1) is stored in X(J). The next step is to find the maximum of X(2), X(3), $\cdots$, X(N) and to interchange this value with X(2). In general, on the Mth step, we find the maximum of X(M), X(M + 1), $\cdots$, X(N) and then we interchange this value with X(M). The flowchart for this procedure is shown in Chapter 1 (see page 21). In FORTRAN, the procedure would be programmed as follows:

```
          DIMENSION  X(100)
               .
               .
               .
          I = 1
     10   J = I + 1
     20   IF (X(I) - X(J)) 40, 40, 30
     30   TEMP = X(I)
          X(I) = X(J)
          X(J) = TEMP
     40   J = J + 1
          IF (J - N) 20, 50, 50
     50   I = I + 1
          IF (I - N) 10, 60, 60
     60   Next Statement
```

Example 6

In recent years there have been many applications of computers in mathematics for testing hypotheses in number theory. A simple example of this is using the computer to test whether or not a particular number is prime. (A positive integer is called prime if it is not divisible evenly by any integer except itself and 1. For instance, 2, 5, 11, 19, and 23 are primes, while 4, 24, 50, and 99 are not.) It can be shown that a number is prime if and only if it is not divisible evenly by any prime less than or equal to its square root.

Suppose we are given an integer N, where $2 \leq N \leq 10^4$. We want to set a variable L equal to zero if N is not prime, and equal to one if N is prime. Since $N \leq 10^4$, we need to test only the primes ≤ 100. We may start by dividing N by 2. If 2 divides N evenly (with no remainder), then N is not prime, so we set L equal to zero and stop; if N is not divisible by 2, we try dividing N by 3. If N is not divisible by 3 either, we try dividing by 5 and so on until we find a prime which divides N or we have tried every prime less than or equal to the square root of N, in which case we set L equal to one and stop.

Specifically, suppose we have an array called NPRM containing the primes from 2 to 100 (there are 25 of them in this range). So

$$NPRM(1) = 2$$
$$NPRM(2) = 3$$
$$\vdots$$
$$NPRM(25) = 97$$

Given any number N such that $2 \leq N \leq 10^4$, we first want to set an integer variable M equal to the integer part of the square root of N. We can do this with the statements

$$AN = N$$
$$M = AN ** 0.5$$

Note that we convert N to the floating-point variable AN before performing the exponentiation.

To test whether or not N is divisible by NPRM(I), we use integer arithmetic to compute

$$J = (N/NPRM(I)) * NPRM(I) - N$$

Then J will equal zero if and only if NPRM(I) divides N. The final flowchart is shown on the following page.

114

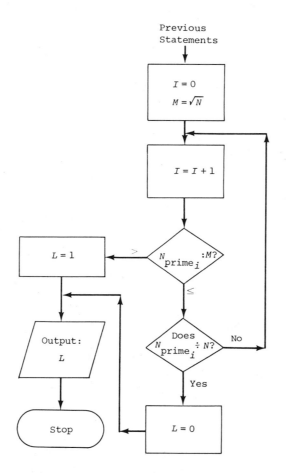

The FORTRAN program that performs this procedure reads:

```
        DIMENSION NPRM(25)

          .
          .

C       ASSUME ALL VARIABLES ARE DEFINED PREVIOUSLY
        I = 0
        AN = N
        M = AN ** 0.5
```

```
 5    I = I + 1
      IF (NPRM(I) - M) 15, 15, 10
10    L = 1
      GO TO 20
15    J = (N/NPRM(I)) * NPRM(I) - N
      IF (J) 5, 20, 5
20    L = 0
      WRITE (2, 30) L
30    FORMAT (I10)
      STOP
      END
```

DOUBLY- AND TRIPLY-SUBSCRIPTED ARRAYS

All of the subscripted variables we have dealt with so far have had one subscript. It is also allowable in FORTRAN to have variables with two or three subscripts. These are handled in an entirely similar manner. A doubly-subscripted array (i.e., a variable with two subscripts) is set up by using a DIMENSION declaration such as

DIMENSION   MATR(3,4)

This would declare that the array MATR consists of

    MATR(1,1), MATR(1,2), MATR(1,3), MATR(1,4)
    MATR(2,1), MATR(2,2), MATR(2,3), MATR(2,4)
    MATR(3,1), MATR(3,2), MATR(3,3), MATR(3,4)

In general, to specify a doubly-subscripted array, we use a statement of the form

DIMENSION   name (m,n)

where "name" is the name of the array, m is an unsigned integer constant giving the maximum value of the first subscript, and n is an unsigned integer constant giving the maximum value of the second subscript. We can then refer to any of the variables' names (I, J) where $1 \leq I \leq m$ and $1 \leq J \leq n$.

For instance, in an accounting job, we might want to know the amount of checks written on each day of the year, and it might be convenient to use two subscripts to do this. If we used the DIMENSION statement

DIMENSION   CHECK (12,31)

then we could take CHECK (I, J) to mean the amount of checks written on the Jth day of the Ith month of the year.

116

Example 7

Suppose there are N students in a class, and for the entire semester there are M test grades, where each grade is 0, 1, 2, 3, or 4. The grades are stored in a doubly-subscripted array called GRADE, where GRADE(I, J) is the Ith student's grade on the Jth test. We want to compute the final grade, FINAL(I), for each student to be the average of all his test grades. We also want to compute the class average CLSAV, which is the overall average of all the final grades. If we know that $N \leq 50$ and $M \leq 10$, we can use the following routine to do this. Assume all variables have been read into the computer.

```
      DIMENSION  GRADE(50, 10), FINAL(50)
      I = 0
      AM = M
      CLSAV = 0.0
   1  I = I + 1
   5  J = 0
      FINAL(I) = 0.0
  10  J = J + 1
      FINAL(I) = FINAL(I) + GRADE(I,J)
      IF (J - M) 10, 20, 20
  20  FINAL(I) = FINAL(I)/AM
      CLSAV = CLSAV + FINAL(I)
      IF (I - N) 1, 25, 25
  25  AN = N
      CLSAV = CLSAV/AN
      Next Statement
```

Example 8

Let us consider a routine for multiplying two 3×3 matrices A and B to give the product matrix C. If

$$A = \begin{bmatrix} a_{11} & a_{12} & a_{13} \\ a_{21} & a_{22} & a_{23} \\ a_{31} & a_{32} & a_{33} \end{bmatrix}$$

$$B = \begin{bmatrix} b_{11} & b_{12} & b_{13} \\ b_{21} & b_{22} & b_{23} \\ b_{31} & b_{32} & b_{33} \end{bmatrix}$$

then by definition, their product AB is

117

$$C = \begin{bmatrix} c_{11} & c_{12} & c_{13} \\ c_{21} & c_{22} & c_{23} \\ c_{31} & c_{32} & c_{33} \end{bmatrix}$$

where

$$c_{11} = a_{11}b_{11} + a_{12}b_{21} + a_{13}b_{31}$$
$$c_{12} = a_{11}b_{12} + a_{12}b_{22} + a_{13}b_{32}$$
$$\vdots \qquad \vdots \qquad \vdots$$
$$c_{mn} = a_{m1}b_{1n} + a_{m2}b_{2n} + a_{m3}b_{3n}$$

This multiplication could be accomplished with the following statements:

```
      DIMENSION  A(3,3), B(3,3), C(3,3)
      I = 0
  5   I = I + 1
      J = 0
 10   J = J + 1
      C(I,J) = A(I,1) * B(1,J) + A(I,2) * B(2,J) + A(I,3) * B(3,J)
      IF (J - 3) 10, 15, 15
 15   IF (I - 3) 5, 20, 20
 20   Next Statement
```

In a similar manner, we can use a triply-subscripted array by giving a DIMENSION statement such as

DIMENSION   name (a,b,c)

where a, b, and c are unsigned integer constants and

a is the maximum value of the first subscript;
b is the maximum value of the second subscript;
c is the maximum value of the third subscript.

We shall see more examples of procedures involving the use of doubly- and triply-subscripted arrays after we learn about the DO statement, which facilitates such procedures.

A EXERCISES

1. Below are examples of FORTRAN expressions and statements. Some are correct, others have errors. If the statement is valid, mark a V next to it. Otherwise, make a suitable correction to make it valid.

   a. JACK (JUMP)
   b. HELLO (5, I)
   c. DIMENSION X(5), Y(J)
   d. ARRAY (5 * JOHN)
   e. ZZZ(II45)
   f. W(JJ - 60)
   g. W(JJ - 60), KK
   h. X(2 * LIM + 800)

   i. DIMENSIONS X(10), ZZ(1000), Y(4)
   j. AAA(IBB, KCC) = I
   k. X = A(J - 5) + BB(I + J)
   l. DIMENSION III(10000)
   m. GO TO 5 = A(I, J)
   n. PRES (MINE, NEVER)
   o. B(IN, OUT)
   p. VARY (IOU) = MONEY

For the following exercises, assume all variables are in storage in the computer, or else include appropriate READ and WRITE statements.

2. A list of 100 variables is called D. Write the FORTRAN to compute the elements of a new array named E where

   $$E_i = D_{i+1} - D_i, \quad i = 1, 2, \ldots, 99$$

3. Write the FORTRAN statements that will calculate an array consisting of the cube roots of the first ten integers. Call the array CUBEROOT.

4. Write a series of FORTRAN statements to correspond to the flowchart shown on page 120.

5. Write the FORTRAN statements to correspond to the following indicated sums:

   $$\begin{aligned}
   \text{SUM } (1) &= 1 + 2 + 3 + \cdots + n \\
   \text{SUM } (2) &= 1 + 5 + 9 + \cdots + (4n - 3) \\
   \text{SUM } (3) &= 1 + 3 + 5 + \cdots + (2n - 1) \\
   \text{SUM } (4) &= 1^2 + 2^2 + 3^2 + \cdots + n^2 \\
   \text{SUM } (5) &= 1^3 + 2^3 + 3^3 + \cdots + n^3
   \end{aligned}$$

6. Make any necessary corrections in the following sequences of statements:

   a.
   ```
         N = 6
         DIMENSION X(N)
         I = 1
       2 Y = X(I) ** 2
         I = I + 1
         IF (I - 6) 2, 2, 3
       3 Z = Y
   ```

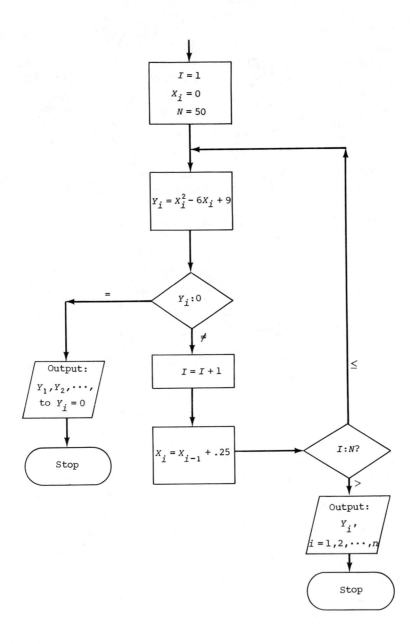

120

6.—*continued*

```
b.          DIMENSION X(5, 5)
            I = 1
            J = 1
         1  X(I, J) = .25 * (X(I + 1, J) + X(I, J - 1))
            J = J + 1
            IF (J - 4) 1, 1, 2
         2  I = I + 1
            IF (I - 4) 1, 1, 3
         3  Y = X(I, J)

c.          DIMENSION A(10, 10)
            I = 1
            J = 1
         4  IF (I - J) 1, 2, 1
         2  A(I, J) = 1.0
            GO TO 3
         1  A(I, J) = 0.0
         3  J = J + 1
            IF (J - 10) 4, 4, 5
         5  I = I + 1
            IF (I - 10) 4, 4, 6
         6  Next Statement

d.          DIMENSION ARRAY (20, 20)
            DIMENSION X(10), Y(10)
            NUMB = 1
       100  ARRAY (NUMB, NUMB + 1) = X(NUMB) - Y(NUMB + 5)
            NUMB = NUMB + 3
            IF (NUMB - 13) 100, 100, 200
       200  Next Statement
```

7. The test results of a large number of students who took both mathematics and English examinations are stored in arrays TMATH and ENGL, respectively. The number of results is less than 1000. Write the FORTRAN to fill up a new array called DIFF, where DIFF(N) is a zero if the difference between the Nth student's mathematics and English scores is less than 20 points and equal to 1 if it is 20 points or more. Let the variable COUNT be equal to the number of 1's in the array DIFF.

8. Draw a flowchart to correspond to Problem 7.

9. Assume that you have two doubly-subscripted arrays A(I, J) and B(I, J), where A and B have the same number of elements. Write the FORTRAN to construct a third array C(I, J), where each element of C is given by C(I, J) = A(I, J) + B(I, J). The maximum size of I and J is 10.

121

10. After the following FORTRAN statements have been executed, what is the value of B?

```
        DIMENSION  A(100)
        I = 1
      3 X = I - 1
        A(I) = X ** 3 - X ** 2 - 10. * X - 8
        I = I + 1
        IF (A(I)) 1, 2, 1
      1 IF (I - 100) 3, 3, 2
      2 B = I
```

11. There are 1000 test results stored in an array called SCORE. Write the FORTRAN to determine how many grades are equal to or greater than 90. Call this number A.

12. Write the FORTRAN for the flowchart on page 21, Chapter 1. Assume that there are 100 variables in the array.

B EXERCISES

1. The Alpha Alpha Alpha fraternity has interviewed every member of the Beta Beta Beta sorority and punched cards for the members as follows:

Columns

1-5	ID	Student's identification number
6-7	HT	Height in inches
8-10	WT	Weight in pounds
11	IAVAIL	A 1 if available for blind dates or a 0 otherwise
12-13	SCORE	A number from 0 to 99, the higher the number the better looking the girl
14	HAIR	Color of the girl's hair: a 1 for blond, 2 for brunette, 3 for red, and 4 for black
15	SPORTS	A 0 if the girl likes sports, a 1 if she hates all sports, and a 2 if no opinion

a. Write a program to find the average weight, height, and SCORE for the Beta Beta Beta sorority.

b. Write a program to see how many Beta Beta Beta sorority members are available for a blind date with a person looking for a girl less than 5'9" in height, weighing more than 110 pounds (but less than 160), having a SCORE greater than 70, and who hates sports. As an exercise in running the program, punch typical cards for 50 sorority members.

122

2. In statistics, the rth moment about the mean, $\overline{X}$, of a set of data is defined as

$$m_r = \frac{\sum\limits_{j=1}^{N} (X_j - \overline{X})^r}{N}, \text{ where } \overline{X} = \frac{\sum\limits_{j=1}^{N} X_j}{N}.$$

Assume that you have less than 1000 of the variable X. Write the FORTRAN to find the mean of X and also first five moments about the mean and store these in an array called XMOM. Try to do this all in one pass, computing X, X^2, X^3, X^4, and X^5 as you go along.

3. Suppose that the following formula has been found to be an accurate index of pollution:

$$P = .01x^2 + .0001y^3 + .05z^2$$

where x = amount of particles of smog/million parts;
y = amount of particles of polluted water/million parts;
z = amount of particles of pollen/million parts of air.

The index is set to be a maximum of 100 even if the value should be higher from the equation. Write a program to calculate P for the following data:

x	y	z
15	50	5
0	100	10
20	30	20
5	25	80
20	40	0
40	16	8
30	30	30
20	30	40

4. The projected growth of a country's population is given by the following equation:

$$A = A_0 (1 + t + \frac{t^2}{2} + \frac{t^3}{6} + \frac{t^6}{24} + \frac{t^5}{60})$$

where A is amount present at any time;
A_0 is amount present at time $t = 0$;
t is time in years divided by ten (i.e., for $t = 1$ year, use .1 in the above).

4.—*continued*

Suppose that a country has 1,000,000 people now. Write a program to predict the population in the next 10 years. How long will it be before the population is 10 million?

5. The standings for teams in a baseball league might be listed as follows:

Team	Wins	Losses	Percent	Games Behind
6	10	2	.833	0
2	9	3	.750	1
1	8	3	.750	1-1/2
3	6	6	.500	4
5	4	8	.330	6
4	0	11	.000	9-1/2

Let $X(I)$ be the six-team array;
  $W(I)$ be the number of wins for team I;
  $XL(I)$ be the losses for team I.

The games behind is given by

$$GB = \frac{(W(I) - XL(I)) - (W(J) - XL(J))}{2}$$

where I stands for the first team and J any other team.

Write a program to read in the team numbers, the wins, and losses and to output a table similar to the above.

6. A ball is dropped from a building 200 feet high and bounces off the ground to 75% of its previous height. It continues bouncing 75% each bounce, until it comes to rest. In theory, this happens only after an infinite number of bounces. In practice, the ball will soon stop after a finite number of bounces. Write a program to print the height of the ball at the top of each bounce for up to 50 bounces. Give the distance traveled during each bounce as well as total distance traveled.

Chapter   6

A group of instructions which is performed over and over again is called a program *loop*. We have seen several examples of this before. For instance, the following instructions will add the integers from 1 to 20.

```
        NSUM = 0
        I = 0
     5  I = I + 1
        NSUM = NSUM + I
        IF (I - 20) 5, 10, 10
    10  STOP
```

In this procedure, notice that we are repeatedly performing the instruction

        NSUM = NSUM + I

while adding 1 to I each time until I equals 20. This sort of situation arises so frequently in programming that a special statement—the DO statement—exists to make it easier.

In general, the DO statement has the form

        DO y I = m_1, m_2, m_3

where y is some statement number; I is an integer variable, called the *control variable*, and m_1 (initial value), m_2 (terminal value) and m_3 (increment) are unsigned integer constants or variables.

Now this statement has the following effects:

1. First of all, the value of I is set equal to m_1.
2. Then all the statements up to and including the statement number y are performed.
3. Then m_3 is added to I. This is compared to m_2.

    a. If the new value of I is greater than m_2, the first statement after the statement number y is performed.
    b. If the new value of I is equal to or less than m_2, control returns to the first statement after the DO statement. If m_3 is omitted, as it often is, it is assumed to be 1.

This procedure is represented in Figure 6-1.

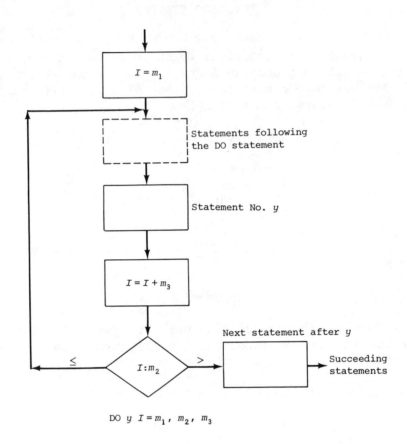

The boxes and diamond are labeled: $I = m_1$; Statements following the DO statement; Statement No. y; $I = I + m_3$; $I:m_2$ with $\leq$ to the left and $>$ to the right leading to Next statement after y and Succeeding statements.

DO y $I = m_1$, m_2, m_3

FIGURE 6-1

Example 1

To perform the program loop given at the beginning of the chapter, using the DO statement, we could have

```
      NSUM = 0
      DO 7 I = 1, 20, 1
  7   NSUM = NSUM + I
      Next Statement
```

In this case, the DO statement specifies that statement 7 be performed, starting with I = 1 and that it be repeatedly performed adding 1 to I each time until I equals 20.

126

Example 2

We know that if the increment m_3 is omitted from the DO statement, it is assumed to be 1. So in the previous example, instead
of

         DO 7 I = 1, 20, 1

we could have put

         DO 7 I = 1, 20

and this would have the same effect.

Example 3

Suppose that at some point in a program we have computed a
value for N and that we want to set B equal to A^N without using
exponentiation. We could accomplish this, using the DO statement:

         B = 1.0
         DO 50 JOE = 1, N
     50 B = B * A

The variable JOE is not used in the procedure itself, and in this
case, the DO statement is used simply to perform statement 50 N
times.

Example 4

In Examples 1-3, we performed only one statement repeatedly
in the DO loop. It is possible to have any number of statements
in the DO loop. For instance, if we wanted to compute

$$NSUM = 1 + 2 + \cdots + 20$$
$$NSQU = 1^2 + 2^2 + \cdots + 20^2$$
$$NCUB = 1^3 + 2^3 + \cdots + 20^3$$

we could have the following statements

         NSUM = 0
         NSQU = 0
         NCUB = 0
         DO 7 I = 1, 20
         NSUM = NSUM + I
         NSQU = NSQU + I ** 2
     7   NCUB = NCUB + I ** 3

This would cause all three of the statements following the DO statement to be performed for I = 1, 2, ⋯, 20.

DO *LOOPS IN THE FLOWCHART*

Probably the most common way to represent a DO loop in a flowchart is to write out the entire process as shown in Figure 6-1. There is, however, an alternative method which shows the DO statement itself. For the DO statement, we use a pointed rectangular box:

To show the range of the DO statement, we write the statement number of the last statement in the DO loop in a small circle after the last instruction box in the loop. Then, to indicate that the loop is performed repeatedly, we use a dotted line to show the return path.

In this notation, the statement

$$\text{DO } y \text{ I} = a, \ b, \ c$$

would be flowcharted as shown in Figure 6-2.

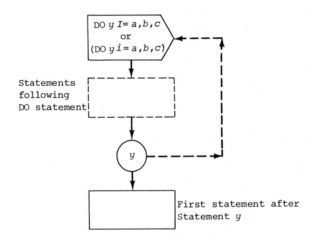

FIGURE 6-2

128

Compare this with Figure 6-1. Figure 6-3 shows how this notation
could be used to draw the flowchart for Example 4.

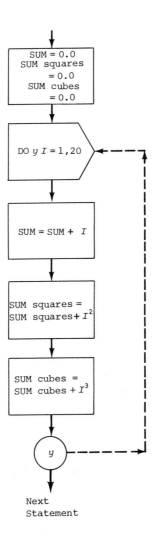

FIGURE 6-3

There are a few restrictions that must be observed when using the DO statement. The purpose of these restrictions is to ensure that the value of the control variable is controlled only by the DO statement.

> *RULE 1:* We must not use any statements within the range of the DO statement that alter the value of the control variable.

This would prevent us from writing statements such as

```
      DO 1 J = 5, 10
      J = 5
    1 M = M + 1
```

Of course, it is easy to see how this might lead to trouble if it were allowable. In this example, the loop would never terminate because the control variable never reaches the final value.

It is perfectly all right to *use* the control variable (as we did in Example 1) just as long as we do not have any statements in the DO loop that *alter* its value.

> *RULE 2:* We must not transfer control into the DO loop from outside the loop.

This would exclude the possibility of such statements as

```
       GO TO 10
       DO 15 J = 1, 6
    10 N = N + J
    15 M = M * N
```

As before, this restriction simply ensures that the value of the variable (J in this case) is controlled by the DO statement. It obviously would not be in the above case.

The above restriction deals with transferring control *into* a DO loop. Transferring control *out of* a DO loop is another matter. It is frequently desirable to use control statements in a DO loop—for performing a certain test over and over, for instance. This is allowable, but there is one restriction which must be observed in such instances.

> *RULE 3:* The last statement in a DO loop must not be one that causes transfer of control.

This restriction causes no real difficulty, however, for it may always be circumvented by using the CONTINUE statement.

The CONTINUE statement is a dummy statement which causes no operation to occur, and consequently can be used anywhere in the program without changing the effect of the program. Its real usefulness, however, is for avoiding the situation described in Rule 3 above. The form of the CONTINUE statement is simply

CONTINUE

We shall use the symbol

to indicate this in a flowchart.

In many cases, the flowchart will not necessarily include the CONTINUE box even though the computer program might have several CONTINUE statements. This is because the programmer can often write the flowchart, which gives the logic of the program, without realizing that in FORTRAN such a statement will be needed. For example, instead of using a control statement as the last statement of a DO loop, we make it the second-to-last statement, and use a CONTINUE statement for the last statement. The CONTINUE statement corresponds merely to an arrow on the flowchart, rather than to a box.

Example 5

Suppose that we want to test to see if I is equal to 2, 5, 8, 11, 14, or 17, and suppose that we want to set J equal to I if I is one of the above numbers, and otherwise we set J equal to 0.

Now, the restriction mentioned before would prevent the following from being acceptable, because an IF statement would be the last statement in a DO loop.

```
 5    DO 10 J = 2, 17, 3
10    IF (J - I) 5, 15, 5
      J = 0
15    Next Statement
```

However, a slight modification, using the CONTINUE statement, resolves the problem:

```
              DO 10 J = 2, 17, 3
              IF (J - I) 10, 15, 10
       10  CONTINUE
              J = 0
       15  Next Statement
```

These statements perform the procedure indicated in the flowchart, and since the last statement in the DO loop is a CONTINUE statement, Rule 3 is not violated.

THE DO STATEMENT AND SUBSCRIPTED VARIABLES

The DO statement is very useful in problems involving subscripted variables. Frequently, situations arise where we want to perform the same operation in some array, using all the elements in succession. The most common way to do this is to set up a program loop, using the control variable of the DO loop as the subscript of an array. Thus, the loop will be performed repeatedly while the subscript is incremented.

Example 6

Suppose we have an array X consisting of the numbers X(1), X(2), $\cdots$, X(50). To set Y equal to the sum of these numbers, using a DO statement, we could have

```
              Y = 0
              DO 1000 I = 1, 50
       1000   Y = Y + X(I)
```

Example 7

In the previous chapter, we saw how to find the average and variance of N numbers X(1), $\cdots$, X(N). This procedure can be somewhat simplified by using the DO statement.

```
              SSQ = 0.0
              SUM = 0.0
              DO 5 I = 1, N
              SUM = SUM + X(I)
       5   SSQ = SSQ + X ** 2
              AN = N
              AV = SUM/AN
```

After finding the sum of the X by performing statement 5 repeated N times, the average is obtained by dividing by N (remembering to convert to a floating-point number). The variance can be computed:

$$VAR = SSQ/AN - AV ** 2$$

Example 8

Another use of the DO statement in connection with sub-scripted variables is for making repeated comparisons.

Suppose we want to see if the number A is equal to any of the numbers B(1), B(2), $\cdots$, B(10). We shall set J equal to 1 if it is and equal to zero if it is not. A flowchart for this procedure is shown in Figure 6-4.

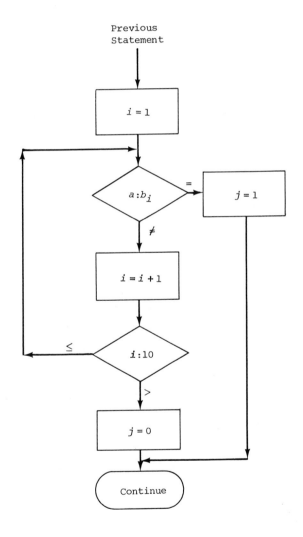

FIGURE 6-4

This could be programmed in FORTRAN as

```
        DIMENSION B(10)
        DO 10 I = 1, 10
        IF (A - B(I)) 10, 20, 10
    10  CONTINUE
        J = 0
        GO TO 30
    20  J = 1
    30  Next Statement
```

Notice that we use a CONTINUE statement to avoid having the IF statement as the last statement in the DO loop.

Example 9

We can use a similar method for the example of the previous chapter where we set XMAX equal to the maximum of X(1), ···, X(N). Using the DO statement, this could be written:

```
        DIMENSION X(100)
        XMAX = X(1)
        DO 15 I = 1, N
        IF (XMAX - X(I)) 10, 15, 15
    10  XMAX = X(I)
    15  CONTINUE
```

NESTED DO LOOPS

A DO statement involves a group of one or more other statements that form the "range" of the DO loop. It is possible to have among these statements another complete DO loop, making a DO loop within a DO loop. This situation is known as nested DO loops. Using a bracket to denote a DO loop, we can represent this pictorially as

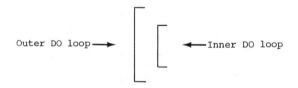

FIGURE 6-5

Each time control passes once through the outer DO loop, the inner DO loop will be completely performed.

Example 10

Say that we have a doubly-subscripted array X consisting of

```
X(1,1)    X(1,2)    ...    X(1,5)
X(2,1)    X(2,2)    ...    X(2,5)
  .
  .
  .
X(10,1)   X(10,2)   ...    X(10,5)
```

Now, suppose that we want to find the sum of the numbers in each row of the array and store the sum of the Ith row in Y(I).   So,

$$Y(I) = X(I,1) + X(I,2) + \cdots + X(I,5)$$

And suppose that we also want to set Z equal to the sum of all the numbers in the array X. So,

$$Z = Y(1) + Y(2) + \cdots + Y(10)$$

This problem may be solved as shown in Figure 6-6.

This is a case of nested program loops. Notice that the loop containing the statement

$$Y(I) = Y(I) + X(I,J)$$

is performed five times, every time the outer loop is performed once. This can be put into FORTRAN, using two DO statements:

```
       DIMENSION X(10,5), Y(10)
       Z = 0.0
       DO 20 I = 1, 10
       Y(I) = 0.0
       DO 10 J = 1, 5
   10  Y(I) = Y(I) + X(I,J)
   20  Z = Z + Y(I)
```

The second DO statement corresponds to the inner loop in the flowchart. The first DO statement corresponds to the outer loop. Statement 10 will be performed first with I = 1 and J = 1, then with I = 1 and J = 2, and so on until I = 1 and J = 5; then it will be performed for I = 2 and J = 1, I = 2 and J = 2, etc., until finally I = 10 and J = 5.

Example 11

Two nested DO loops can end on the same statement. For instance, if we wanted to set each X(I,J) in the array of Example 10 equal to zero, we could have

135

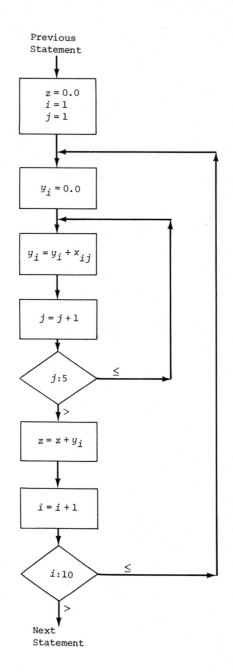

FIGURE 6-6

136

```
           DO 300  I = 1, 10
           DO 300  J = 1, 5
      300  X(I,J) = 0.0
```

As before, the inner DO loop is performed more often than the
outer DO loop. Thus, these statements would cause statement
300 to be executed 50 times, starting with I = 1 and J = 1,
then I = 1 and J = 2, etc., until I = 10 and J = 5.

The restrictions given before, which apply to single DO
loops, apply to *each* DO loop in a set of nested loops. So,
for example, we could *not* have

```
           DO 300  I = 1, 10
           GO TO 300
           DO 300  J = 1, 5
      300  X(I,J) = 0.0
```

As far as the first DO statement is concerned, the GO TO statement is all right. But as far as the second statement is concerned, the GO TO statement is illegally transferring control
to within a DO loop.

As another example, we *could* have

```
           DO 300  I = 1, 10
           J = 0
           DO 300  J = 1, 5
      300  X(I,J) = 0.0
```

But we could *not* have

```
           DO 300  I = 1, 10
           I = 0
           DO 300  J = 1, 5
      300  X(I,J) = 0.0
```

In the first case, we alter the value of J, but we do so
externally to the DO loop which controls the value of J. In
the second case, we alter the value of I, but now we are doing
so within the range of the DO loop that varies I. This violates
Rule 1.

Such restrictions forbid certain ways of nesting DO loops.
We have seen that we can nest DO loops as shown in Figure 6-7.
It is illegal, however, to try to nest DO loops as shown in
Figure 6-8. An attempt to execute such statements would amount
to an illegal transfer of control into the range of a DO loop.

137

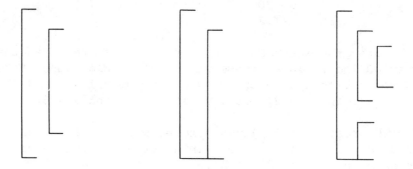

FIGURE 6-7. *Some acceptable ways to nest DO loops*

FIGURE 6-8. *Unallowable "nested" DO loops*

The following statements, then, would not be allowable.

```
        DO 10 I = 1, 10
        DO 20 J = 1, 10
   10   A = A + 1.0
   20   B = B + 1.0
```

There is no sensible way to interpret the meaning of these
statements. Of course, if we were to interchange Statements 10
and 20, there would be no problem of interpretation.

One final restriction is that we must use different control
variables in DO statements forming nested DO loops. Actually,
this is just to avoid the restriction that we cannot alter the
variable of the DO statement within the DO loop. The following
statements would be illegal:

```
        DO 5   I = 1, 5
        DO 5   I = 1, 10
    5   A = A + 1.0
```

1. Various FORTRAN statements are given below. Some are
    correct, but others violate a basic rule. If the statement
    is valid, mark a V next to it. Otherwise, make a suitable
    correction to make it valid. Some of the statements have
    been covered in previous chapters.

    a. DO 31 KXX = J, K, 3   h. A(I,3) = M2 + J
    b. DO N K6 = S, J, 2   i. DO 3 A = 1, N4A2, 2
    c. DO 2 X = J, N, N   j. DO 17 FEW = 1, N
    d. DO 100 K = N, M, N   k. DO 21 I = J, J, J
    e. DIMENSIONS X(10), Y(3), Z(100) l. DO 10 IX2 = N, N + M
    f. DO 176 IJX2 = JC2K, LAST   m. DO 3 Y = 10, 1
    g. DO 21 I = 37   n. DO 8 I = 1, 2, 3

2. Sequences of FORTRAN statements are given below. Some are
    valid and will be executed with no error. Others have errors.
    Do the same as you did in Exercise 1.

    a.   DO 3 JIM = 1, 4, 2   d.   DO 101 LIM = 1, N
            X = JIM   X = A + B
            GO TO 4   DO 9 LIM 2 = 1, M
        3   Y = X ** 2   90   Y = X + Z
        4   Y = X ** 3/2.   9   CONTINUE
                                    101   A = 0.0
    b.   DO 100 J = 1, 10
              X = J + 5   e.   DIMENSION X(100)
      100   GO TO 76   DO 5 I = 1, 20
       76   CONTINUE   ZZ = 5 * I - 6
                                            J = ZZ
    c.   DO 6 I = 1, 10   5   X(J) = J - 4
            DO 6 J = M, N, L
            X = J + I   f.   DO 22 K = 1, 20, 4
            Y = X ** 2   DO 22 L = 1, 16, 3
        6   CONTINUE   X = K
                                            Y = L - 8
                                            Z = X + Y
                                            IF (Z - 10.0) 10, 10, 12
                                       10   CONTINUE
                                       22   CONTINUE
                                       12   GO TO 9
```
```

3. After the following statements have been executed, what is
    the value of K?

                DO 700 I = 1, 100
                X = I - 1
                DO 700 J = 1, 10
                Z = J + 4
                IF (X ** 2 - 2. * X - Z) 700, 600, 700
        700 CONTINUE
                GO TO 800
        600 K = I + J
        800 CONTINUE

4. Write the FORTRAN to correspond to the following flowchart.
    Use a DO loop.

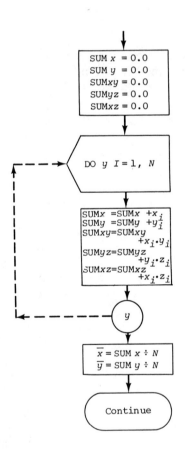

5. In the study of statistics, one frequently needs to calculate quantities known as the *variance* and the *standard deviation*. We defined the variance on page 111. The standard deviation is given by

$$S_x = \sqrt{\frac{\sum_{j=1}^{N} (X_j - \overline{X})^2}{N}}, \text{ where } \overline{X} \text{ is the mean.}$$

   Add the necessary FORTRAN statement to those in Problem 4 to calculate both the variance and the standard deviation.

6. Assume that in 1970 the population figures for the United States and Canada were 200,000,000 and 25,000,000, respectively. Assume also that the annual rate of growth for the United States was 1.10 percent and for Canada 4.75 percent. If these growth rates remain constant, will the population of Canada equal or excel that of the United States in the next 100 years? What year? Construct a flowchart to solve the problem. The flowchart should include a DO loop.

7. A deck of cards is punched with the following data:

Column	Name	
1-5	ID	Student's identification number
6	SEX	1 if male, 2 if female
7-8	HT	Height in inches
9-11	WT	Weight in pounds
12	CLASS	1 if first year, 2 if second, etc.
13	ATH	Students have been given a number from 1 to 9 depending on athletic ability, with 9 being the best.

   Write a program to determine how many prospective athletes are in a school. A prospective football player must be a male, of height greater than 60 inches, weight greater than 180 pounds, cannot be a freshman, and must have athletic ability of 7 or more. Use a DO loop to do this. Your output should include a student's identification number.

8. Write a program to handle a person's bank checking account. Assume that for each deposit you have a card punched:

Column	Name	
1-3	NDEP	The deposit number starting with 001
4-8	IDEP	A 5-digit number referring to the depositer (does not change) as a floating-point constant
9-16	DEP	Amount of deposit

8.—*continued*

For each check you have:

Column	Name	
1-5	IDEP	Same as above
6-9	NCHK	Check number
10-17	AMT	Amount of the check

The first data card contains the following information

Column	Name	
1-3	NUMDEP	Number of deposits to be read in
4-6	NUMCHK	Number of checks to be read in
7-14	BAL	Previous balance

Write a program to input the above data and output the listing of your transactions. For sample input data, use your own check book and check records.

9. Modify the program written in Problem 8 to handle not only your checks and deposits but also anyone else's. Rather than count the number of deposits and checks, add a test at the end of the data deck to stop the computer from reading cards. This can be done by assigning a number of 99999 in the space on the last card where IDEP is and making a similar test for the checks.

B EXERCISES

1. The following results for the sum of the first n numbers, the sum of the squares of the first n numbers, and the sum of the cubes of the first n numbers are proven in nearly every elementary algebra text.

$$1 + 2 + 3 + \cdots + n = 1/2 [n(n+1)]$$
$$1^2 + 2^2 + 3^2 + \cdots + n^2 = 1/6 [n(n+1)(2n+1)]$$
$$1^3 + 2^3 + 3^3 + \cdots + n^3 = (1 + 2 + 3 + \cdots + n)^2$$

Suppose, however, that we did not know this and we wanted to calculate the three sums. Write a flowchart to do this that uses a single DO loop.

2. Write the FORTRAN for Problem 1 that corresponds to the DO loop.

3. Given the three sides of a triangle, a, b, c. The area is given by *Heron's formula* to be

$$AREA = \sqrt{s(s - a)(s - b)(s - c)},$$

where $s = 1/2(a + b + c)$.

a. Write the flowchart to input three sides of a triangle, calculate the area, and output the answer.

b. Generalize your flowchart to calculate the areas for n triangles.

4. The atmospheric pressure, p, in inches of mercury, is given approximately by $p = 29.9(10)^{-.093m}$, where m is the altitude in miles above sea level. Write a program to give the pressure at intervals of 1/4 mile starting from 1 mile below sea level to 10 miles above sea level.

5. A popular example of elementary probability theory is to determine the probability that two people out of a randomly selected group of m people have the same birthday. Ignoring leap years, the probability of any two people *not* having the same birthday is 364/365. The probability that a third person's birthday will differ from the first two is 363/365; a fourth person's is 362/365, etc. For 10 people we have nine such fractions to be multiplied together to obtain the probability that all 10 birthdays are different. Write a program to generate the probabilities that two people out of a group of m have the same birthday where m varies from 2 to 80. (If you have never seen this problem, the results may surprise you.)

6. A deck of data cards is punched as follows:

Column	Name	
1-5	IDEN	Student's identification number
6	COLL	Student's college, assume 6 colleges, numbered 1 through 6
7-11	GPA	Student's grade average as a number (4.00 is the highest and 0.00 the lowest)
12	CLASS	The year a student is in, 1 for freshman 2 for sophomore, etc. A student is a senior (graduating) if he is a fourth year or higher student.

Write a program to input the above data and output the graduating students who are to graduate with honors (a GPA of 3.5 or more).

143

7. Modify Problem 6 to output all the graduating seniors according to rank in class starting with the top GPA and going down.

8. An outdoor movie screen is 15 feet above the eye level and is itself 40 feet high. The best spot to park your car is at the point P, where the angle (α) your eye makes with the screen is the largest. Let x be the distance measured from the screen. It can be shown that the tangent of α is given by the formula

$$\tan \alpha = \frac{40x}{x^2 + 825}$$

The value of x that maximizes $\tan \alpha$ also maximizes x. Write a program to find this value, starting with $x = 0$ and incrementing x by 1. For each increment of x, $\tan \alpha$ should increase until it reaches the desired maximum. When $\tan \alpha$ starts to decrease, the problem is solved, correct to the nearest foot.

Chapter 7

In this chapter, we shall present other forms of the READ, WRITE, and FORMAT statements. We shall also discuss other statements that may be used for obtaining input and output data from a computer.

REPEAT SPECIFICATIONS IN FIELD DESCRIPTORS

Consider the statements

            READ (2, 10) A, B, C, D
    10 FORMAT (F5.0, F5.0, F5.0, F5.0)

In this case, a series of identical field descriptors come one after another in the FORMAT statement. In such cases, there is a shorter way of writing the FORMAT statement. This consists of FORMAT statements using *repeat specifications*. In the statement

        10 FORMAT (4F5.0)

the number 4 is called a repeat count. It means that the F5.0 field descriptor which follows is to be repeated four times. So, both of the above FORMAT statements mean exactly the same thing. The repeat specification may be used with any of the field descriptors we have mentioned. For example, the statements

            READ (1, 54) I1, I2, J, A1, A2, B1, B2, B3
    54 FORMAT (3I4, 2F10.0, 3E7.0)

mean that the first three fields read (for I1, I2, and J) are read with an I4 field descriptor; the following two fields (for A1 and A2) use an F10.0 field descriptor; and the last three fields on the card (for B1, B2, and B3) use an E7.0 field descriptor. This form of the FORMAT statement is a shorthand way of writing

    54 FORMAT (I4, I4, I4, F10.0, F10,0, E7.0, E7.0, E7.0)

Suppose now that we have a whole group of field descriptors that is repeated. For instance, in the statement

        5 FORMAT (I6, F10.2, I6, F10.2, I6, F10.2)

the group I6, F10.2 is repeated three times. This sort of

situation can also be abbreviated, using a *group repeat count*. We place parentheses around the whole group and then we write the repeat factor in front of the parentheses to specify how many times the group is to be repeated. This would be written

```
5  FORMAT (3(I6, F10.2))
```

The use of repeat counts in a FORMAT statement is quite general; repeated descriptors or groups of descriptors can be used anywhere, and the meaning will be the same as if the whole group were written out the long way. The following are some further examples of repeat specifications:

```
12  FORMAT (I5, F5.2, 4(I3, E4.0))
55  FORMAT (3(I2, I4), 3F10.0)
 7  FORMAT (2(I3, F5.1, E8.0, I4), I2, 2(F5.0, I2))
14  FORMAT (F11.4, 2(I2, F6.0, I3), 3F5.2)
```

THE SLASH (/) IN THE FORMAT *STATEMENT*

The slash (/) means division in a FORTRAN arithmetic expression. In a FORMAT statement, it has a different meaning. Here it means to skip to the beginning of the next card (for input) or the next line (for output). The slash can be used anywhere in the FORMAT statement. Commas are used optionally to separate it from adjacent field descriptors. Thus, the statements

```
    WRITE (2, 11) X, NED, ZAP
11  FORMAT (F10.1/I10/F10.1)
```

mean to write X with an F10.1 field, skip to the next line, write NED with an I10 field, skip to the next line, and write ZAP with an F10.1 field. So, if X = 12.2, NED = 100, and ZAP = 520.8, the resulting output would be

```
12.2
100
520.8
```

We can also skip more than one line, using the slash. There are two ways to do this. The first way is just to write a series of slashes in a row, such as ////. The second way is to use a repeat factor and enclose the slash in parentheses: $n(/)$. For instance, 4(/) means the same thing as ////. In both cases, each time a slash is encountered it means to skip to the beginning of the next line (or card). For example,

```
   WRITE (2, 3) M, L
3  FORMAT (I5////I5) or 3 FORMAT (I5,////,I5)
```

146

means to write M under an I5 format, skip to the beginning of the next line, skip to the beginning of the next line three more times, then write L with an I5 format. Thus, three lines in all are skipped between the two numbers printed. Notice that *n* slashes means that *n* - 1 lines are skipped between the numbers printed. This is because the slash means "skip to the beginning of the next line," and not "skip a line." Note this difference. For example, if N = 11 and M = 22,

```
        WRITE (2, 1) N, M
     1  FORMAT (I5/I5)
```

will print out

```
        11
        22
```

There is one slash, but no lines are skipped *between* the two numbers printed; it is just that the second number is printed on the next line.

Used for input, the slash means to skip to the beginning of a new card. This enables us to read more than one card with a single READ statement. For instance, suppose that A(I) and B(I) are punched in columns 1-10 and 11-20 of a card. To read three such cards and store the values read in the first three elements of each array, we could use the statements

```
        READ (1, 7) A(1), B(1), A(2), B(2), A(3), B(3)
     7  FORMAT (2F10.0/2F10.0/2F10.0)
```

Then A(1) and B(1) are read from the first card, each with an F10.0 format. The slash means to ignore the rest of the first card and go on to the beginning of the next card. A(2) and B(2) are then read from the second card, and A(3) and B(3) are read from the third card. Actually, we can shorten this FORMAT statement somewhat, using a repeat specification:

```
     7  FORMAT (2(2F10.2/), 2F10.2)
```

Of course, we could do the same thing by performing the READ statement three times, since each time the READ statement is executed, a new card is read. In this case, we could have put

```
        DO 10 I = 1, 3
    10  READ (2, 7) A(I), B(I)
     7  FORMAT (2F10.0)
```

In many cases, however, the use of the slash is more convenient.

147

OUTPUT AND PUNCHED CARDS

We mentioned earlier that output from a computer can be in
the form of punched cards. This is often very desirable since
the data can then be immediately used in subsequent programs.
Let us assume that the unit number in the WRITE statement for the
punch is 7.   The following FORTRAN statement

```
          WRITE (7, 10) X
     10   FORMAT (10X, F10.4)
```

will result in a card being punched. This card will have the
first 10 columns blank and the value of X punched in columns
11-20 with four decimal places. The rest of the card will be
blank.

Since punched cards have only 80 columns, care must be taken
not to exceed this field length. For example, the FORTRAN statement

```
          WRITE (2, 100) A, B, C
     100  FORMAT (3F40.8)
```

is correct, but the statement

```
          WRITE (7, 100) A, B, C
```

could not punch A, B, and C on a single card.

ALTERNATE TO THE H FIELD DESCRIPTOR

One of the most time-consuming aspects of writing a program
comes in the writing of the FORMAT statements using Hollerith
specifications. At one time, this was the only way to obtain
printed headings. This is still a satisfactory method and has
the advantage that it will work in all FORTRAN systems. However,
other convenient methods are now being used. Unfortunately, they
are not uniform from computer to computer. One such method is
to use asterisks in the FORMAT statements. Everything between
asterisks is simply printed out as is. (Another computer system
uses a quote mark. Before attempting this, check with the
instruction manual for the particular computer.)

For example,

```
          WRITE (2, 500)
     500  FORMAT (* THE ANSWER IS AS FOLLOWS *)
```

results in the message

being printed out. But if one desires an asterisk to be printed, the H field must be used.

IMPLIED DO LOOPS IN THE VARIABLE LIST

Consider the statement

READ (1, 5) X(1), X(2), X(3), X(4), X(5), X(6), X(7), X(8)

In this statement, we are reading in the first eight elements of the array X. Obviously, it is a bit tedious to have to explicitly write out each element of the array that is to be read. It would be considerably more tedious if we wanted to read the first 100 values of an array in a similar fashion. Fortunately, however, there is a method in FORTRAN that solves this problem. The notation is somewhat similar to the DO statement, and is called the *implied DO loop*. This is used only in the list of variables in a READ or WRITE statement. For a one-dimensional array, the form is

$$(\text{Name}(I), \ I = m_1, \ m_2, \ m_3)$$

where

Name is any array name,
I is any integer variable name,
m_1, m_2, m_3 are integer constants or variables;
m_1 is the initial value,
m_2 is the terminal value, and
m_3 is the increment.

The last of these, m_3, can be omitted, and in that case it is assumed to be 1. When this form is encountered on the list of an input or output statement, the following occurs:

First, the variable I is set equal to m_1, and the array element Name(I) is read or written.

Second, m_3 is added to I.

Third, I is compared to m_2; if I is greater than m_2, the implied DO loop is finished; otherwise, Name(I) is read or written, and then the process goes back to the second step.

In other words, writing (Name(I), I = m_1, m_2, m_3) in the list of variables of a READ or WRITE statement is like writing Name(m_1), Name($m_1 + m_3$), Name($m_1 + m_3 + m_3$), $\cdots$, Name(m_2).

Suppose we want to read in a value for a variable Z, and then the values for the subscripted variables A(3), A(5), A(7),

A(9), A(11), A(13), A(15), and A(17), and finally the value of the variable Q. We could use the statement

READ (I, 87) Z, (A(IDEN), IDEN = 3, 18, 2), Q

After reading Z, the integer variable IDEN is set to 3 and A(3) is read, then 2 is added to IDEN and since IDEN is still less than 18, A(IDEN) [that is, A(5)] is read. IDEN is then incremented again by 2, and A(7) is read, and so on until A(17) has been read. After this, we are through reading values for A, and so Q is read. Of course, an appropriate FORMAT statement must be used. In this case, since ten values in all (Z, 8 A's, Q) are being read, if they were all punched with an F5.0 format, we could use the statement

87 FORMAT (10F5.0)

As always, there is one field descriptor for each variable.

As mentioned before, if the increment (m_3) is omitted from the implied DO loop form, it is assumed to be 1, just as with the DO statement. So, to rewrite the statement

READ (1, 5) X(1), X(2), X(3), X(4), X(5), X(6), X(7), X(8)

using this form it would suffice to put

READ (1, 5) (X(JIK), JIK = 1, 8)

The limits in the implied DO loop can be integer variables as well as constants, provided, of course, that their values are valid as subscripts for the array involved. The above statement, for instance, is equivalent to

        L = 1
        LL = 8
        READ (1, 5) (X(JIK), JIK = L, LL)

More than one variable name can appear in the implied DO loop. In the more general case, the form is

(Name1(I), Name2(I), $\cdots$, NameN(I), I = m_1, m_2, m_3)

This form is equivalent to writing out Name1(m_1), Name2(m_1), $\cdots$, NameN(m_1), Name1($m_1 + m_3$), Name2($m_1 + m_3$), $\cdots$. That is, the implied DO loop is performed for all variables enclosed in parentheses. For instance, if A, B, and C are arrays, we can write out their values in the order A(1), B(1), C(1), A(2), B(2), C(2), $\cdots$, C(7) by using the statement

150

$$\text{WRITE } (2, 87)(A(I), B(I), C(I), I = 1, 7)$$

There is one further simplification that is allowed in reading or writing an array: If the whole array is to be read or written, it is necessary to put only the name of the array in the variable list. By the "whole array" we mean all the elements of the array, as defined by the DIMENSION statement. If an array YYY is declared by

$$\text{DIMENSION } \text{YYY}(10)$$

then the whole array is the list of variables YYY(1), YYY(2), YYY(3), $\cdots$, YYY(10). In this case, the above rule means that putting just the array name YYY in the list of an input or output statement is the same as writing out all the elements, or using an implied DO list which specifies all the elements. Thus,

$$\text{READ } (1, 2) \text{ YYY}$$

would mean the same thing as

$$\text{READ } (1, 2) \text{ (YYY(I), I = 1, 10)}$$

Doubly-subscripted arrays can also be handled with an implied DO loop. The general form in this case is

$$((\text{Name}(I, J), I = m_1, m_2, m_3), J = n_1, n_2, n_3)$$

where

Name is the name of a two-dimensional array;
I, J are integer variables;
m_1, m_2, m_3, n_1, n_2, n_3 are integer constants or variables.

This form is similar to a pair of nested DO loops, with the innermost variable varying most rapidly. That is, the above form is equivalent to writing out

$\text{Name}(m_1, n_1)$, $\text{Name}(m_1 + m_3, n_1)$, $\text{Name}(m_1 + 2m_3, n_1)$, $\cdots$, $\text{Name}(m_2, n_1)$,

$\text{Name}(m_1, n_1 + n_3)$, $\text{Name}(m_1 + m_3, n_1 + n_3)$, $\cdots$, $\text{Name}(m_2, n_1 + n_3)$, $\cdots$,

$\text{Name}(m_1, n_2)$, $\text{Name}(m_1 + m_3, n_2)$, $\cdots$, $\text{Name}(m_2, n_2)$

In other words, J is set first to n_1, and then the whole inner loop is performed just as in the one-dimensional case. Then J is incremented by n_3, and if J is not greater than n_2, the inner implied DO loop is performed again, and so on until finally J is greater than n_2. If either m_3 or n_3 is omitted, it is assumed to be 1.

For example, the statement

```
            READ (1, 3)  ((A(N, M), N = 1, 2), M = 1, 3)
```

is equivalent to

```
    READ (1, 3) A(1, 1), A(2,1), A(1,2), A(2,2), A(1,3), A(2,3)
```

An implied DO loop does not, however, have to apply to both
subscripts of a two-dimensional array. We can vary only one
subscript, if desired, while holding the other one fixed. For
example,

```
            WRITE (2, 17)  (MAT(L, J), J = 2, 10, 2)
```

would write out the values of

```
    MAT(L, 2), MAT(L, 4), MAT(L, 6), MAT(L, 8), MAT(L, 10)
```

(The variable L is understood to have been previously defined.)

As with singly-subscripted arrays, if we put just the array
name of a doubly-subscripted array in the variable list of a READ
or WRITE statement, this automatically specifies all the elements
of the array, as defined in the DIMENSION statement. In this
case, the first subscript varies the most rapidly. Thus, if XEL
is a doubly-subscripted array defined by the statement

```
            DIMENSION XEL (2,4)
```

then if we put just the name XEL in an input-output variable list,
it would mean the same thing as if we had written

```
            ((XEL(I, J) I = 1, 2), J = 1, 4)
```

So, if we had the statement

```
            READ (1, 4) XEL
```

it would read in all the elements of the array XEL in the order

```
    XEL(1,1), XEL(2,1), XEL(1,2), XEL(2,2), XEL(1,3), ···, XEL(2,4)
```

The implied DO loop notation can be used advantageously with
the slash and repeated field descriptors for reading or writing
subscripted variables. To see how this is done, suppose that we
want to read in the values of a doubly-subscripted array called Z.
If Z(1,1), Z(2,1), ···, Z(7,1) are punched on the first card, each
with an F10.0 format, we can read these values with the statements

```
            READ (1,5) (Z(I, 1), I = 1, 7)
        5   FORMAT (7F10.0)
```

If the next four cards are similarly punched, the second card containing the values of Z(1, 2), Z(2, 2), $\cdots$, Z(7, 2), the third card containing the values of Z(1, 3), Z(2, 3), $\cdots$, Z(7, 3), and so on, we could read all five cards with the statements

```
      READ (1, 5) ((Z(I, J), I = 1, 7), J = 1, 5)
    5 FORMAT (5(7F10.0/))
```

These statements mean that seven numbers are read from the first card and stored in Z(1, 1), Z(2,1), $\cdots$, Z(7, 1). Now there are still ten blank columns left over on the first card, so the slash means to go on and read the next number from the second card. Notice that the group repeat count five repeats the slash as well as the 7F10.0, so that this process continues for all five cards. If it so happened that the array Z were dimensioned to be exactly 7 by 5, that is, that it were declared by the statement

```
    DIMENSION Z(7, 5)
```

then we could omit the implied DO loops and just write the array name Z in the READ statement

```
    READ (1, 5) Z
```

Since the whole array is being read, this would mean the same thing.

As another example, suppose that X, JOHN, and ZIP are one-dimensional arrays, and we want to print out X(1), JOHN(1), and ZIP(1) on the first print line, X(2), JOHN(2), and ZIP(2) on the second print line, and so on for all 20 values of each array. This can be done, using a DO statement:

```
      DO 23 I = 1, 20
   23 WRITE (2, 7) X(I), JOHN(I), ZIP(I)
    7 FORMAT (F10.5, I10, F10.5)
```

We could do this just as well, using an implied DO loop notation:

```
      WRITE (2,7) (X(I), JOHN(I), ZIP(I), I = 1, 20)
    7 FORMAT (F10.5, I10, F10.5)
```

In this example, the number of field specifications (3) and the number of variables (20) are not the same. The rules governing this are given next.

When the list is shorter than the FORMAT specifications, the additional numeric field specifications are ignored. But any field specifications that are not numeric are executed up to either the last right-hand parenthesis or the next numeric field specification, whichever comes first. The statements

```
        WRITE (2, 8) A, B
      8 FORMAT (F20.4,/,F20.4,//,F20.4)
```

will result in the following output: The value of A is printed
out according to the field specification of F20.4; the printer
skips to the next line; the value of B is printed in an identical
field; then the *printer skips to a new line twice* (leaving one
actual line skipped) before execution of the original input or
output statement is terminated. The DO loop

```
        DO 100 I = 1, 20
    100 WRITE (2, 101) X(I)
    101 FORMAT (2F15.4)
```

is another example of having more field specifications than
variables. In this case, there will be 20 lines of print, one
value of X on each line.

   If there are more variables in the list than specifications
in the FORMAT statement, the format control will revert to one of
two places determined as follows:

   CASE 1: If there are no nested parentheses, control
             reverts to the start of the FORMAT statement.

   CASE 2: If there are nested parentheses, control
             reverts to the *right-most left parenthesis.*

   In both of these cases, every time the control reverts to a
new position, the system demands a new record start (i.e., read
another card, print on a new line).

   The statements written as the implied DO loop

```
        WRITE (2, 101) (X(I), I = 1, 20)
    101 FORMAT (2F10.5)
```

will now result in 10 lines of printed output. The statements

```
        WRITE (2, 200) I, A, B, C, D, E
    200 FORMAT (I10, (F10.3))
```

will print the value of I, according to the field specification
I10 and then the values of A, B, C, D, and E according to the
field specification F10.3. The value of A will be on the same
line as the value of I but the other values will be on separate
lines.

154

OTHER FORMS OF INPUT-OUTPUT[1]

There are several other statements that can be used for input and output. These vary with the computer and so care must be exercised before attempting to use them. If you understand the principle behind the READ and WRITE statements discussed in the preceding sections, there will be no difficulty in adapting the statements to be presented here.

The READ Statement. A statement that can also be used to read data into the computer is the READ statement. It differs from our previous READ statement in that the form is

$$\text{READ } n, \text{ var}_1, \text{ var}_2, \cdots, \text{ var}_n$$

where n is a number referring to a FORMAT statement and var_1, var_2, $\cdots$, var_n are a list of n variables. Notice that a comma is inserted between the format number and the first variable name. No unit number is specified—the card reader is implied by the form of the statement.

Several examples of this together with the FORMAT statement are:

Statement	*Explanation*
READ 6, A 6 FORMAT (10X, F10.2)	A variable A is read into the computer. The variable is punched on a card in columns 11-20.
READ 100, YES, NO 100 FORMAT (F20.8/I3)	Two variables YES and NO are read into the computer. YES is on the first card in columns 1-20 and NO is on the next card in the first three columns.
READ 20, (ARRAY (I), I = 1, 40) 20 FORMAT (7F10.3)	Forty values of the variable ARRAY are read in. They are punched seven to a card with field widths of 10. A total of six cards are read, seven values from each of the first five cards and five from the last card.

---

[1]The statements presented here are not necessarily ANSI standard FORTRAN. They are, however, still very commonly used and will work on most computer systems.

Statement	Explanation
DO 20 I = 1, 40 20 READ 30, ARRAY (I) 30 FORMAT (7F10.3)	Again, 40 values of the variable ARRAY are read. This time 40 data cards are needed. (Why?)

The PRINT Statement. For output, the PRINT statement can sometimes be used. It is analogous to the WRITE statement we learned about before. However, the unit is assumed to be the printer, and hence need not be specified in the statement. Its general form is

$$\text{PRINT } n, \text{ var}_1, \text{ var}_2, \cdots, \text{ var}_n$$

where n is a statement number referring to a FORMAT statement and var_1, var_2, $\cdots$, var_n are a list of variables to be printed out.

A few examples of this are given below:

Statement	Explanation
PRINT 1000, A, B, C, I, J, K 1000 FORMAT (3F20.3, I4, I5, I6)	The values of six variables A, B, C, I, J, K are printed out. A, B, and C take 20 spaces each; I, J, and K take 4, 5, and 6 spaces, respectively.
PRINT 7, X, Y 7 FORMAT (1H1, 20X, 3HX =, 1 F6.2, 10X, 3HY =, F6.2)	First, the printer skips to a new page, 20 columns are skipped, the characters Xb = are printed, then the value of X is printed. Then 10 columns are skipped and characters Yb = are printed. Next, the value of Y is printed.

On many systems, all input and output must be done using magnetic tapes. For some computers, this requires READ and WRITE statements that have the following form:

$$\text{READ INPUT TAPE } n, \text{ } m, \text{ var}_1, \text{ var}_2, \cdots, \text{ var}_n$$
$$\text{WRITE OUTPUT TAPE } n, \text{ } m, \text{ var}_1, \text{ var}_2, \cdots, \text{ var}_n$$

The meaning of the above should be clear:

n refers to the tape used for input (output). This depends on the particular tapes being used. Some computers require only certain tapes for these operations, and in others the programmer can select his own.

m is the statement number corresponding to a FORMAT statement.

var_1, var_2, $\cdots$, var_n are a list of variables to be input or output.

There are even alternate forms to the above statements that are actually a shorthand method of writing them. They are

RIT *n*, *m*, var_1, var_2, $\cdots$, var_n for READ INPUT TAPE
WOT *n*, *m*, var_1, var_2, $\cdots$, var_n for WRITE OUTPUT TAPE

Their meanings are exactly the same as discussed above.

The PUNCH Statement. An alternate FORTRAN statement for obtaining punched cards for output is the PUNCH statement. The general form of it is

PUNCH *n*, var_1, var_2, $\cdots$, var_n

where *n* refers to a FORMAT statement number and var_1, var_2, $\cdots$, var_n are a list of variables to be punched.

For example,

PUNCH 101, LIST, ARRAY
101   FORMAT (I3, F10.2)

will result in the values of the two variables LIST and ARRAY being punched on a card according to the form as specified in Statement 101.

157

A EXERCISES

1. Examples are given below of Input-Output statements. If the statement is correct, mark a V next to it; if not, make a suitable correction to make it valid.

   a.   READ (1, 2) JUMP, OVER
        2 FORMAT (10X, I6, 2X, F10.8)

   b.   WRITE (2, 90) THE, ANSWER
      90 FORMAT (25X, ////, 5X, 2F11.3)

   c.   WRITE (2, 80)
      80 FORMAT (1H1, 20X, 14H THE ANSWER IS)

   d.   READ (1, 1) I, (X(J), J = 1, I)
       1 FORMAT (I8/ (8F10.2))

   e.   WRITE (2, 30) ALPHA, BETA, GO
      30 FORMAT (4F, 10.8)

   f.   READ (1, 10), X, Y, ZZ
      10 FORMAT (2F10.0)

   g.   DIMENSION X(10, 100)
           WRITE (2, 800) ((X(I, J), (= 1, 4), J = 1, 60)
    800 FORMAT (10X, 4F30.8)

   h.   N = 4
           DIMENSION X(N)
           READ (1, 11) (X(I), I = 1, 2)
      11 FORMAT (10F4.2)

   i.   DIMENSION X(20), Y(20)
       7 FORMAT (F8.2)
           DO 12 J = 1, 20, 2
      12 READ (1, 7) X(J)
           DO 5 J = 1, 20
       5 Y(J) = X(J) * X(J)

2. Below are a few examples of the READ statement. Determine how many data cards are actually used for each case.

   a.   READ (1, 2) A, C, B, D
       2 FORMAT (3F10.4)

   b.   READ (1, 80) I, J, X, Y, Z
      80 FORMAT (I3, I4/2F10.2/F20.8)

```
c.          DO 10 I = 1, 4
            DO 10 J = 1, 4
      10    READ (1, 11) X(I, J)
      11    FORMAT (2F10.6)

d.          READ (1, 100) (X(I), I = 1, 19)
     100    FORMAT (6F10.3)

e.          READ (1, 99) (Y(I), I = 1, 20)
      99    FORMAT (4F8.2/3F8.1/2F10.2/(3F10.3))

f.          READ (1, 10) ((ARRAY (I, J), I = 1, 10), J = 1, 9)
      10    FORMAT (7F10.4)
```

3. Write the FORTRAN to correspond to the flowchart on page 21, Chapter 1.

4. Write the FORTRAN to correspond to the flowchart on the following page.

5. Write the FORTRAN statement that will result in the following inputs or outputs.

a. Skip to a new page, skip 10 lines, output the values of X and Y in a field F20.8.

b. Skip 5 lines, skip 20 spaces, print the heading X-VALUE, skip 10 spaces, print the heading Y-VALUE, skip a line, then print the values of X and Y under the headings, according to a field of F20.4.

c. Assume a 132-column printer. The 20 values of the two arrays A and Y are to be printed with headings X-ARRAY and Y-ARRAY. The arrays are to be centered on the page.

d. Read in 800 values of Z into an array. The data are punched 8 to a card, each value 10 columns long.

e. The variable array Z is to be read in from punched cards, one value per card. Each card is punched according to field E20.4. The last card has -.999E + 3 in this field. This is *not* a data card, but will be used to control the input statement. There are fewer than 1000 values of Z. Write the FORTRAN to input the array and let N be the number of cards read in.

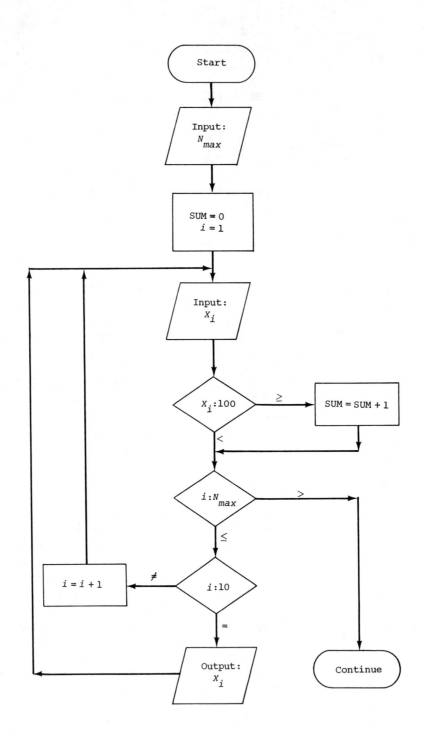

5.—*continued*

    f.   Output on a printer according to format F30.4
       the values just read into the computer in Part e.
       Make appropriate headings and include the subscript
       along with the variable.

6.   Write the FORTRAN to read in 30 values of X and Y, find
    their sum, called SUMXY, their difference, DIFXY, and
    their products, PRDXY. The output is to be both in tabled
    form and punched cards.

7.   Write the FORTRAN statements to input three numbers, N, Al,
    and D. Then calculate

$$SN = \frac{N}{2}\left[2Al + (N - 1)D\right]$$

and output the results. This is to be repeated until a
value of N is input that is either zero or negative.

B EXERCISES

1.   A hallway 6 feet wide meets another that is 4 feet wide at
    a right angle. What is the longest length of a perfectly
    straight ladder that can be carried around the corner.
    It can be shown that the length L is given in terms of x as

$$L = x + \frac{6x}{\sqrt{x^2 - 16}}$$

Find L correct to the nearest
.1 foot by setting $x = 4.1$
and incrementing it until the
maximum L is found. Have your
output include a sketch of the
problem to be solved as follows:

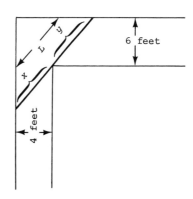

1.—*continued*

LADDER PROBLEM FIND LONGEST LENGTH TO FIT AROUND CORNER

```
        X
        X                    . . . . . . . .  .
        X                    .
        X                    .          6  ft.
        X                    .  . . . . . . .  .
        X                    .  .
        X                  .   4   .
        X                  .  ft.  .
        X                    .     .
        X                    .     .
        X                    .     .
```

LADDER LENGTH   CORNER SKETCH

2. A company keeps its monthly billing statements on computer
    cards. On each card the following data is punched:

Columns

1–20	Person's name (to be ignored in INPUT-OUTPUT for now)
21–25	NUMB	Five-digit account number
26–31	AMTOLD	Amount of money owed
32–37	AMTPD	Amount paid this month

To figure out a new balance for each person, the following
equation is used:

$$BAL = AMTPD - AMTOLD \ (1.015)$$

Write a program to read in any amount of cards and print a
statement for each card read. This statement will simply
read (for a typical case)

ACCT. NO.	OLD BALANCE	AMT. PAID	NEW BALANCE
05213	$126.00	$50.00	$77.89

THANK YOU FOR YOUR PROMPT PAYMENT. NEXT PAYMENT IS DUE
BY THE FIRST OF THE MONTH.

If no amount was paid, the new balance is still figured but
a message is also printed warning what happens to people who
do not pay their bills. If the old balance was zero, nothing
is output.

3. Generalize Problem 1 for any two hallways *a* and *b* feet wide.

4. The Pythagorean theorem states that the sum of the squares of a right-angled triangle is equal to the square of the hypotenuse. The most common such triangle is the one whose sides are 3, 4, and 5. Other such triangles are (5, 12, 13), (7, 24, 25), and (15, 8, 17). There are, of course, an infinite number of such triangles. To generate these, the following formulas can be used:

$$\text{One side:} \quad X = m^2 - n^2$$
$$\text{Other side:} \quad Y = 2mn$$
$$\text{Hypotenuse:} \quad Z = m^2 + n^2$$

where n is any positive integer and m is any integer larger than n. The student can readily verify that, using the above, one does obtain a triangle satisfying the Pythagorean theorem.

Write a program to construct a table of 100 such triangles. Since m and n are arbitrary, take $n = 1$ and let m start with $m = 2$ and increment it by one. Your output should include an appropriate table heading as well as a listing of m, n, X, Y, and Z.

5. The results of an English and mathematics examination are punched on cards as follows:

Columns

1-20	NAME	Name of student (not used in this problem)
21-23	IENGL	Score on English test (0 to 100)
24-26	MATH	Score on mathematics test

Write a program to draw one bar graph for the grades as follows:

```
        BAR GRAPH FOR 21 STUDENTS'
          GRADES IN MATHEMATICS

        . . . . . . . . . . . . . .
        . 1 1 1 1 1
        . 1 1 1 1 1
  50-60 . 1 1 1 1 1
        . 1 1 1 1 1
        . 1 1 1 1
        . 1 1 1 1
  60-70 . 1 1 1 1
        . 1 1 1 1
        . 1 1 1 1 1 1 1 1
        . 1 1 1 1 1 1 1 1
```

163

BAR GRAPH—*continued*

```
        . . . . . . . . . . . . . .
70-80   . 1 1 1 1 1 1 1
        . 1 1 1 1 1 1 1
        .
        .
80-90   .
        .
        .
        . 1 1 1 1
90-100  . 1 1 1 1
        . 1 1 1 1
        . 1 1 1 1
        . . . . . . . . . . . . .
```

6. In order for a space ship to be launched from the earth and reach the moon, it must be launched with sufficient velocity to escape the earth's gravitational field. This minimum velocity is called the *escape velocity* and one expression for it is

$$Vo^2 = 2gRe - \frac{200gRe^2}{81(a + Rm + Re)} + \frac{2gRe^2}{81(a + Rm)}$$

where Re = radius of earth (the earth is assumed to be a sphere)
     Rm = radius of moon
      a = distance between earth and moon
      g = acceleration due to gravity on earth

Write a program to evaluate the above for the following values:

      a = 240,000 miles
   Re = 4000 miles
      g = 32 ft/sec^2
   Rm = 1/4 Re

If there were no moon (or any other heavenly body attracting the space ship), the escape velocity would be given by

$$Vo^2 = 2gRe$$

By how much do your two answers differ?

If the rocket is fired from the earth with velocity equal to the escape velocity, its velocity at any distance r is given by

164

6.—*continued*

$$V = \frac{2gRe^2}{r + Re}$$

(again neglecting all heavenly bodies).

Tabulate V for r going from 0 to 240,000 miles in increments of 10,000 miles.

PART TWO

Additional FORTRAN

Chapter 8

SUBPROGRAMS

It is often necessary in a program to perform some procedure several times. Such a procedure may be regarded as a *subprogram*. In general, a subprogram is any part of a program that we want to consider separately. There are several statements in FORTRAN that we can use to create subprograms and relate them to a main program. In this chapter, we shall see how they are used.

As an example of a subprogram, suppose we want a program to read in a number and print out its absolute value. A flowchart for this procedure is shown in Figure 8-1.

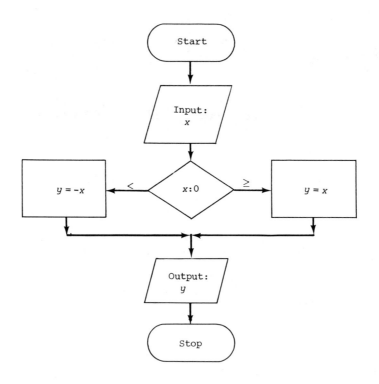

FIGURE 8-1

The procedure used to calculate Y in this flowchart may be regarded as a subprogram. We can flowchart this subprogram separately, as shown in Figure 8-2. Here we have given the name Sub 1 to the entire procedure represented by the flowchart.

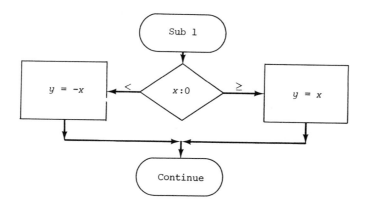

FIGURE 8-2

Now, any time we want to set Y equal to the absolute value of X in a flowchart, we can use the flowchart box shown in Figure 8-3.

FIGURE 8-3

This box represents the whole procedure defined by Figure 8-2. Using this method, we can rewrite Figure 8-1 as shown in Figure 8-4.

FIGURE 8-4

169

While this example may seem trivial, we shall see examples later on where the use of subprograms is extremely useful. The point is that once we have defined a subprogram, we can use it again and again without writing it out each time. In a flowchart, this is done by using a six-sided box like the one shown in Figure 8-3. In FORTRAN, there are four basic types of subprograms: statement functions; intrinsic functions; external functions; and external subroutines. We shall consider each of these in this chapter.

STATEMENT FUNCTIONS

A statement function is used to evaluate an arithmetic expression. Suppose that in some program we are going to want to evaluate the expression $X**2+X+1.0$ several times for different values of X. We can set up a statement function Y(X) by putting the following statement at the beginning of the program:

$$Y(X) = X**2+X+1.0$$

This statement is *not* an assignment statement. The equals sign here does *not* have its usual meaning to evaluate the right-hand side and assign the value to the left-hand side. Instead, this statement serves to define a function Y. Actually, the statement does three things:

1. It tells that Y is a function;
2. It tells that the function Y involves one variable, X;
3. It tells how Y is to be evaluated.

What we are actually doing is defining the *expression* Y(X) to be equivalent to the *expression* $X**2+X+1.0$. In the rest of the program, every time we write the expression Y(X), it will mean the same as though we had written the expression $X**2+X+1.0$. For example, consider the program:

$$Y(X) = X**2+X+1.0$$
$$X = 3.0$$
$$Z = Y(X)$$

The first statement serves to define the function Y. The second statement sets X = 3.0, and the third statement evaluates the function Y for this value of X. That is, the statement Z = Y(X) assigns Z the value 13.0, just as though we had put Z = 3.0**2+3.0+1.0.

The expression Y(X) must not be confused with a subscripted variable. Although it looks like one, it is something entirely different. A subscripted variable is always defined by a DIMENSION statement, while a statement function is always defined in a statement like the one above.

170

A statement function involves one or more variables in its definition. The function Y(X) defined above is a function of the variable X. These variables are the "dummy arguments" of the function. When we evaluate a function, we replace each dummy argument with an expression, called an "actual argument." For example, suppose we define a function F(X) by the statement

F(X) = X + 3.0

Then later on in the program, we could have the statements

A = F(1.0)
B = F(2.0)
C = F(3.0)

The statement A = F(1.0) will replace the dummy argument X in the definition of F with the actual argument 1.0 and evaluate A = 1.0 + 3.0 = 4.0.

Similarly, B will be set equal to 5.0, and C will be set equal to 6.0. The value of whatever expression appears in the parentheses of the function will replace the variable in the definition of the function. If we had the statements

X = 2
A = F(X ** 2)

then A would be evaluated as A = F(X ** 2) = X ** 2 + 3.0 = 7.0.

In general, to define a statement function in a program, we use a statement of the form

$$f(x_1, x_2, \cdots, x_n) = e$$

where

f is any FORTRAN variable that will serve as the name of the function;

$x_1, x_2, \cdots, x_n$ are FORTRAN variables that are the dummy arguments, telling what variables the function involves;

e is any arithmetic expression involving the variables $x_1, x_2, \cdots, x_n$.

This type of statement must come at the beginning of the program, before the first instruction. If a DIMENSION statement is used in the program, the function definition would come after the DIMENSION statement.[1]

Now, what this statement does is to define the expression $f(x_1, x_2, \cdots, x_n)$ to be equivalent to the expression e in the definition. Once a function has been defined in this way, we can *evaluate* it by writing the expression $f(y_1, y_2, \cdots, y_n)$. This expression has a value which is obtained by replacing each x_i with y_i in the defining expression e. The following rules must be observed:

RULE 1: Each actual argument may be any arithmetic expression.

RULE 2: Each actual argument must be the same type as the corresponding dummy argument; if x_1 is an integer variable, y_1 must be an integer expression. Also, there must be the same number of actual arguments as dummy arguments.

RULE 3: The mode of the function is determined by the first letter of its name, the same as for a variable.

As an example of these rules, suppose that the statement function

    POW (X, N) = X ** N

is used to define a function of two variables. Later in the program we could evaluate this function, replacing the variables with constants. The statement

    Y = POW(3.0, 2)

would set Y equal to POW(3.0, 2) = 3.0 ** 2 = 9. By Rule 1, the quantities in parentheses may be any arithmetic expressions. For instance, the statements

    X = 3.0
    N = 2
    Y = POW(X + 1.0, N ** 2)

would set Y equal to (X + 1.0) ** (N ** 2) = 4.0 ** 4 = 256.

---

[1] To be exact, all statement function definitions come before the first instruction (executable statement) in the program, and after all the declarations, such as DIMENSION, COMMON, and LOGICAL.

Evaluating the function in this manner simply substitutes the expressions in parentheses for the items in the definition of the function. By Rule 2, it would be incorrect to have the statement

        Y = POW(X)

since the definition of the function POW requires that it is a function of two variables. Also, by Rule 2, it would be incorrect to have the statement

        Y = POW(4, 3.0)

The first variable in the definition of the function is the floating-point variable X, so the first item in parentheses when we are evaluating the function must also be a floating-point quantity.

Rule 3 means that since POW is a floating-point name, the value of the function POW(X, N) will be a floating-point number. If we define a function by the statement

        NSUM(M, N) = M + N

then the value of this function will be an integer. NSUM(1, 2) would have the integer value 3. The function HAT(Y) = Y - 6.0 would be a floating-point function since HAT is a floating-point variable name.

Once a function has been defined, we can use it as a part of any arithmetic expression. If we define the function SUM by

        SUM(Z,Y,Z) = Z + Y + Z

then later in the program we could have the statement

        Y = 2.0 * SUM(P, Q, 1.0) ** 2 + 10.0

This would mean the same thing as the statement

        Y = 2.0 * (P + Q + 1.0) ** 2 + 10.0

The following table gives some more examples of statement functions.

Definition	Example	Value
DIF(X,Y) = X - Y	DIF(1.0,(A ** 2))	1.0 - A ** 2
CUBE(X) = X ** 3	CUBE(X + 1.0)	(X + 1.0) ** 3
MPROD(I,J,K) = I * J * K	MPROD(2,M,1/N)	2 * M * 1/N
SQ(X) = X ** 0.5	SQ(9.0)	3.0
APB(I,J) = A(I) + B(J)	APB(1,2)	A(1) + B(2)
DEG(THETA) =180.0 * THETA/3.1416	DEG(2.0 * 3.1416)	360.0

Example 1

Let us see how statement functions may be used to solve a quadratic equation in a program. Recall that the equation $Ax^2 + Bx + C = 0$ has solutions

$$X_1 = (-B + \sqrt{B^2 - 4AC})/2A$$

$$X_2 = (-B - \sqrt{B^2 - 4AC})/2A$$

The quantity $B^2 - 4AC$ is called the "discriminant" of the equation. If it is negative, the solutions will be complex numbers. For this example, we shall stop in this case after printing out the message "COMPLEX SOLUTIONS." The program will read numbers A, B, and C and print out the values for X1 and X2. Four statement functions are used in the program, which is given below:

```
        DISC(A, B, C) = B ** 2 - 4.0 * A * C
        D(A, B, C) = DISC(A, B, C) ** 0.5
        X1(A, B, C) = (-B + D(A, B, C))/(2.0 * A)
        X2(A, B, C) = (-B - D(A, B, C))/(2.0 * A)
        READ (1, 5) A, B, C
    5   FORMAT (3F10.1)
        IF (DISC(A, B, C)) 10, 20, 20
   10   WRITE (2, 15)
   15   FORMAT (17H COMPLEX SOLUTIONS)
        STOP
   20   X = X1(A, B, C)
        Y = X2(A, B, C)
        WRITE (2, 25) X, Y
   25   FORMAT (2F10.3)
        STOP
        END
```

Note that the function D uses the function DISC in its definition. This is all right, since DISC (A, B, C) just represents an arithmetic expression. Reasonable care must be exercised in defining function statements. Consider the statements

$$A(X) = B(X) + 1.0$$
$$B(X) = A(X) - 1.0$$

These statements define the function B in terms of the function A, and the function A is defined in terms of the function B. Obviously, nothing is defined at all in this way, and the statements would be illegal in FORTRAN as function definitions.

To output the solutions in the program, note that we must use the variables X and Y to store the values computed for X1 and X2. We could *not* use the statement

WRITE (2, 25) X1(A, B, C), X2(A, B, C)

since the list of the WRITE statement is composed of variable names. X1(A, B, C) and X2(A, B, C) are function references, which are expressions, and so would be illegal in this context.

Example 2

We already know how to declare a doubly-subscripted array by using a DIMENSION statement. We shall see now how we can treat a singly-subscripted array as though it were doubly-subscripted by using a statement function. Consider the function NSUB, defined as

$$NSUB(I, J) = I + 3 * (J - 1)$$

If I and J are both between 1 and 3, then each pair of numbers I, J will determine a unique number between 1 and 9:

NSUB(1, 1) = 1	NSUB(1, 2) = 4	NSUB(1, 3) = 7
NSUB(2, 1) = 2	NSUB(2, 2) = 5	NSUB(2, 3) = 8
NSUB(3, 1) = 3	NSUB(2, 3) = 6	NSUB(3, 3) = 9

Now, suppose that A and B are arrays defined by the statement

DIMENSION A(9), B(3, 3)

We can use the function NSUB to treat A as a doubly-subscripted array. For example, to set each element of A equal to a corresponding element of B, we could use the statements

```
      DO 10 I = 1, 3
      DO 10 J = 1, 3
      N = NSUB(I, J)
   10 A(N) = B(I, J)
```

175

As a matter of fact, all doubly-subscripted arrays are set up in a similar way in the computer. FORTRAN does this same procedure automatically every time a doubly-subscripted array is used in a program.

In the above case, it would undoubtedly be simpler just to declare A as a doubly-subscripted array. Suppose, however, that we wanted to use a quadruply-subscripted array in some program. This is not always permissible in FORTRAN, but we can accomplish the same thing by defining a function of four variables in a way similar to the above. If we want to set up an "array" B of dimension $3 \times 3 \times 3 \times 3$, we would make B an array of 81 elements, and use the function NSUB, defined by

$$NSUB(I, J, K, L) = I + 3 * (J - 1) + 9 * (K - 1) + 27 * (L - 1)$$

Then the statements

    N = NSUB(I, J, K, L)
    B(N) = X

would, in effect, set B(I, J, K, L) equal to X.

FORTRAN-SUPPLIED FUNCTIONS

Statement functions are just one type of function subprogram. In the next section, we shall learn how to define more complicated functions, which may involve many statements in their definitions. Some common functions arise so frequently in applications that they are "built-in" features of FORTRAN. An example is the function ABS, which finds the absolute value of a floating-point expression. The definition of this function is supplied automatically by FORTRAN, so we can use it in a program without having to define it first. For example, a program may contain the statement

    Y = ABS(X + 1.)

This statement will set Y equal to the absolute value of X + 1. The function ABS is used just like a statement function, but it is defined by FORTRAN, and so we do not have to define it in a program in order to use it. Another example is the function SIN. This function finds the trigonometric sine of an expression. Since this function is supplied by FORTRAN, we can use it in a program without having to define it ourselves. So, a program could contain the statement

    CC = 1.0 - (SIN(PHI)) ** 2

This statement would find the sine of PHI, square it, and subtract the result from 1.0.

176

Some FORTRAN-supplied functions, like ABS, are "intrinsically" defined by the compiler itself. Others, like SIN, are called "external" functions. When they are used in a program, they are called in from a library of function subprograms. This distinction does not usually concern us, however, since all FORTRAN-supplied functions are used in the same way in a program. If f is the name of any FORTRAN-supplied function, we can reference this function at any point in a program by writing the expression

$$f(y_1, y_2, \cdots, y_n)$$

Here $y_1, y_2, \cdots, y_n$ are expressions which are *actual arguments* of the function f. This usage must conform to the same rules as for statement functions.

RULE 1: Each actual argument may be a constant, a variable name, an array element name, or an arithmetic expression.

RULE 2: The actual arguments must agree in number and type with the dummy arguments in the definition of the function.

RULE 3: The value of the function is an integer or real number, depending on the first letter of the name.

For example, ABS finds the absolute value of a single floating-point expression. Thus, by Rule 2, it would be incorrect to write ABS(N), since N is an integer variable. Similarly, it would be incorrect to write ABS(A, B), since the function ABS is defined for one variable only. Rule 3 means that since SIN is a floating-point variable name, the value of the expression SIN(X) is a floating-point number.

A partial table of FORTRAN-supplied functions is given on the following page. Notice that there are two functions for use in finding absolute values. The difference is the type of argument they take. IABS takes an integer argument and returns an integer number. Thus, N = IABS(-3) would set N equal to the integer value 3. It is incorrect to write N = IABS(-3.0). To find the absolute value of the floating-point number -3.0, we would have to use the function ABS.

The function FLOAT just converts an expression to floating-point form. If we wanted to add two variables N and X in floating-point form, we could use the statements

$$A = N$$
$$Y = A + X$$

or we could do this directly, using the function FLOAT, by writing

Function	Definition	Type of Argument
ABS(X)	Absolute value of X	Real
IABS(N)	Absolute value of N	Integer
FLOAT(N)	Convert to floating point	Integer
INT(X)	Convert to integer and truncate	Real
AMOD(X, Y)	X modulo Y	Real
MOD(M, N)	M modulo N	Integer
EXP(X)	Exponential function, e^x	Real
ALOG(X)	Natural logarithm, $\log_e x$	Real
ALOG 10(X)	Common logarithm, $\log_{10} x$	Real
SIN(X)	Trigonometric sine, $\sin x$	Real
COS(X)	Trigonometric cosine, $\cos x$	Real
TANH(X)	Hyperbolic tangent, $\tanh x$	Real
ATAN(X)	Arctangent, $\arctan x$	Real
ATAN2(Y,X)	Arctangent, $\arctan (Y/X)$	Real
SQRT(X)	Square root, $x^{1/2}$	Real

$$Y = X + FLOAT(N)$$

The counterpart of FLOAT is the function INT, which converts a floating-point expression to integer form, truncating the decimal "part." For instance, the statement

$$N = INT (4.999)$$

would set N equal to the integer value 4.

The functions MOD and AMOD are used for determining remainders. MOD(N, M) is the remainder when N is divided by M. The exact definition can be given in terms of integer arithmetic as

$$MOD(N, M) = N - (N/M) * M$$

For example, MOD(10, 4) has the value 2. MOD(N, 3) would be equal to zero if and only if N were divisible by 3. The function AMOD is defined similarly for floating-point numbers. The exact definition is

$$AMOD(X, Y) = X - FLOAT(INT(X/Y)) * Y$$

For example,

$$
\begin{aligned}
AMOD(9.1, 3.0) &= 9.1 - FLOAT(INT (9.1/3.0)) * 3.0 \\
&= 9.1 - 3.0 * 3.0 \\
&= 0.1
\end{aligned}
$$

As with MOD, AMOD(X, Y) will be zero if and only if X is an integral multiple of Y. Notice that the second argument must not be zero.

The trigonometric functions SIN and COS assume that the argument is given in radians. Thus, SIN(3.14159/2.0) = 1.0. Similarly, the function ATAN will return the value of the arc-tangent in radians, so ATAN(1.0) would have the value $\pi/2$. (The value of ATAN(X) will be between $-\pi/2$ and $\pi/2$. For other angles, ATAN2 must be used.)

The functions in the previous table should be available in every version of FORTRAN. Some computer systems will have other standard functions available as well. One commonly available group of functions is used to find maximum and minimum values of a list of arguments. For example, the function MINO will find the minimum value of any number of arguments. MINO(1, 2, 3) has the value 1. MINO(1, 2, 3, 4, -5) has the value -5. These functions are unusual because they can take any number of arguments. Some related functions are given in the table below.

Function	Type of Arguments	Type of Function
AMAX0	Integer	Real
AMAX1	Real	Real
MAX0	Integer	Integer
MAX1	Real	Integer
AMIN0	Integer	Real
AMIN1	Real	Real
MIN0	Integer	Integer
MIN1	Real	Integer

Each of these functions can take any number of arguments greater than or equal to two. To find the maximum value of five real variables A, B, C, D, and E and set this equal to a real number, we use the expression AMAX1(A, B, C, D, E). The expression MAX1(A, B, C, D, E) would do the same thing, except that the value of the function would be an integer number, since MAX1 is an integer variable name. The expression MIN0(I, J, K) would have the integer value equal to the minimum value of I, J, and K.

FUNCTION SUBPROGRAMS

Often we want to use a function that is either not supplied by FORTRAN or else too complicated to write as a single statement used in defining a statement function. We can define functions by using a *function subprogram*.

179

A function subprogram is a self-contained program segment. It has an END statement of its own, and it is independent of the main program. To use a function subprogram with a program, we arrange the program input deck with all the cards of the main program coming first. After the last card of the main program (the END card), we put the first card of the function subprogram This card will contain the (declaration) statement

$$\text{FUNCTION } f(x_1, x_2, \cdots, x_n)$$

Then come the statements that tell how to evaluate this function. Finally, the function subprogram has an END card of its own. When the input cards are arranged in this way, the main program can evaluate the function f at any point by using the expression $f(y_1, y_2, \cdots, y_n)$. This setup is shown in Figure 8-5.

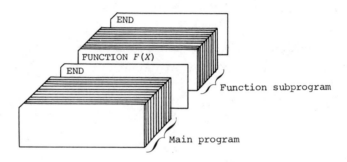

FIGURE 8-5. Relative positions of main program and function subprogram

Each function subprogram must include three things: a FUNCTION statement (declaration); an assignment statement; and a RETURN statement. The FUNCTION statement is always the first statement in the function subprogram. This statement has the form

$$\text{FUNCTION } f(x_1, x_2, \cdots, x_n)$$

Here f is the name of the function. It has the same form as a FORTRAN variable name. The dummy arguments $x_1, x_2, \cdots, x_n$ are FORTRAN variables that tell what the function involves.

The function name should not be the same as any variable name in the main program in which it is used. We could not, for instance, use an array AA and a function AA in the same program, for then the expression AA(I) would be ambiguous.

180

A function subprogram is referenced in the main program in the usual way by writing $f(y_1, y_2, \cdots, y_n)$ as part of an expression. When this expression is evaluated, it will cause the whole function subprogram to be executed with the actual argument values $y_1, y_2, \cdots, y_n$. Once this has been done, we want to branch back into the main program. To accomplish this, we use a RETURN statement in the function subprogram. This statement has the form

RETURN

When this statement is encountered in the function subprogram, it tells the computer that the evaluation of the function is complete, and control returns to the main program whence the function was called.

The function name must also appear as a variable somewhere in the function subprogram. There must be an assignment statement of the form

$f = e$

where f is a variable identical to the function name and e is some arithmetic expression. There may be more than one such statement in a function subprogram, and any such statement may be executed more than once in a subroutine. Whatever value is assigned to f on the last execution of this statement will be the value of the function that is returned to the main program.

Example 3

We know that the absolute value of an expression can be found by using the FORTRAN-supplied function ABS, but for this example, let us write a function subprogram of our own to do this. We shall call the function AB. It will be a function of one floating-point variable, called X, so the first statement in the subprogram will be

FUNCTION AB(X)

Next, we shall want an IF statement to determine whether X is negative or positive. If X is negative, we shall set AB equal to -X; otherwise, we shall set AB equal to X. In either case, after we assign a value to AB, we shall write a RETURN statement to branch back to the main program. The complete subprogram would be:

```
        FUNCTION AB(X)
        IF (X) 10, 20, 20
   10   AB = -X
        RETURN
   20   AB = X
        RETURN
        END
```

A flowchart for this function is shown in Figure 8-6.

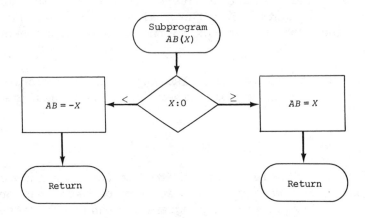

FIGURE 8-6

   To see how this function can be used by a program, let us
write a program to read five values into an array A and write
out the absolute value of each. A flowchart for this program
is shown in Figure 8-7. Here we have used a six-sided box to
represent the function AB defined in Figure 8-5. This tells
us to replace the six-sided box with the entire function subprogram. To do this in FORTRAN, we write the main program
first, followed by the function subprogram. Each time the
expression AB(Y) occurs in the main program, it will be evaluated by branching to the subprogram for AB and executing the
subprogram, replacing the dummy argument in the definition of
AB with the actual argument in the main program. This may be
any expression. In this case, the actual argument will be the
name of an array element. When a RETURN statement is executed
in the subprogram, the main program will continue from where it
left off. The complete job is shown following the flowchart in
Figure 8-7.

182

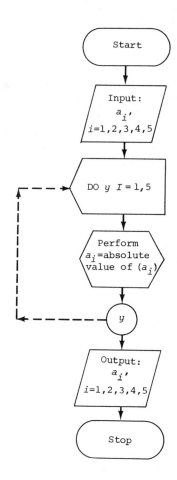

FIGURE 8-7

```
      DIMENSION A(5)
      READ (1, 2) (A(I), I = 1, 5)
    2 FORMAT (5F10.3)
      DO 10 I = 1, 5
   10 A(I) = AB(A(I))
      WRITE (2, 2) (A(I), I = 1, 5)
      STOP
      END
      FUNCTION AB(X)
      IF (X) 10, 20, 20
```

183

```
10    AB = -X
      RETURN
20    AB = X
      RETURN
      END
```

Notice that Statement 10 is utilized both in the main program and in the function subprogram. This is perfectly acceptable, since they are separate programs. We can use the same statement or variable names in the function subprogram as we use in the main program, and they will not mean the same thing. For example, we could have used an array X instead of the array A in the main program. This would not have been confused with the variable X in the function AB. The only way that the main program communicates with the function AB is by means of the arguments. Other than this, they are like two entirely different programs. Declarations such as the DIMENSION statement are "local" to main programs or subprograms and may need to be repeated.

A program may use more than one function subprogram. In fact, a function subprogram may itself use one or more function subprograms. When this is done, the program deck is arranged with the main program first, then all of the function subprograms used (either by the main program, or by the other function subprograms). It does not matter what order the functions come in, as long as all functions referenced are included. This is illustrated in our next example.

Example 4

First,we define a function NPROD of two integer variables

$$NPROD(N, M) = (N + 1) * (N + 2) * \cdots * (M - 1) * M$$

If N and M are equal, we define NPROD to be 1. If N is greater than M, we set NPROD equal to 0 and return. Otherwise, we continue with the calculations. The FORTRAN function program is as follows:
```
      FUNCTION NPROD(N, M)
      IF (M - N) 10, 20, 30
10    NPROD = 0
      RETURN
20    NPROD = 1
      RETURN
30    L = N + 1
      NPROD = 1
      DO 40 I = L, M
40    NPROD = NPROD * I
      RETURN
      END
```

184

The flowchart for this program is shown in Figure 8-8.

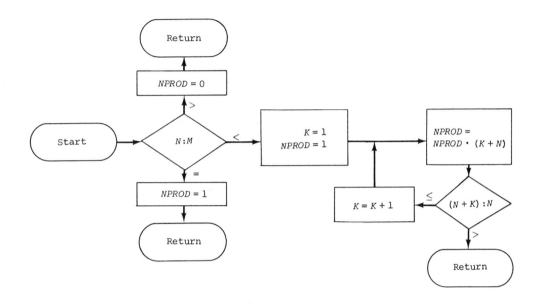

FIGURE 8-8

If M is less than N, the subprogram assigns the value zero to NPROD and then returns. If M and N are equal, the subroutine assigns the value 1 to NPROD and returns. If N is less than M, the DO loop is performed. Statement 40 illustrates the fact that the function name may be used in the function subroutine just like any other variable name. This statement is executed M - N times, assigning a different value to NPROD each time. As far as the main program is concerned, it is only the last time Statement 40 is executed that is important; this last value of NPROD is the value that the function assumes in the main program.

We can use the function NPROD to define two other functions. NFAC(N) will compute factorial N or, as it is written, N!. It is defined in the function subprogram:

```
FUNCTION NFAC(N)
NFAC = NPROD(1, N)
RETURN
END
```

The function C(N, M) will give the binomial coefficient

185

$$ {}^nC_m \equiv C_m^{\,n} \equiv \frac{n!}{m!\,(n-m)!} = \frac{n\,(n-1)\,(n-2)\,\cdot\,\cdots\,\cdot\,(n-m+1)}{m!} $$

This function may be defined by the statements

```
FUNCTION C(N, M)
C = NPROD(M, N)/NFAC(N - M)
RETURN
END
```

Now, suppose we want to write a simple program to read in three numbers N, X, and Y, and compute P = (X + Y) ** N, using the binomial formula

$$ (x+y)^n = \sum_{i=0}^{n} C_i^{\,n}\, x^i\, y^{n-i} $$

This could be done using the functions defined above with the program:

```
      READ (1, 5) N, X, Y
  5   FORMAT (I5, 2F10.0)
      P = Y ** N
      DO 10 I = 1, N
 10   P = P + C(N, I) * X ** I * Y ** (N - I)
      WRITE (2, 15) P
 15   FORMAT (F12.4)
      STOP
      END
```

Since this program uses the function C, when we execute the program we must furnish the subprogram for C as well. Since the function C uses the functions NPROD and NFAC for its definition, we must also include these subprograms. The three subprograms may appear in any order as long as they follow the main program, and as long as they are all there. Thus, the input deck of cards for the computer would be set up as follows:

```
      READ (1, 5) N, X, Y
      ...
      (main program)
      ...
      END
      FUNCTION C(N, M)
      ...
      END
      FUNCTION NPROD(N, M)
      ...
      END
```

186

```
FUNCTION NFAC(N)
...
END
[(data card) to be read by main program]
```

Example 5[2]

Function subprograms are often used to compute functions
which are defined in terms of power series. This is how the
exponential function EXP is computed. Of course, this function is supplied by FORTRAN. Suppose that we want to compute
the hyperbolic sine of a number, and that there is no FORTRAN-
supplied function available to do this. We shall write a function subprogram SINH to compute this function. The hyperbolic
sine, $\sinh x$ is defined as

$$\sinh(x) \equiv x + \frac{x^3}{3!} + \frac{x^5}{5!} + \cdots$$

This is the sum of an infinite number of terms, and so it
cannot be computed exactly. A common procedure is to agree to
compute enough terms so that the absolute value of the last term
$x^n/n!$ is less than some small number, say 10^{-8}. Also, in case X
is very large, we should agree to compute no more than, say, fifteen
terms at most.

The computational procedure we shall use makes use of the
fact that

$$\frac{x^{n-2}}{(n-2)!} \cdot \frac{x^2}{(n-1) \cdot n} = \frac{x^n}{n!}$$

Thus, if TERM = $x^3/3!$, then the next term may be computed by

$$\text{TERM} = \text{TERM} * X ** 2/(5. * (5. - 1.))$$

In the program, we shall set XSQ = X * X, and we shall define
a statement function D(N) = FLOAT(N * N - N). Then if TERM is the
value of the N-2nd term in the series, the Nth term may be computed by TERM = TERM * XSQ/D(N).

After computing each term, we add it to SINH. Then we test
to see if the absolute value of TERM is less than 1.0E - 8. If so,
we branch to a RETURN statement; otherwise, we see if we have
computed more than the allowable number of terms. For our particular problem, we arbitrarily test N with 15. If $N \geq 15$, we branch
to a RETURN statement.

---

[2]This example may be omitted by those not familiar with
hyperbolic functions.

187

A flowchart for this program is shown in Figure 8-9.

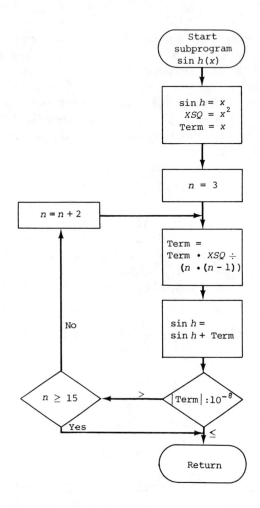

FIGURE 8-9

The FORTRAN subprogram is given below:

```
FUNCTION SINH(X)
D(N) = FLOAT (N * N - N)
SINH = X
XSQ = X * X
TERM = X
DO 25 N = 3, 15, 2
```

```
         TERM = TERM * XSQ/D(N)
         SINH = SINH + TERM
         IF (ABS(TERM) - 1.0E - 8) 50, 25, 25
    25   CONTINUE
    50   RETURN
         END
```

SUBROUTINES

The function subprograms we have been discussing give us a way of linking up two programs. On the one hand, we have the main program; and on the other, we have the function subprogram. These are separate and constitute two independent programs except for the fact that the main program can execute the function subprogram to evaluate the function, communicating only by means of the arguments.

A *subroutine* subprogram in FORTRAN is, in a sense, a more general form of a function subprogram. Like a function, a subroutine is separate from the main program, and is almost a program in itself. Also, like a function, a subroutine can be executed under the control of a main program. The difference is that while a function has the specific job of finding a value for some expression, a subroutine does not have this restriction.

Subroutines can be useful in many ways. For one thing, instead of writing one long program to do a job, we can break it down into several shorter subroutines. The job could then be done by a short main program that executes the various subroutines. Another advantage is that when it is necessary to perform the same procedure in several programs, the procedure could be written as a subroutine. Instead of having to write out the whole procedure in each of the programs, we could make a copy of the subroutine and just include a statement in each program.

In FORTRAN, there are certain statements that are used to define and reference subroutines. The procedure is similar to using function subprograms.

A subroutine is defined with a SUBROUTINE declaration statement. This statement has the form

$$\text{SUBROUTINE name } (x_1, x_2, \cdots, x_n)$$

where "name" is any FORTRAN variable name and $x_1, x_2, \cdots, x_n$ are FORTRAN variables that are dummy arguments.

The first statement in any subroutine subprogram must always be a SUBROUTINE statement of this form. After this statement, we

189

can write any instructions to tell what the subroutine is to do. These statements will be followed by an END statement.

To execute a subroutine, we use a CALL statement in the main program. This statement has the form

$$\text{CALL name } (y_1, y_2, \cdots, y_n)$$

where "name" is the name of some subroutine, as defined in a SUBROUTINE statement, and $y_1, y_2, \cdots, y_n$ are any FORTRAN expressions.

What this statement does is to transfer control from the main program to the first executable statement in the subroutine "name." The expressions $y_1, y_2, \cdots, y_n$ correspond to the dummy variable names $x_1, x_2, \cdots, x_n$ in much the same way as for function subprograms. The subroutine will be executed with each y_i taking the place of the corresponding x_i in the definition of the subroutine. As with functions, the y's must agree in number and type with the x's. The computer continues to execute the subroutine until a RETURN statement in the subroutine is executed. When this happens, control returns to the first statement after the CALL statement which called the subroutine.

To illustrate, we shall write a simple subroutine called ADD. This subroutine will involve three variables. The purpose of the subroutine will be to add the first two variables and store the result in the third variable. This subroutine can be defined with the statements

```
SUBROUTINE ADD (A, B, C)
C = A + B
RETURN
END
```

Now, say we want to write a program which uses two arrays X and Y. For each I, we want to set Y(I) = X(I) + 2.0. This could be done using the subroutine ADD in the following manner:

```
      DIMENSION X(10), Y(10)
      DO 5 I = 1, 10
      CALL ADD(X(I), 2.0, Y(I))
    5 CONTINUE
      STOP
      END
```

When this program is read into the computer, the cards for the subroutine ADD would follow the cards for the main program. The CALL statement in the program calls this subroutine and causes the entire subroutine ADD to be performed. Every time

190

A, B, and C appear in the subroutine, they are replaced by X(I), 2.0, and Y(I), respectively. Thus, the subroutine would set Y(I) = X(I) + 2.0. The RETURN statement in the subroutine caused control to return to the main program.

The variables that appear in the SUBROUTINE statement are "dummy" variables, or arguments, which do not correspond to any actual variables in the main program. The "actual" arguments are the expressions that appear in the CALL statement. As with function subprograms, the actual parameters of a subroutine may be any expressions, and not just simple variable names. The only restriction is that the actual arguments in the CALL statement must correspond exactly to the dummy arguments in the SUBROUTINE statement that defines the subroutine. Each argument in the CALL statement must be of the same type (integer or real) as the corresponding argument in the SUBROUTINE statement. Thus, in the above example, we could not use the statement

        CALL ADD(N, A, B)

since N is an integer variable.

A dummy argument in a SUBROUTINE statement may also be an array name. When this is done, the subroutine must contain a DIMENSION statement for the array. For instance, the following subroutine will set Y equal to the sum of the first five elements in an array X.

              SUBROUTINE SIGMA (X, Y)
              DIMENSION X(5)
              Y = 0.0
              DO 10 I = 1, 5
        10   Y = Y + X(I)
              RETURN
              END

In a main program, if A is any array with five or more elements, the statement

        CALL SIGMA(A, B)

will set B equal to the sum of the first five elements of A.

This subroutine has the drawback that the size of the dummy array X is fixed. A very useful feature of subroutines is that we can use arrays with *variable* dimensions. If L, M, and N are any integer variables, we can use the statement

        DIMENSION X(L, M, N)

191

in a subroutine. The variables L, M, and N, as well as the array
name, X, *must* appear in the parameter list of the SUBROUTINE
statement, and their values may not be changed within the subroutine. Since the array name X is also a dummy argument in the
SUBROUTINE statement, the subroutine can be called using any
array as the actual argument. When this is done, the actual
arguments corresponding to L, M, and N should be set equal to
the actual dimensions of the array when executing the CALL statement. For example, we could rewrite the subroutine SIGMA shown
above to make X an array of variable dimension. This is done
below:

```
          SUBROUTINE SIGMA(N, X, Y)
          DIMENSION X(N)
          Y = 0.0
          DO 10 I = 1, N
    10    Y = Y + X(I)
          RETURN
          END
```

Then if A is an array in the main program that is defined by the
statement

```
          DIMENSION A(100)
```

we can set B equal to the sum of all the elements of A by using
the statement

```
          CALL SIGMA (100, A, B)
```

Example 6

For this example, we shall write a subroutine which will
multiply two matrices to give the resulting product matrix. If
X is an array having L rows and M columns, and Y is an array
having M rows and N columns, then the product Z = XY is an array
having L rows and N columns with elements defined by

$$z_{ij} = \sum_{k=1}^{m} x_{ik} y_{kj} \qquad \begin{pmatrix} i = 1, \cdots, L \\ j = 1, \cdots, N \end{pmatrix}$$

We can calculate Z easily using a subroutine with a variable
DIMENSION statement. The subroutine will be called

```
          MULT (X, Y, Z, L, M, N)
```

We first set all the elements of Z equal to zero, and then
calculate Z(I, J) from the above formula. This is done using
three nested DO loops. The complete subroutine is as follows:

192

```
          SUBROUTINE MULT (X, Y, Z, L, M, N)
C         X IS AN L X M ARRAY
C         Y IS AN M X N ARRAY
C         Z IS THE L X N PRODUCT ARRAY
          DIMENSION X(L, M), Y(M, N), Z(L, N)
          DO 10 I = 1, L
          DO 10 J = 1, N
   10     Z(I, J) = 0.0
          DO 20 I = 1, L
          DO 20 J = 1, N
          DO 20 K = 1, M
   20     Z(I, J) = Z(I, J) + X(I, K) * Y(K, J)
          RETURN
          END
```

Example 7

Let us write a subroutine to evaluate a polynomial. If $p(x)$ is the polynomial, it can be written as

$$p(x) = a_1 + a_2 x + a_3 x^2 + \cdots + a_n x^{n-1}$$

For our program, it is convenient to write the above as

$$p(x) = a_1 + \{[a_n x + a_{n-1}) x + a_{n-2}] x + \cdots + a_2\} x$$

This looks strange, but will greatly assist in the programming. To illustrate the above, suppose we have a cubic equation given by

$$p(x) = a_1 + a_2 x + a_3 x^2 + a_4 x^3$$

We evaluate it by the above scheme as follows. Define polynomials p_1, p_2, p_3, and p_4. Then

$$p_1(x) = a_4$$
$$p_2(x) = p_1(x) \cdot x + a_3 = a_4 x + a_3$$
$$p_3(x) = p_2(x) \cdot x + a_2 = a_4 x^2 + a_3 x + a_2$$
$$p_4(x) = p_3(x) \cdot x + a_1 = a_4 x^3 + a_3 x^2 + a_2 x + a_1$$

Clearly,

$$p(x) = p_4(x)$$

The FORTRAN subroutine will find the value of $p(x)$ for any given x, knowing the coefficients a_1, a_2, $\cdots$, a_n. Let A be the array giving these. A flowchart for the evaluation procedure is shown in Figure 8-10.

193

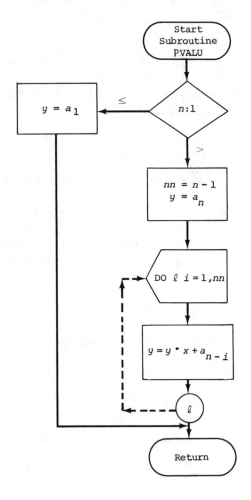

FIGURE 8-10

194

The FORTRAN subroutine will be called PVALU (A, N, X, Y).
Here N is the number of coefficients in the array A, X is the
variable, and Y is the result. The complete subroutine is:

```
      SUBROUTINE PVALU (A, N, X, Y)
      DIMENSION A(N)
      IF (N - 1) 10, 10, 20
10    Y = A(1)
      RETURN
20    NN = N - 1
      Y = A(N)
      DO 30 I = 1, NN
30    Y = Y * X + A(N - I)
      RETURN
      END
```

THE COMMON *STATEMENT*

A As we have seen, a subroutine is compiled as a separate
program from the main program, and also from any other subprograms
it uses. This means that we can use a variable name in both the
main program and a subprogram and it will refer to two different
variables. For instance, in Example 7, we used the variable name
NN. In a main program, which calls the subroutine PVALU, we can
also use variable NN, and it will be a different variable from
the I, J, and K of the subroutine.

Sometimes it is desirable to use the same storage locations
for some of the variables in a subroutine as the variables in the
main program or another subroutine. This can be done by using
the COMMON statement. This statement has the form

COMMON A, B, $\cdots$, N

where A, B, $\cdots$, N are variable, or array, names. When this
statement is used in a program, it must be among the first group
of statements in the program. In a function or subroutine subprogram, it should be the first statement after the FUNCTION or
SUBROUTINE statement. This statement allows a main program and
a subprogram to share storage in the following manner. If the
main program contains the statement

COMMON A1, A2, A3

and a subprogram contains the statement

COMMON B1, B2, B3

then the variable B1 is assigned the same location in storage as the variable A1; B2 is assigned the same location as A2, and B3 is assigned the same location as A3. If another subroutine contains the statement

COMMON C1, C2

then C1, B1, and A1 all share the same location in storage as do C2, B2, and A2.

The items in the list of the COMMON statement may be arrays. We can give dimension information in the COMMON statement when this is done. For instance, the statement

COMMON X(10)

would specify an array, X, of ten elements in common storage. If a subroutine then contained the statement

COMMON Y(10)

the array Y would be stored in the same location as the array X.

In general, what the COMMON statement does is to specify the arrangement of computer memory called common storage. The first variable in the list of the COMMON statement is stored in the first memory location in common storage; the second variable is stored in the second location, and so on. When another subprogram uses a COMMON statement, the first variable in the list is also stored in the first location in common storage, and so on, so that the corresponding variables in the lists of the two COMMON statements share the same storage locations in common storage.

If a main program contains the statement

COMMON X(3), Y, Z

and a subroutine contains the statement

COMMON A, B, C, D, E

then the variable A and the variable X(1) are both stored in the first location in common storage. The variables B and X(2) are both stored in the second location in common storage, and the variables C and X(3) are both stored in the third location in common storage. Also, then D corresponds to Y and E to Z.

Example 8

If A is a 3 × 3 array, the determinant D of A is defined by
$D = a_{11}(a_{22}a_{33} - a_{23}a_{32}) - a_{21}(a_{12}a_{33} - a_{13}a_{32}) + a_{31}(a_{12}a_{23} - a_{13}a_{22});$

the following subroutine DET(D, A) will compute the determinant of a 3 × 3 array A and store it in D.

```
SUBROUTINE DET(D, A)
DIMENSION A(3, 3)
D1 = A(2, 2) * A(3, 3) - A(2, 3) * A(3, 2)
D2 = A(1, 2) * A(3, 3) - A(1, 2) * A(3, 2)
D3 = A(1, 2) * A(2, 3) - A(1, 3) * A(2, 2)
D = A(1, 1) * D1 - A(2, 1) * D2 + A(3, 1) * D3
RETURN
END
```

Now, let us see how we can use the subroutine DET to write a subroutine SOLV which we can use to solve a system of three linear equations in three unknowns. The equations are

$$a_{11} x_1 + a_{12} x_2 + a_{13} x_3 = b_1$$

$$a_{21} x_1 + a_{22} x_2 + a_{23} x_3 = b_2$$

$$a_{31} x_1 + a_{32} x_2 + a_{33} x_3 = b_3$$

These equations can be solved by Cramer's rule, which says that x_1, x_2, and x_3 are given by

$$X_1 = \frac{1}{D} \begin{vmatrix} b_1 & a_{12} & a_{13} \\ b_2 & a_{22} & a_{23} \\ b_3 & a_{32} & a_{33} \end{vmatrix} \qquad X_2 = \frac{1}{D} \begin{vmatrix} a_{11} & b_1 & a_{13} \\ a_{21} & b_2 & a_{23} \\ a_{31} & b_3 & a_{33} \end{vmatrix} \qquad X_3 = \frac{1}{D} \begin{vmatrix} a_{11} & a_{12} & b_1 \\ a_{21} & a_{22} & b_2 \\ a_{31} & a_{32} & b_3 \end{vmatrix}$$

where

$$D = \begin{vmatrix} a_{11} & a_{12} & a_{13} \\ a_{21} & a_{22} & a_{23} \\ a_{31} & a_{32} & a_{33} \end{vmatrix}$$

Each of the determinants D_i is just the determinant of the matrix obtained by replacing the ith column of the matrix A with the elements b_1, b_2, and b_3. If the determinant D is zero, then the equations do not have a unique solution.

The FORTRAN subroutine SOLV will first compute the determinant D. If $D = 0$, the subroutine will print a message to this effect and then stop, since there are no solutions for x_1, x_2, and x_3. If D is not zero, then each x_i is found by setting an array C equal to the array A, and then replacing the ith column of C by b_1, b_2, and b_3. We first call DET(X(I), C) and then set X(I) = X(I)/D. This procedure is shown in the flowchart of Figure 8-11.

197

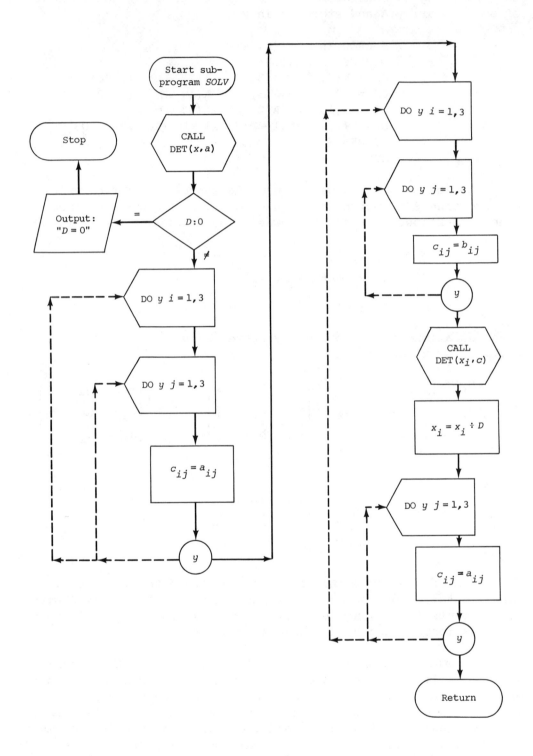

FIGURE 8-11

In the FORTRAN subroutine, we could make the arrays A, B, and X parameters of the subroutine with the statement

SUBROUTINE SOLV (A, B, X)

However, we shall be using these same arrays in a main program. But it does take time to establish the correspondence whenever the subroutine is called. A more efficient method is to place the arrays A, B, and X in common storage. The subroutine would then contain the statement

COMMON A(3, 3), B(3), X(3)

The main program would contain an identical statement, and the same storage areas would be used for the arrays in the subroutine as for the arrays in the main program. Since by using this method, the subroutine does not need any variables, the variable list can be omitted altogether, and the subroutine can be declared with the statement

SUBROUTINE SOLV

The complete subroutine is shown below:

```
      SUBROUTINE SOLV
      COMMON A(3, 3), B(3), X(3)
      DIMENSION C(3, 3)
      CALL DET (D, A)
      IF (D) 20, 10, 20
   10 WRITE (2, 15)
   15 FORMAT (6H D = 0)
      STOP
   20 DO 25 I = 1, 3
      DO 25 J = 1, 3
   25 C(I, J) = A(I, J)
      DO 50 I = 1, 3
      DO 30 J = 1, 3
   30 C(I, J) = B(J)
      CALL DET(X(I), C)
      X(I) = X(I)/D
      DO 40 J = 1, 3
   40 C(I, J) = A(I, J)
   50 CONTINUE
      RETURN
      END
```

The following program will read in values for A and B, compute X by calling SOLV, then write out the values for X. Notice that the COMMON statement is identical to the one used in the subroutine SOLV. To execute this program, we must remember to include the subroutines SOLV and DET after the end of the program as shown below:

```
      COMMON A(3, 3), B(3), X(3)
      READ (1, 5) A, B
   5  FORMAT (4(3F10.0/))
      CALL SOLV
      WRITE (2, 10) X
  10  FORMAT (1X, 5H X1 =, E13.4, 5H X2 =, E13.4, 5H X3 =, E13.4)
      STOP
      END
      SUBROUTINE SOLV
      COMMON A(3, 3), B(3), X(3)
      ...
      ...
      END
      SUBROUTINE DET (D, C)
      ...
      END
```

A EXERCISES

1. Examples of function subprograms are given below. If the statements are correct, mark a V next to them; otherwise, make suitable corrections to make them valid.

   a. F(A, B, C) = A + B - C
       X = Z - F(Y(1), 2.0)

   b. ZERO(A, C, D, 4) = A - C * D/4.0
       X = ZERO(1.0, 2.0, 3.0, 4.0)

   c. PRINC(A, R, N) = A * (1. - R ** N)
       AMT = SUM - PRINC(100., .06, 30)

   d. FUNCTION ANS(A, B, C)   e. FUNCTION DIST(A, B, TNETA)
       SUM = A + B + C   C = A ** 2 + B ** 2
       PROD = A * B * C   C = -2. * A * B * COS(TNETA)
       D1 = A - B   IF (C - D) 5, 6, 6
       ANS = SUM + PROD - D1   6 DIST = SQRT(C - D)
       RETURN   RETURN
       END   5 DIST = 0.0
                                          RETURN
                                          END

1.—*continued*

f.   SUBROUTINE BIG (X, N, XMAX)
        DIMENSION X(N)
        XMAX = X(1)
        DO 10 I = 2, N
        IF (X(I).LT.XMAX) GO TO 10
        XMAX = X(I)
     10 CONTINUE
        RETURN
        END

g.   N = 6
        PAY (AMT, XINT) = AMT * (XINT * (1. + XINT) ** N)
        Y = PAY (100.0, .05)

h.   FUNCTION FLOW (AREA, RADIUS, SLOPE, COEF)
        Q = 1.49 * AREA * (RADIUS ** (2./3.)) * SQRT(SLOPE)
        FLOW = Q/COEF
        RETURN
        END

i.   SUBROUTINE LIST (X, Y, N)
        DIMENSION X(N), Y(N)
        DO 100 I = 1, N
    100 WRITE (2, 101) X(I), Y(I)
    101 FORMAT (1H1, 20X, N(2F20.4))
        RETURN
        END

2. The equation

$$M = \frac{Ai(1+i)^n}{(1+i)^n - 1}$$

gives the monthly payment to repay an amount of money, where

M = monthly payment,
A = principal amount,
n = number of monthly payments,
i = annual interest rate.

Write the formula for the above as a

a. statement function
b. FUNCTION subprogram
c. SUBROUTINE

3. Write a FUNCTION subprogram to determine the average of N numbers.

4. The formula for the length C of a triangle, given two sides A and B and the included angle c, is

$$C^2 = A^2 + B^2 - 2AC \cos c$$

   a. Write a FUNCTION subprogram to calculate the above.
   b. Write a SUBROUTINE to calculate the above.

5. Write a subroutine to draw a large number, either a 1, a 2, or a 3, in the center of the page. The number printed is to be determined through the CALL statement. Have the number surrounded by a rectangular border consisting of all asterisks.

6. Suppose an object falls vertically off of a building 1000 feet above the cab of a truck. Its distance above the ground is given by $s = 1000 - 16t^2$, where t is in seconds. The same time that it starts to fall, a truck located 200 feet away from the building drives to intercept it before it hits the ground. This truck moves with constant velocity v_0 until it reaches the building and then instantaneously stops and waits for the object to fall on top of it. Its distance is given by $s = v_0 t$. Write a program to output the following table. (The first line of output is filled in.)

Time (Seconds)	D1—Object from Ground in Ft	D2—Truck from Intercept in Ft	D3—Truck from Object in Ft
0	1000.000	200.000	1019.804
.	.	.	.
.	.	.	.

Use FUNCTION subprograms as much as possible. Input an arbitrary velocity so that the truck will not necessarily make it to the intercept point every time. In these cases, have a message printed out as follows:

YOU DROVE TOO SLOW - THE OBJECT HIT THE GROUND ALREADY

B EXERCISES

1. For the two functions $f_1(x) = x^2 + 3x - 2$ and $f_2(x) = x^4 - x$, we wish to evaluate their sum $F = f_1 + f_2$ for values of $x = 0, .5, 1, \cdots, 20$. Write a FORTRAN program to do this, using function statements.

2. Do Problem 1, using a FUNCTION subprogram.

3. Write a subroutine, called STD, that finds the standard deviation of a set of N numbers. (See Problem A5, Chapter 6.)

4. Write a FUNCTION subprogram to evaluate

$$f(d, m, s) = \sin(d, m, s)$$

where d, m, and s represent an angle in degrees, minutes, and seconds.

5. A *subfactorial* is defined as follows:

$$!N = N \cdot !(N - 1) + (-1)^N$$

with $!0 = 1$. Several of these are $!1 = 0$, $!2 = 1$, $!3 = 2$, etc. Write a FUNCTION subprogram to calculate subfactorials.

6. Write a program to calculate the first 20 subfactorials using the subprogram from Problem 5.

7. For an $n \times n$ array, A, write subroutines to calculate new matrices:

   a. B, where each element of B is x times the value of each element of A.
   b. C, where each element of C, c_{ij}, is related to A in the following manner:

$$a_{ij} = c_{ji}$$

   c. D where each element of D, d_{ij}, is obtained by

$$d_{ij} = \sum_{k=1}^{n} a_{ik} a_{kj}.$$

8. A particle moves in a plane along the circumference of a circle in a counterclockwise manner. The circle is of radius 4 and is centered at (0, 10). At time $t = 0$, the particle is at (0, 14), and it takes five minutes to make a complete revolution. Also, at time $t = 0$, another particle is at the origin. It moves in a straight line with constant velocity to the point (10, 10). It takes 10 minutes for it to do this.

   Write a program using a subroutine to give the distances between the two particles for any time t. When are they closest together? (See Figure 8-12.)

203

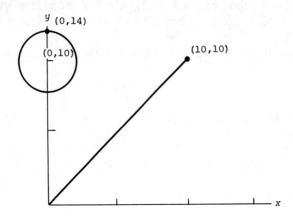

FIGURE 8-12

Chapter   9

LOGICAL EXPRESSIONS AND CONDITIONAL STATEMENTS

LOGICAL CONSTANTS AND VARIABLES

In addition to the integer and real constants we have been using, there is a type of constant in FORTRAN called a *logical constant*. These constants are not numeric; that is, they do not have values that are numbers. In fact, there are only two values for a logical constant: .TRUE. and .FALSE. . Notice that they are always written with a period preceding and following them.

We may also use *logical variables* in a computer program. The only value which a logical variable can assume is one of the two logical values, .TRUE. and .FALSE. . Such variables are not used in arithmetic statements like integer or real variables; that is, we would not add or multiply two logical variables. Instead, they are used in logical expressions such as P .OR. (Q .AND. R), consisting of logical variables and constants, connected by logical operators, in a manner analogous to the connections of real and integer variables and constants by arithmetic operators to form arithmetic expressions. In this chapter, we shall see how such expressions are developed and used to form statements.

In order to specify that a certain variable is going to be used as a logical variable, we must use a LOGICAL (declaration) statement at the beginning of the program. This statement has the form

$$\text{LOGICAL name}_1, \text{ name}_2, \cdots, \text{ name}_n$$

where name_1, name_2, $\cdots$, name_n are variable names. This statement must come before the first executable statement in the program. It will cause the variables which appear in the list to be treated as logical variables throughout the program.

Logical variables must conform to the usual rules for naming variables in FORTRAN:

1. The name must consist of no more than six characters.[1]

---

[1] See footnote, page 32.

2. It must contain only letters and numbers (no
   punctuation marks).
3. It must begin with a letter.

However, it makes no difference whether the names have the
form of real or integer variables, since they will not be used
as either one; the *LOGICAL declaration overrides the usual rule
for determining the variable type, and all variables in the list
of the LOGICAL statement will be used only as logical variables.*
For example, the variables

$$I1, LOGO, MA3$$

would normally be of integer type, and A, B, C would be variables
of floating-point type. But if the statement declaration

$$LOGICAL \; I1, \; LOGO, \; MA3, \; A, \; B, \; C$$

appeared at the beginning of a program, then all of these variables would be treated as logical variables throughout the program, so each of them would be allowed to assume only one of the
two values .TRUE. and .FALSE. . Thus, we could have the
statements

$$I1 = .TRUE.$$
$$C = .FALSE.$$
$$LOGO = B$$

but it would be incorrect to have the statements

$$I1 = 6$$

or

$$B = 3.1$$

since a logical variable cannot assume a numeric value.

LOGICAL OPERATORS

Logical variables can be combined to form more complicated
logical expressions. This is done by using logical operators.
An example is the expression

$$P \; .AND. \; Q$$

where P and Q are logical variables. The characters .AND.
(with the periods preceding and following AND) comprise the
logical operator which connects the two variables. Depending on
the values of P and Q, the expression P .AND. Q will have either

the value .TRUE. or the value .FALSE. . In this case, if P
and Q both have the value .TRUE., then the expression P .AND. Q
will have the value .TRUE. . If R is another logical variable,
the statements

$$P = .TRUE.$$
$$Q = .TRUE.$$
$$R = P .AND. Q$$

will assign the value .TRUE. to R.

The use of logical operators in logical expressions is
analogous to the use of arithmetic operators in arithmetic
expressions. Just as

$$I + J$$

is an integer arithmetic expression which takes on integer values,
depending on the values of the integer variables I and J,

$$P .AND. Q$$

is a logical expression which takes on logical values, depending
on the values of the logical variables P and Q.

Three logical operators are used in FORTRAN. They are
.NOT., .AND., and .OR. . We shall see how each of these is
used.

The operator .NOT. changes the value of the expression following it to the complement value of the expression; that is, it
changes .TRUE. to .FALSE. and vice versa. Thus, the expression
.NOT. .X. has the value .FALSE. if .X. is .TRUE.; if .X. is
.FALSE., it has the value .TRUE. .

If the statements

```
LOGICAL M, N, A, B
A = .TRUE.
B = .FALSE.
M = .NOT. A
N = .NOT. B
```

were encountered in a program, then M would be assigned the value
.FALSE., and N would be assigned the value .TRUE. .

The operator .NOT. can be used in this way by placing it in
front of any logical expression (that is, a logical constant,
variable, or more complex combination of these). If E is any
logical expression, then the value of .NOT. E is given by the
table:

E	.NOT. E
.TRUE.	.FALSE.
.FALSE.	.TRUE.

Whatever the expression E may be, its value will be either .TRUE. or .FALSE., and placing the operator .NOT. in front of the expression will change the value as above.

The logical operator .AND. takes two logical expressions and connects them to form a logical expression whose value is determined as in the following table:

P	Q	P .AND. Q
.TRUE.	.TRUE.	.TRUE.
.TRUE.	.FALSE.	.FALSE.
.FALSE.	.TRUE.	.FALSE.
.FALSE.	.FALSE.	.FALSE.

Here P and Q may be any logical constants, variables, or other expressions. So, the logical expression P .AND. Q has the value .TRUE. if and only if both P and Q have the value .TRUE. . If P has the value .FALSE. and Q has the value .TRUE. (as in the third line of the table), then the expression P .AND. Q has the value .FALSE. . The expressions

```
.FALSE.  .AND.  .TRUE.
.TRUE.   .AND.  .FALSE.
.FALSE.  .AND.  .FALSE.
```

will have the value .FALSE., while .TRUE. .AND. .TRUE. has the value .TRUE. .

The operator .OR., like .AND., connects two expressions to form a logical expression whose value is determined as in the table below:

P	Q	P .OR. Q
.TRUE.	.TRUE.	.TRUE.
.TRUE.	.FALSE.	.TRUE.
.FALSE.	.TRUE.	.TRUE.
.FALSE.	.FALSE.	.FALSE.

We see from this table that if at least one of the expressions P or Q has the value .TRUE., then P .OR. Q will have the value .TRUE. . The only case in which P .OR. Q is .FALSE. is when

both P and Q have the value .FALSE. . For example, the
expressions

.TRUE. .OR. .FALSE.

and

.TRUE. .OR. .TRUE.

both have the value .TRUE. . The statements

```
LOGICAL P, Q, R, S
P = .TRUE.
Q = .FALSE.
R = P .OR. .TRUE.
S = Q .OR. R
```

would assign the value .TRUE. to R and S.

EVALUATION OF EXPRESSIONS

The operators .NOT., .AND., and .OR. can be used in the same
logical expression to form more complicated constructions. For
example,

(.NOT. P) .AND. Q

contains the two operators .NOT. and .AND. . To evaluate such an
expression, we proceed a step at a time. Suppose P is .TRUE. and
Q is .FALSE., then the values of the above expression would be
found as follows:

```
(.NOT. P) .AND. Q
(.NOT. .TRUE.) .AND. .FALSE.
.FALSE. .AND. .FALSE.
        .FALSE.
```

The order in which the operations are grouped is important.
The expression .NOT. (P .AND. Q) is *not* the same as (.NOT. P) .AND. Q.
Note that for P is .TRUE. and Q is .FALSE.,

.NOT. (P .AND. Q)

has the value
```
.NOT. (.TRUE. .AND. .FALSE.)
.NOT. .FALSE.
      .TRUE.
```

For the same values of P and Q, the expression (.NOT. P) .AND. Q
is .FALSE. . The order in which the operations in any expression
are evaluated may be determined by the following rules:

209

RULE 1: Any part of the expression enclosed in parentheses is evaluated completely before proceeding to evaluate any part of the expression outside the parentheses. This rule applies to each set of parentheses. For example, in evaluating the expression

((P .AND. Q) .OR. R) .AND. S

P .AND. Q would be evaluated first, then (P .AND. Q) .OR. R, and finally the whole expression.

RULE 2: Unless otherwise grouped by parentheses, occurrences of the operator .NOT. are evaluated before evaluating the operators .AND. or .OR. . In the expression

.NOT. P .OR. Q

the .NOT. P would be evaluated first. Thus, this expression is assumed to mean (.NOT. P) .OR. Q, rather than .NOT. (P .OR. Q).

RULE 3: Unless otherwise grouped by parentheses, the operator .AND. is evaluated before the operator .OR. . This means that P .OR. Q .AND. R would be interpreted as P .OR. (Q .AND. R) rather than as (P .OR. Q) .AND. R.

RULE 4: The expression is evaluated from left to right, unless otherwise specified by the above three rules.

As an illustration of these rules, consider the expression

.NOT. P .AND. Q .OR. R .AND. S

In evaluating this expression, the .NOT. P is evaluated first, then the .AND. operator in (.NOT. P) .AND. Q, next the .AND. operator in R .AND. S, and finally the .OR. operator connecting these parts.

So, the whole expression is evaluated as though it were written

((.NOT. P) .AND. Q) .OR. (R .AND. S)

Of course, there is nothing wrong with using parentheses. Just as with arithmetic statements such as $A/B - C$, the rules remove the ambiguity which might otherwise result from omitting parentheses.

TRUTH TABLES

Given a fairly complicated expression such as

.NOT. (P .AND. .NOT. Q)

the question sometimes arises for what values of P and Q will the expression have the value .TRUE.? This question can best be answered by making what is known as a *truth table*. This is just a convenient way of evaluating an expression for all possible values of the variable involved. The above expression involves two variables, P and Q. Each of these may have either the value .TRUE. or .FALSE., so there are four combinations which have to be considered.

P = .TRUE. and Q = .TRUE.
P = .TRUE. and Q = .FALSE.
P = .FALSE. and Q = .TRUE.
P = .FALSE. and Q = .FALSE.

For the purpose of making a truth table, it will be convenient to use the letter T for the value .TRUE., and F for .FALSE. .

To make a truth table, we first list in a column the possible values of the variables involved. Then, using the rules of the preceding section, we find the first operation performed in evaluating the expression and write this part of the expression at the top of a column in the table. Then we find the next operation to be evaluated, and write this part of the expression at the top of the next column of the table. We continue this until finally we have the whole expression to be evaluated at the top of the last column of the table.

For example, the first operation to be evaluated in the expression

.NOT. (P .AND. .NOT. Q)

would be the occurrence of .NOT. within the parentheses. So we would write .NOT. Q at the top of a column. The next operation performed would be the evaluation of the operator .AND. . Finally, the .NOT. outside the parentheses is evaluated. Writing each of these steps at the top of the next columns, the table looks like this:

211

P	Q	.NOT. Q	P .AND. .NOT. Q	.NOT. (P .AND. .NOT. Q)
T	T			
T	F			
F	T			
F	F			

Now that the expression is broken down into parts, it is easy to fill in the values in the three blank columns. In the first row, P and Q are both .TRUE., so .NOT. Q is .FALSE. . We can write an F in column three. Then to evaluate P .AND. .NOT. Q, we substitute .TRUE. for P and .FALSE. for .NOT. Q, and we see that this part of the expression is .FALSE. . We write an F in column four. In the last column of the first row, .NOT. (P .AND. .NOT. Q) is just .NOT. operating on the value in the next-to-last column, so we have a T in the last column. Continuing in this manner for the other three rows, we arrive at the table below.

P	Q	.NOT. Q	P .AND. .NOT. Q	.NOT. (P .AND. .NOT. Q)
T	T	F	F	T
T	F	T	T	F
F	T	F	F	T
F	F	T	F	T

Since we have included each intermediate step in the calculation, it is necessary to evaluate only one operator at a time as we proceed from column to column.

Now, if we want to know what the value of the expression .NOT. (P .AND. .NOT. Q) is for P = .TRUE. and Q = .FALSE., we look in the second row of the table and find from the last column that the expression is .FALSE. . We can also see that this is the only case in which the expression will be .FALSE. .

This method of constructing a truth table will work for any expression. The intermediate steps can be omitted, but it is easier to put them in. In case the expression contains more than two variables, additional rows will be needed. For three variables, there are eight combinations of values. An illustration of this is given in the following truth table for the expression (P .OR. Q) .AND. R.

P	Q	R	P .OR. Q	(P .OR. Q) .AND. R
T	T	T	T	T
T	T	F	T	F
T	F	T	T	T
T	F	F	T	F
F	T	T	T	T
F	T	F	T	F
F	F	T	F	F
F	F	F	F	F

RELATIONAL EXPRESSIONS

A relational expression is a type of logical expression used in FORTRAN to make comparisons between arithmetic quantities. Such an expression consists of two arithmetic expressions connected by a *relational operator*. For example, one such relational operator is .EQ., which means "equal to." A relational expression using this operator is LIMA .EQ. 9. This expression has a *logical value*, i.e., either .TRUE. or .FALSE. . If LIMA has the value 9, then this expression takes on the value .TRUE. . If this LIMA is not equal to 9, then the expression has the value .FALSE. .

There are six relational operators which may be used in FORTRAN:

Operator	Meaning
.EQ.	Equal to (=)
.NE.	Not equal to ($\neq$)
.GT.	Greater than (>)
.LT.	Less than (<)
.GE.	Greater than or equal to ($\geq$)
.LE.	Less than or equal to ($\leq$)

The periods before and after each operator are considered to be part of the operator.

The general form of a relational expression is

A .R. B

where .R. is one of the six relational operators above, and A and B are arithmetic expressions. A and B may be either integer or floating-point arithmetic expressions, but they should be of the

213

same mode, either both integer or both floating point. This expression is evaluated as follows:

1. The arithmetic expressions A and B are evaluated in the usual way.
2. The value of A is compared to the value of B.
3. If the values satisfy the relation, the relational expression takes on the value .TRUE.; otherwise, it takes on the value .FALSE. .

Consider, for instance, the statements

```
LOGICAL Z
I = 10
Z = I .LT. 5
```

When the relational expression is evaluated, I has the value 10, so I does not satisfy the relation I .LT. 5 (meaning "I is less than 5"), and the expression takes the value .FALSE. . So, Z is .FALSE. . Similarly, the statements

```
LOGICAL Z
G = 4.1
H = 5.3
Z = H - 1.0 .GE. G
```

would assign the value .TRUE. to the logical variable Z, since H - 1.0 is, in fact, greater than or equal to G.

Some other examples of relational expressions are given below:

$$A = 1.0, \quad B = 2.0, \quad C = 3.0$$

Expression	Value
A - 1.0 .GE. 0.0	.TRUE.
A - 1.0 .LT. 0.0	.FALSE.
3.0 .LT. 2.0 * C	.TRUE.
(A - B) * C .EQ. B	.FALSE.
A .NE. B	.TRUE.
B .LT. C	.TRUE.
1.5 .LT. B	.TRUE.
B - 2.1 .GT. C - 3.0	.FALSE.
C .EQ. A + B	.TRUE.
5.2 .NE. 5.2	.FALSE.

Using the logical operators .AND. and .OR., we may connect relational expressions with other logical expressions. For instance, suppose that P is a logical variable, and we want to assign the value .TRUE. to P if $0 \le X < 1.0$, and .FALSE. otherwise. Since $0 \le X < 1.0$ is really a shorthand way of writing the two statements $0 \le X$ and $X < 1.0$, we whall need to use two relational operators. This may be done with the single statement P = (0.0 .LE. X) .AND. (X .LT. 1.0).

When compound statements such as this are evaluated, the relational operators are evaluated before the logical operators. If X = 2.0, the above expression would be evaluated:

    0.0 .LE. X is assigned the value .TRUE.
    X .LT. 1.0 is assigned the value .FALSE.
    .TRUE. .AND. .FALSE. is assigned the value .FALSE.
    P is assigned the value .FALSE.

In general, expressions are evaluated in the following order:

    1. Arithmetic expressions;
    2. Relational operators;
    3. Logical operators.

Thus, if we write

$$3.0 * A - 1.0 \ .LT. \ B \ .AND. \ B \ .LT. \ 3.0 * A + 1.0$$

it would be interpreted as

$$((3.0 * A - 1.0) \ .LT. \ B) \ .AND. \ (B \ .LT. \ (3.0 * A + 1.0))$$

which is the FORTRAN equivalent of the statement $(3A - 1) < B < (3A + 1)$.

THE LOGICAL IF STATEMENT

The most important use of logical expressions is in connection with the logical IF statement. This statement has the same purpose as the arithmetic IF statement studied in Chapter 3, but it has a different form that is sometimes more convenient to use.

The general form of the logical IF statement is

                          IF (E) S

where E is any logical expression, and S is any executable FORTRAN statement except a DO statement or another IF statement. When this statement is executed, the logical expression E is evaluated, and then if E has the value .TRUE., Statement S is performed. If E has the value .FALSE., Statement S is *not* executed.

215

For example, we know that, using an arithmetic IF statement, the procedure shown in Figure 9-1

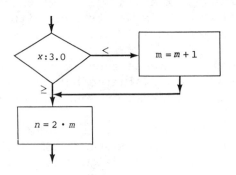

FIGURE 9-1

could be programmed with the statements

```
    IF (X - 3.0) 5, 10, 10
  5 M = M + 1
 10 N = 2 * M
```

Using a logical IF statement, this could be written

```
    IF (X .LT. 3.0) M = M + 1
    N = 2 * M
```

If the relational expression X .LT. 3.0 has the value .TRUE., then the statement M = M + 1 will be performed before the statement N = 2 * M. If X .LT. 3.0 has the value .FALSE., then the statement M = M + 1 will be by-passed and the next statement performed is N = 2.0 * M.

The ability to use any logical expression in the parentheses of the logical IF statement can often be quite useful. For one thing, tests that require two or more arithmetic IF statements can often be combined in a single logical IF statement. For instance, Figure 9-2 shows a procedure that will set X = 0 if 0 < X < 1, leave the value of X unchanged otherwise, and then set Y = X. Using arithmetic IF statements, this could be programmed as

```
    IF (X - 1.0) 5, 20, 20
  5 IF (X) 20, 20, 10
 10 X = 0.0
 20 Y = X
```

216

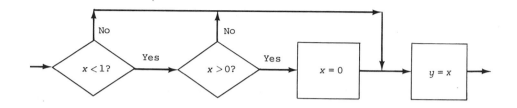

FIGURE 9-2

The same thing can be accomplished with the statements

    IF (0.0 .LT. X .AND. X .LT. 1.0) X = 0.0
    Y = X

Similarly, Figure 9-3 shows a procedure that will set X = 0 if
either X > 1 or X < 0. This would also require two arithmetic
IF statements, but it can be done with one logical IF statement:

    IF (X .GT. 1.0 .OR. X .LT. 0.) X = 0.0
    Y = X

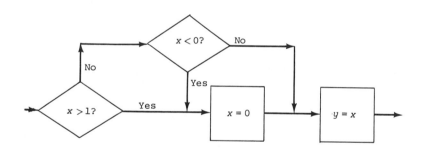

FIGURE 9-3

Anything that can be programmed using logical IF statements can
be programmed with arithmetic IF statements. The logical form
is quite versatile, however, and can sometimes make the program
easier to write. Furthermore, the logical form reduces the
proliferation of statement numbers, which can sometimes be confusing or make the program look messy. The following examples
will demonstrate the use of logical variables and the logical IF
statement in complete programs.

Example 1

A certain teacher uses the following system in grading
tests:

217

TEST SCORE	GRADE
91-100	4
81-89	3
71-79	2
61-69	1
59 & below	0

Now, for borderline cases with scores of 60, 70, 80, or 90, he promised his class that "homework would count." If a student is a borderline case and he has turned in all three homework assignments, he gets the higher grade; otherwise, he gets the lower grade.

Suppose that there are N students and that the test score for student I is stored in an array element NSCOR(I). The number of homework assignments turned in by student I is stored in NHMWK(I). The problem is to write a program to compute each student's grade NGRAD(I).

A solution to this problem is shown in the flowchart in Figure 9-4. Just for comparison, consider how this flowchart could be programmed, using the arithmetic IF statement. The first part would look something like this:

```
        DO 100 I = 1, N
        IF (NSCOR(I) - 91) 10, 4, 4
   10   IF (NSCOR(I) - 90) 20, 15, 20
   15   IF (NHMWK(I) - 3) 20, 4, 20
    4   NGRAD(I) = 4
        GO TO 100
   20   IF (NSCOR(I) - 81) 25, 3, 3
        .               .
        .               .
        .               .
```

The first three IF statements correspond to one phase of the testing. We shall see that these three arithmetic IF statements can be replaced by a single logical IF statement. There are several advantages to doing so. First, since the four IF statements above are interconnected, they must have statement numbers. Using the logical operator, .OR., we shall be able to avoid having to use so many statement numbers, and the program will be easier to construct. Second, it is more difficult to follow a program with multiple IF statements like the above. It is hard to look at the program and tell what it is supposed to do. With the use of logical IF statements, the operation of the program will be clearer.

The program corresponding to the given flowchart is presented following Figure 9-4.

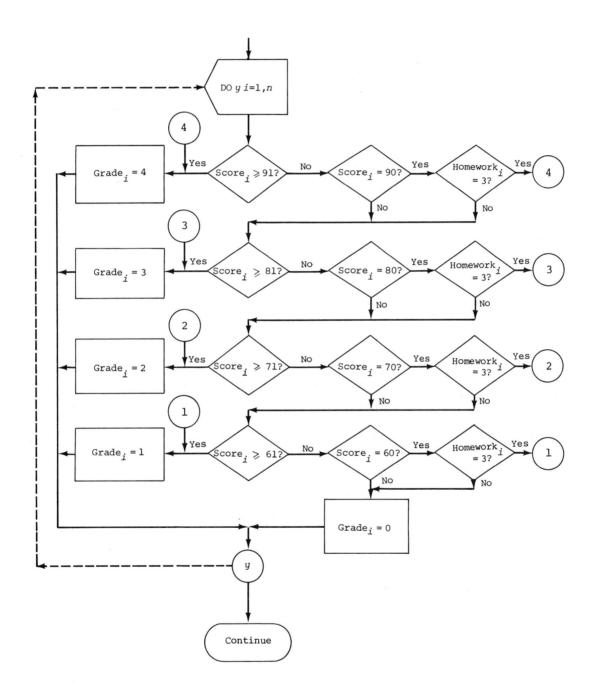

FIGURE 9-4

219

```
        LOGICAL H
        DIMENSION NSCOR (100), NGRAD (100), NHMWK (100)
              :                    :
              :                    :
        DO 100 I = 1, N
        H = NHMWK(I) .EQ. 3
        M = NSCOR(I)
        IF (M .GE. 91 .OR. M .EQ. 90 .AND. H) GO TO 4
        IF (M .GE. 81 .OR. M .EQ. 80 .AND. H) GO TO 3
        IF (M .GE. 71 .OR. M .EQ. 70 .AND. H) GO TO 2
        IF (M .GE. 61 .OR. M .EQ. 60 .AND. H) GO TO 1
        NGRAD(I) = 0
        GO TO 100
    1   NGRAD(I) = 1
        GO TO 100
    2   NGRAD(I) = 2
        GO TO 100
    3   NGRAD(I) = 3
        GO TO 100
    4   NGRAD(I) = 4
  100   CONTINUE
        STOP
        END
```

Here we have set the logical variable H equal to the condition NHMWK(I) .EQ. 3, and we set M - NSCOR(I). This was done to make the writing shorter in the IF statements. Each of the IF statements above corresponds to three of the arithmetic IF statements used before. Notice that the logical expressions within the IF statements have been written without parentheses. Because of the precedence of the operator .OR. over .AND., they will be interpreted as though they had been written:

(M .GE. 91) .OR. ((M .EQ. 90) .AND. H), etc.

which is the same as

(NSCOR(I) .GE. 91 .OR. ((NSCOR(I) .EQ. 90) .AND. NHMWK(I) .EQ. 3)

The student can easily verify that this is exactly the condition under which the NGRAD(I) is set equal to 4 in the flowchart.

Example 2

The following table shows a hypothetical schedule for figuring the income tax for a married person. For an unmarried person, the tax is 2% greater than this (i.e., 1.02 times whatever tax a married person with the same income pays).

If Income Is at Least	But Less Than	Tax Is
0.00	1000.00	5% of income
1000.00	2000.00	50.00 plus 15% of excess over 1000.00
2000.00	3000.00	200.00 plus 20% of excess over 2000.00
3000.00	4500.00	400.00 plus 30% of excess over 3000.00
More than 4500.00		850.00 plus 40% of excess over 4500.00

Suppose that the data for each person is punched on cards in the following format:

```
    Column 1:   1 if person is unmarried; 2 if married
Columns 2-10:   Social security number
Columns 11-19:  Income (with two assumed decimal places)
```

After the last card in the data set, there is a card with a zero punched in column 1. Write a program to read each card, compute the tax, and output the social security number and the tax for each person.

This problem can easily be solved using the method shown in the flowchart in Figure 9-5. First, the marital status MS, social security number NSS, and income X are read in. If MS = 0, then we have already read the last data card, so we stop. Otherwise, we compute the tax as though the person were married, and then multiply the tax by 1.02 if the person is single. Finally, we output the results and begin anew with another card.

The following program shows a simple way to write this procedure in FORTRAN, using the logical IF statement:

```
 1   READ (1, 5) MS, NSS, X
 5   FORMAT (I1, I9, F9.2)
     IF (MS .EQ. 0) STOP
     IF (X .LT. 1000.0) TAX = .05 * X
     IF (X .LT. 2000.0) TAX = 50.0 + .15*(X - 1000.0)
     IF (X .LT. 3000.0) TAX = 200.0 + .20 * (X - 2000.0)
     IF (X .LT. 4500.0) TAX = 400.0 + .30 * (X - 3000.0)
     IF (X .GT. 4500.0) TAX = 850.0 + .40 * (X - 4500.0)
     IF (MS .EQ. 1) TAX = 1.02 * TAX
     WRITE (2, 10) NSS, TAX
10   FORMAT (I10, F8.2)
     GO TO 1
     END
```

Note, however, that this program does not exactly correspond to the flowchart shown in Figure 9-5. According to the flowchart,

221

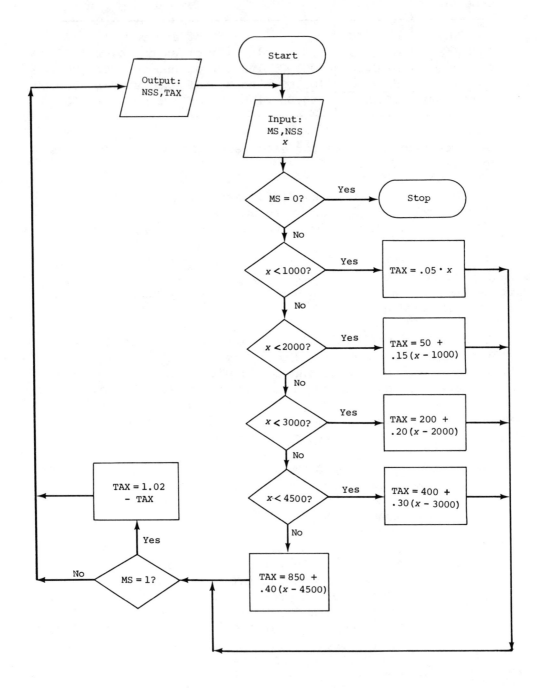

FIGURE 9-5

if X is less than 1000, the tax will be comptued by the formula
TAX = .05 * X, and then the next statement executed will be the
comparisons of MS to 1 by the decision box at the bottom of the
flowchart. In the program above, if X is less than 1000, then
after computing the tax, the next statement performed will be
the comparison of X to 2000 by the statement

$$\text{IF (X .LT. 2000.0) TAX} = 50.0 + .15 * (X - 1000.0)$$

In fact, all the IF statements in the above program will be
performed no matter what X is. This is really unnecessary.
The problem is that only one executable statement can follow
the logical expression in a logical IF statement. In the flowchart, we actually want to execute two statements if X is less
than 1000: one statement to compute the tax and a GO TO statement to jump to the last decision box.

   In order to do this using a logical IF statement, we would
need statements such as

```
      IF (X .GE. 1000.0) GO TO 20
      TAX = .05 * X
      GO TO 75
   20 IF (X .GE. 2000.0) GO TO 30
```

   Here the condition in the first IF statement is
X .GE. 1000.0. If this is .TRUE., then X is greater than or
equal to 1000, so we jump to the next IF statement. If
X .GE. 1000.0 is .FALSE., then X is less than 1000, so the
tax is computed and then the program jumps to Statement 75,
which will correspond to the last decision box of the flowchart.
The complete program, written this way, would be:

```
    1 READ (1, 5) MS, NSS, X
    5 FORMAT (I1, I9, F9.2)
      IF (MS .EQ. 0) STOP
      IF (X .GE. 1000.0) GO TO 20
      TAX = .05 * X
      GO TO 75
   20 IF (X .GE. 2000.0) GO TO 30
      TAX = 50.0 + .15 * (X - 1000.0)
      GO TO 75
   30 IF (X .GE. 3000.0) GO TO 40
      TAX = 200.0 + .20 * (X - 2000.0)
      GO TO 75
   40 IF (X .GE. 4500.0) GO TO 50
      TAX = 400.0 + .30 * (X - 3000.0)
      GO TO 75
   50 TAX = 850.0 + .40 * (X - 4500.0)
```

```
75   IF (MS .EQ. 1) TAX = 1.02 * TAX
     WRITE (2, 80) NSS, TAX
80   FORMAT (I10, F8.2)
     GO TO 1
     END
```

This is longer to write but faster to execute.

This example illustrates a fact which should be kept in mind. When using logical IF statements in a program instead of using the statements

$$\text{IF (E) } S_1$$
$$S_2$$

where E is a logical expression and S_1 and S_2 are statements, it may be more convenient to use the form

$$\text{IF (.NOT. E) } S_2$$
$$S_1$$

which will accomplish the same thing in a slightly different manner.

Example 3

The mess sergeant at a military base is faced with the problem of ordering food for the month. He generally serves either potatoes or macaroni with the meals, and he wants to buy some of each but there are certain restrictions that he must observe.

The first restriction is that there is enough money in the mess fund to buy at most 160 sacks of potatoes or 80 boxes of macaroni. If he buys some of each, then the total number of sacks of potatoes plus twice the number of boxes of macaroni must be less than 160. Letting P be the number of sacks of potatoes and M be the number of boxes of macaroni, this condition can be expressed as $P + 2M \leq 160$.

The second restriction is that in order to be able to provide enough meals for the month, he must buy at least 70 boxes of macaroni or 70 sacks of potatoes. If he buys some of each, this restriction is $P + M \geq 70$.

The third restriction is that since macaroni is less expensive than potatoes, he wants to buy more macaroni than potatoes, so $M > P$. Finally, he always serves potatoes on weekends, so he needs at least 20 sacks of potatoes; thus, $P \geq 20$.

The problem is to find some possible quantities of potatoes and macaroni that meet the requirements. That is, we want to find numbers P and M that satisfy all four of the following inequalities:

1. $P + 2M \leq 160$.
2. $P + M \geq 70$.
3. $M > P$.
4. $P \geq 20$.

This problem can be solved graphically. To do this, we set up axes for P and M, and show the graphs of the equations

a. $P + 2M = 160$;
b. $P + M = 70$;
c. $M = P$;
d. $P = 20$.

Each of these graphs is a straight line, and they are plotted in Figure 9-6.

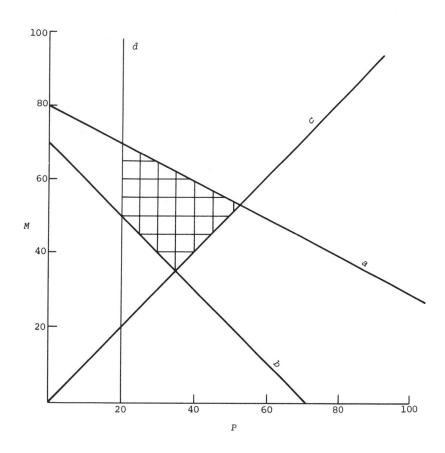

FIGURE 9-6

225

Line a is the graph of the equation $P + 2M = 160$. We are interested in points for which $P + 2M \leq 160$, and this corresponds to the region on or below line a. In other words, if P and M are the coordinates of any point below line a, then $P + 2M \leq 160$.

Similarly, line b is the graph of the equation $P + M = 70$, and any points on or above this line will satisfy $P + M \geq 70$. Thus, any point with coordinates P and M which lies on or above line b and on or below line a will satisfy both conditions $P + 2M \leq 160$ and $P + M \geq 70$.

Continuing this reasoning for the other two conditions, we arrive at the conclusion that the coordinates of any point which lies on or below line a, on or above line b, to the left of line c, and on or to the right of line d will satisfy all four given conditions. This set of points consists of the shaded region in Figure 9-6. For instance, $P = 30$ and $M = 60$ is a possible solution.

This method of solution is easy to visualize, but we are more interested in programming the problem for a computer solution. While we are at it, we might as well find several solutions. Suppose that the sergeant wants to buy five sacks of potatoes or five boxes of macaroni at a time. This means that we shall want to find all the pairs of integers P and M that satisfy the conditions and are also divisible by five.

A simple way to do this is to try out various combinations such as $P = 5$ and $M = 5$, $P = 5$ and $M = 10$, etc., and to write out any combinations that satisfy the conditions. This can easily be done by using nested DO loops. We first note that the first condition implies that P will be no greater than 160 and M will be greater than 80. So, we can try out all combinations with the nested DO statements

```
DO 500  NP = 5, 160, 5
DO 500   M = 5, 80, 5
```

Here we have used NP instead of P since we want an integer variable. These statements will provide all combinations of NP and M in the range $5 \leq NP \leq 160$ and $5 \leq M \leq 80$, stepping up by five each time on each variable.

In order to test each combination, it will be convenient to have four logical variables in the program. We shall call them A, B, C, and D. We first set A equal to the value of the relational expression corresponding to the first condition:

```
A = NP + 2 * M .LE. 160
```

226

If A is .FALSE., NP and M do not satisfy the first condition and there is no need to continue. So we shall branch to the end of the DO loops and start again with a different set of values for NP and M. This can be done with the logical IF statement

IF (.NOT. A) GO TO 500

If the first condition is satisfied, then A is .TRUE., and .NOT. A is .FALSE.; this IF statement will not cause the program to branch to Statement 500. The next thing we do is to set the logical variable B equal to the second condition

B = P + M .GE. 70

Once again, if B is .FALSE., we branch to the end of the DO loops by using the statements IF (.NOT. B) GO TO 500.

This same procedure is carried out for the other two conditions. If NP and M satisfy all four conditions, we output their values before continuing with the DO loops.

The complete program is:

```
      LOGICAL A, B, C, D
      DO 500 NP = 5, 160, 5
      DO 500 M = 5, 80, 5
      A = NP + 2 * M .LE. 160
      IF (.NOT. A) GO TO 500
      B = NP + M .GE. 70
      IF (.NOT. B) GO TO 500
      C = M .GT. NP
      IF (.NOT. C) GO TO 500
      D = NP .GE. 20
      IF (.NOT. D) GO TO 500
      WRITE (2, 10), NP, M
   10 FORMAT (5X, 4HP = , I4, 3X, 4HM = , I4)
  500 CONTINUE
      STOP
      END
```

While this example was a rather simple problem, this sort of problem arises frequently, and it can be of immense practical importance. One aspect, which is quite common, is this: suppose that potatoes cost $2.00 per sack and macaroni costs $1.15 per box. Find the solution that satisfies the given conditions and that costs the least. This is an example of what is called the *general linear programming problem*. Much work has been done on the subject to develop efficient algorithms for finding such solutions, and the subject is too complex to go into here. Imagine, however, what it would be like if our mess sergeant were trying to find the least expensive way to buy 100 different items, subject to, say, 200 conditions about the minimum quantity of each needed, the maximum funds available for each item, the maximum amount of each item that could be kept on hand, etc. Such problems can become very complicated, and a computer is definitely needed to compute a solution. However, we could add a few statements to find an approximate "best solution" among the points covered during the search. (See Problem 47 at the end of this chapter.)

LOGICAL ARRAYS

We can form logical arrays in much the same way that we formed integer or floating-point arrays. The difference is that each variable associated with a logical array is a logical variable.

Recall that the statement DIMENSION A(10) sets up an array of ten elements A(1), A(2), $\cdots$, A(10), and that each of these is a floating-point variable. If we write the statements

> LOGICAL A
> DIMENSION A(10)

then A will be set up as a logical array consisting of ten elements, each of which is a logical variable. So the value of A(1) will be either .TRUE. or .FALSE. . The LOGICAL statement specifies that A is of logical type and the DIMENSION statement specifies that A is an array.

There is a shorter way of writing the above two statements, which is often more convenient to use. We can combine the DIMENSION statement with the LOGICAL statement and write

> LOGICAL A(10)

This means the same thing as the above two statements: that A is a logical array of ten elements. In the general statement

> LOGICAL var_1, var_2, $\cdots$, var_n

each of the variable's names may be either a simple variable or a subscripted variable with the dimensions given. For example, the statement

> LOGICAL A, B, P(10), Q(3)

would specify that A and B are logical variables and P and Q are logical arrays of size 10 and 3, respectively. So P(1), P(2), $\cdots$, P(10), Q(1), Q(2), and Q(3) are all logical variables.

We can also use two- and three-dimensional logical arrays. The statement

LOGICAL XL (2, 5)

would establish XL as a logical array consisting of the ten elements

XL(1,1), XL(1,2), XL(1,3), XL(1,4), XL(1,5)
XL(2,1), XL(2,2), XL(2,3), XL(2,4), XL(2,5)

Logical arrays can be useful when repeated tests must be made and the results stored. For instance, suppose that A and B are floating-point arrays and that L is a logical array. We might want to set L(I) = .TRUE. if A(I) is greater than B(I). This can be done as follows:

```
      DIMENSION A(50),B(50)
      LOGICAL L(50)
      DO 5 K = 1, 50
    5 L(K) = A(K) .GT. B(K)
```

Sometimes iterative procedures involving logical variables are required. This is another case where logical arrays can be useful. Suppose that L is a logical array of size 50. We want to assign values to the logical variables P and Q by

P = L(1) .OR. L(2) .OR. L(3) .OR. $\cdots$ .OR. L(50)
Q = L(1) .AND. L(2) .AND. L(3) .AND. $\cdots$ .AND. L(50)

Rather than write out the whole expressions, we can use an iterative procedure. One way would be to use the statements

```
      P = .FALSE.
      Q = .TRUE.
      DO 9 K = 1, 50
      P = P .OR. L(K)
    9 Q = Q .AND. L(K)
```

Since P is .FALSE. to start with, P .OR. L(1) will have the same value as L(1). On the next time through the DO loop, P .OR. L(2) will have the same value as L(1) .OR. L(2), etc.

In the same way, since Q is .TRUE. to start with, Q .AND. L(1) will have the same value as L(1). On the second time through the DO loop, Q .AND. L(2) will have the same value as L(1) .AND. L(2). At the completion of the DO loop, P and Q will have the desired values.

We have seen that when complicated tests must be made in a program, logical variables and the logical IF statement can be

229

of great help in programming. When many similar tests involving
logical variables are required, logical arrays can be useful. We
shall see an application of logical arrays in the next example.

Example 4

In a certain city all the streets downtown are one-way.
The city planners were thoughtful enough so that even with this
system one could travel from any one place to any other. The
trouble is that some of the streets pass under low bridges, and
so cannot be used by large trucks. Figure 9-7 shows the six
major intersections in the city (identified by the numbers 1-6),
and the lines in the figure show the roads between the intersections that can be used by trucks with the directions of travel
indicated by arrows.

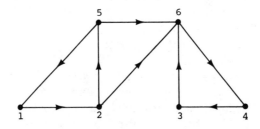

FIGURE 9-7

A trucking firm wants to know from which points to which a
truck can travel. For instance, a truck can get from 1 to 3 by
going from 1 to 2, from 2 to 6, from 6 to 4, and from 4 to 3.
But a truck could not get back from 6 to 1 by any route.

Before trying to program a solution to this problem, let
us consider the method to be used. For our method, we shall
construct a "tree" diagram for each starting point, which will
show what points can be reached from the starting point.

We begin with point 1. The only point that can be reached
from point 1 by a direct route (i.e., along a straight line) is
point 2. We write this diagrammatically as shown in Figure 9-8.

FIGURE 9-8

Now from point 2, there are two direct routes which can be taken: one leading to 5 and the other leading to 6. This we write as shown in Figure 9-9.

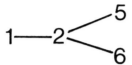

FIGURE 9-9

From each of these points, we show in Figure 9-10 the points that can be reached by a direct route.

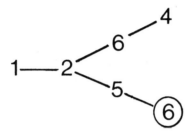

FIGURE 9-10

On the bottom branch, we note that the only point that can be reached from 5 is 6. But we have already succeeded in reaching 6 at an earlier step (on the top branch). So, by continuing the bottom branch, we can reach no points which have not already been reached. To indicate that we are at the "end of a limb" on this branch, we circle the 6. We continue the top branch until we arrive at a point which is already in the diagram. When all branches have been terminated in this way, the diagram is complete. This is shown in Figure 9-11.

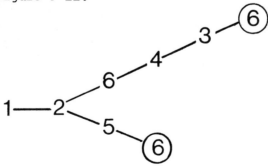

FIGURE 9-11

Any point that appears in this diagram can be reached from point 1 (the starting point), and all points that can be reached

231

from point 1 appear in this diagram. Starting now from point 5, we obtain the diagram shown in Figure 9-12.

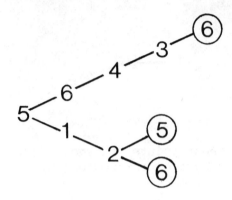

FIGURE 9-12

As before, this diagram contains all the points 1, 2, 3, 4, 5, and 6. This means that starting from point 5, any other point may be reached.

Starting from point 3, we obtain the diagram shown in Figure 9-13.

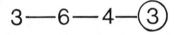

FIGURE 9-13

This diagram shows that points 6 and 4 may be reached from point 3, but 1, 2, and 5 may not be reached by any route starting at point 3. We have made diagrams for the cases of starting at points 1, 3, and 5. If we also make diagrams starting with points 2, 4, and 6, we will have a complete solution to the problem. To determine whether a truck can travel from point I to point J, we look at the diagram starting with I and see if J is in I.

To program this in FORTRAN, we will use several logical arrays. The first array we will call RT (short for route). It will be a 6 × 6 logical array which will represent Figure 9-7. We will define RT (I, J) to be .TRUE. if there is a direct route from point I to point J. If there is no such route, RT (I, J) = .FALSE. . By a direct route, we mean a straight-line route in Figure 9-7. Thus, RT will have the values shown in Figure 9-14. In this figure, T stands for .TRUE., and a blank square stands for .FALSE. . The student should convince himself that this array conveys the same information as Figure 9-7.

232

	1	2	3	4	5	6
1	T	T				
2		T			T	T
3			T			T
4			T	T		
5	T				T	T
6				T		T

FIGURE 9-14.   Values of the Array RT

(We would probably want to read in these values from cards, but we will ignore this for the moment since input and output of logical variables is taken up in the next section.)

What we want to find in this problem is whether or not there is any path (not necessarily a direct route) from point I to point J.   We shall set up a 6 × 6 logical matrix PATH, and the program will have to set PATH (I, J) = .TRUE. if there is a path from I to J, and .FALSE. if there is no path.

Now, we shall need some way to represent the process of making the diagrams we used to solve the problem.   To represent this process in a FORTRAN program, it will be convenient to use three logical arrays, which we will call POINT, PRES, and NEXT.   These will be one-dimensional logical arrays.

At each step of constructing a tree, PRES tells which points are under consideration in the present step.   For example, in the third step of making the diagram starting with 5, the diagram looks like Figure 9-15.

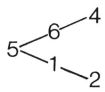

FIGURE 9-15

The points under consideration in this step are 2 and 4.   To indicate this, we shall set PRES (2) and PRES (4) equal to .TRUE.; PRES (1), PRES (2), PRES (5), and PRES (6) will be .FALSE. .

The array POINT tells which points are already in the diagram. In the third step of making the diagram beginning with 5 (see Figure 9-15), the points 1, 2, 4, 5, and 6 have already been reached in the diagram, so POINT (1), POINT (2), POINT (4), POINT (5), and

233

POINT (6) will be .TRUE. and POINT (3) will be .FALSE. at this step.

To go from the present step to the next step, we shall set NEXT (I) = .TRUE. if point I can be reached by a direct route from any of the points under consideration in the present step. To do this, we can use the statements

```
         DO 25 I = 1, 6
         IF (.NOT. PRES(I)) GO TO 25
         DO 25 J = 1, 6
         IF (RT(I,J)) NEXT(J) = .TRUE.
      25 CONTINUE
```

The first DO loop will examine each of the points to see if it is in the present step. If not, the second DO loop is not performed for that value of I. If point I is in the current step [i.e., if PRES (I) = .TRUE.], the second DO loop determines which points can be reached from I by a direct route, and sets NEXT(J) = .TRUE. for these points. In the step corresponding to Figure 9-15, PRES (2) and PRES (4) are the only elements of PRES which are .TRUE., so we examine

$$RT(2, 1), \ RT(2, 2), \ \cdots, \ RT(2, 6)$$
$$RT(4, 1), \ RT(4, 2), \ \cdots, \ RT(4, 6)$$

Of these, only RT(4, 3) and RT(2, 5) and RT(2, 6) are .TRUE., so we set NEXT (3), NEXT (5), and NEXT (6) equal to .TRUE., to show that the points 3, 5, and 6 are in the next step. This corresponds to drawing the next branches in the diagram, as shown in Figure 9-16.

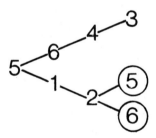

FIGURE 9-16

Of the new points 3, 5, and 6, we want to see which ones have already been reached in the diagram. To do this, we compare NEXT (I) with POINT (I). If they both are .TRUE., this means that point I is in the present step or some previous step, as well as in the next step. We shall set NEXT (I) = .FALSE., since there is no need to consider point I again. This corresponds to circling the 5 and 6 in Figure 9-16 to show that they are already in the diagram.   This process can be carried out by the statements

```
        DO 30 I = 1, 6
        IF (NEXT(I) .AND. POINT(I)) NEXT(I) = .FALSE.
    30  CONTINUE
```

Next, we test to see if we are finished with the diagram.   To do this in the program, we test to see if there are any points in the next step which were not already reached.   Since we have already set NEXT (I) = .FALSE. if point I has been reached, we set L = NEXT (1) .OR. NEXT (2) .OR $\cdots$ .OR. NEXT (6) and then if L is .TRUE., we are not finished, so we reinitialize the arrays involved and repeat the above procedure.

If L is .FALSE., we are finished with a diagram, so we fill in a row of the array PATH by setting PATH (N, J) = .TRUE. if POINT (J) is .TRUE. .   After this is done, we reinitialize the various arrays and begin again with a different starting point N.

The complete program is:

```
        LOGICAL RT(6, 6), PATH(6, 6), POINT(6), PRES(6), NEXT(6),L
C       INITIALIZE PATH
        DO 1 I = 1, 6
        DO 1 J = 1, 6
    1   PATH(I, J) = .FALSE.
C       BEGIN TREE STARTING WITH POINT N
        DO 100 N = 1, 6
        DO 5 I = 1, 6
        POINT(I) = .FALSE.
    5   PRES(I) = .FALSE.
        POINT(N) = .TRUE.
        PRES(N) = .TRUE.
   10   DO 15 I = 1, 6
   15   NEXT(I) = .FALSE.
C       FOR EACH POINT IN THE PRESENT STEP, SET
C       NEXT(J) = .TRUE. IF J CAN BE REACHED
C       BY A DIRECT ROUTE FROM I
        DO 25 I = 1, 6
        IF (.NOT. PRES(I)) GO TO 25
        DO 25 J = 1, 6
        IF (RT(I, J)) NEXT(J) = .TRUE.
   25   CONTINUE
C       SET NEXT(I) = .FALSE. IF I HAS
C       ALREADY BEEN REACHED ON A PREVIOUS
C       STEP
        DO 30 I = 1, 6
        IF (NEXT(I) .AND. POINT(I)) NEXT(I) = .FALSE.
   30   CONTINUE
C       IF NO NEW POINTS HAVE BEEN REACHED,
```

```
C       THE DIAGRAM BEGINNING WITH N IS
C       COMPLETE
        L = .FALSE.
        DO 35 I = 1, 6
   35   L = L .OR. NEXT(I)
        IF (.NOT. L) GO TO 50
C       SET POINT(I) = .TRUE. IF I HAS BEEN
C       REACHED ON THIS STEP.  NEXT STEP BECOMES
C       CURRENT STEP
        DO 40 I = 1, 6
        IF(NEXT(I)) POINT(I) = .TRUE.
   40   PRES(I) = NEXT(I)
        GO TO 10
C       THE DIAGRAM BEGINNING WITH N IS
C       COMPLETE.  FILL IN THE NTH ROW
C       OF PATH AND BEGIN A NEW DIAGRAM
   50   DO 60 J = 1, 6
        IF(POINT(J)) PATH(N, J) = .TRUE.
   60   CONTINUE
  100   CONTINUE
        STOP
        END
```

At the completion of this program, the array PATH will have the values shown in Figure 9-17 (T stands for .TRUE. and blank stands for .FALSE.).

	1	2	3	4	5	6
1	T	T	T	T	T	T
2	T	T	T	T	T	T
3			T	T		T
4			T	T		T
5	T	T	T	T	T	T
6			T	T		T

FIGURE 9-17

From Figure 9-17, we see that there is a path from point 1 to any other point, but that starting at point 3 only points 3, 4, and 6 can be reached.

INPUT AND OUTPUT OF LOGICAL VARIABLES

Values for logical variables can be read or written in FORTRAN just as numeric data are. To do this, the L field description is used. The L field description is used in a FORMAT statement just like the other field descriptions discussed in Chapter 6. The general form is where *n* is an unsigned integer constant giving the length of the field.

When the value of a logical variable is written under an L*n* specification, *n* - 1 blanks will be printed, followed by the character T or F according to whether the value is .TRUE. or .FALSE. . For example, if P, Q, and R are logical variables with values .TRUE., .FALSE., and .TRUE., respectively, then the statements

```
        WRITE (2, 11) P, Q, R
11  FORMAT (L3, L2, L1)
```

would print out the data bbTbFT. The L3 field for P prints two leading blanks before the T, the L2 field for Q prints one leading blank, and the L1 field for R does not print any leading blanks.

Used for input, the L*n* field will cause *n* characters to be read. Blank spaces may precede the data if desired. Only the first nonblank character in the field is interpreted. It must be either T or F, and the variable will be assigned a value .TRUE. or .FALSE. accordingly. If the statements

```
       READ (1, 5) P
5  FORMAT (L6)
```

were used to read the characters bbTbbb from a card, then the variable P would receive the value .TRUE. since the first nonblank character in the input field is T. The data Tbbbbb or bbbbbT would also be read as .TRUE. . If the input field contained the characters bbTRUE, this again would cause a value of .TRUE. to be read, since the first nonblank character is T, and it is only the first nonblank character in the field that is used to determine the value of the data. Actually bbTOMb or bbFRED would also work but, in practice, L1 field is usually used for input of logical variables.

Example 5

In this example, we shall write a program to grade a true-false test. The test consists of 20 questions (each question being worth five points). The input data consists of one card for each student. The student's matriculation number is punched in columns 1-6, and columns 7-26 contain his answers (each answer being a T or an F) and the questions. The first card read will have zeros in columns 1-6 and the correct answers to the questions in columns 7-26. The last card read will have all 9's in columns 1-6. For each student, the program must print out the matriculation number, his answers, and his score.

To solve this problem, we shall first read the correct answers into a logical array called CA (for correct answers). This will be a one-dimensional array of size 20 with CA(I) equal to the correct answer for question I. This read operation is accomplished with the statements

```
        READ (1, 5) MAT, (CA(I), I = 1, 20)
    5   FORMAT (I6, 20L1)
```

The implied DO loop in the READ statement reads in all 20 answers, each under an L1 format. We have also read in the value of the matriculation number MAT, which should be zero on the first card. Just to make sure that it is, we can test as follows:

```
        IF (MAT .NE. 0) STOP
```

Then if the correct answer card is accidentally left out of the data set, the program would stop rather than give everyone the wrong scores. To read in the first student's answers, we use the statement

```
        READ (1, 5) MAT, (SA(I), I = 1, 20)
```

SA is another logical array in which the student's answers are stored.

The next thing to be done in the program is to see if MAT is 999999, for if it is, we are finished. For any other value of MAT, we compute the student's score by comparing each SA(I) to each CA(I). If they are the same, we shall add five points to the score NSC. This is done, using a logical IF statement. Note that SA(I) and CA(I) are the same if they are either both .TRUE. or both .FALSE. . So, the expression

```
        CA(I) .AND. SA(I) .OR. .NOT. CA(I) .AND. .NOT. SA(I)
```

will be .TRUE. if and only if CA(I) and SA(I) have the same value.

To output the results, we use the statements

```
        WRITE (2, 20) MAT, (SA(I), I = 1, 20), NSC
    20  FORMAT (/, 1X, I6, 20L2, 8H SCORE =, I4)
```

The initial slash will double-space the output, and the L2 output fields will skip a space between each consecutive answer. A sample line of output would be

```
        142200 T F F T ... T SCORE = 50
```

The flowchart for this program is shown in Figure 9-18.

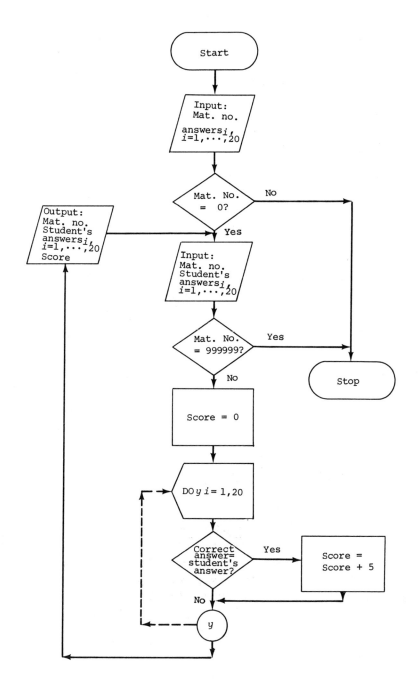

FIGURE 9-18

239

The complete program is:

```
       LOGICAL SA(20), CA(20)
       READ (1, 5) MAT, (CA(I), I = 1, 20)
   5   FORMAT (I6, 20L1)
       IF (MAT .NE. 0) STOP
  10   READ (1, 5) MAT, (SA(I), I = 1, 20)
       IF (MAT .EQ. 999999) STOP
       NSC = 0
       DO 50 I = 1, 20
    1  IF (CA(I) .AND. SA(I) .OR. .NOT. CA(I) .AND. .NOT. SA(I))
       NSC = NSC + 5
  50   CONTINUE
       WRITE (2, 60) MAT, (SA(I), I = 1, 20), NSC
  60   FORMAT (/, 1X, I6, 20L2, 8H SCORE =, I4)
       GO TO 10
       END
```

We conclude this chapter with a final example showing again the power of logical variables and the logical IF statement in dealing with multiple tests in a fairly involved program.

Example 6

We want to program the machine to play the game tic-tac-toe. The game is played on a 3 × 3 board like the one shown in Figure 9-19.

11	12	13
21	22	23
31	32	33

FIGURE 9-19

The machine moves first by printing one of the numbers on the board to indicate its move. The player then selects a number to indicate his move and this number is read into the machine. The machine then prints out its second move, and so forth until one player wins or until the game is a draw. A player wins if he gets three moves in a row, either horizontally, vertically, or diagonally. If all the cells have been moved in and neither player has three in a row, the game is a draw.

A little experimentation will show that, properly played, the game will always result in a draw. What we want to do is to program the machine so that the game will result in a draw unless the second player makes a mistake, in which case the machine should win if possible.

240

Although this game is very simple in nature, it turns out to be rather complicated to program the machine to play it because there are so many possibilities to be considered. The first thing we have to do is to decide on a strategy for the machine to follow. That is, we need a set of rules so that when the machine knows what moves have been made, it will be able to determine what its next move will be.

There are several possible strategies which could be used. We shall use the following rules for determining the machine moves.

RULE 1: The machine's first move will be in the center (cell 22).

RULE 2: If the machine can get three in a row on its move, it should do so.

RULE 3: If the machine cannot get three in a row, but the second player has two moves in a row, the machine should block by moving to the vacant cell in that row.

RULE 4: If the machine cannot win on its move, and it is not necessary to block as in Rule 3, then the machine should move to get two moves in the same row.

RULE 5: If this can be done by moving in a corner, the machine should do so.

RULE 6: If none of the above rules apply, the machine should move in any vacant cell.

To illustrate these rules, consider an example. Rule 1 says that the first move is in the center. Suppose the second player's first move is in cell 11 (see Figure 9-20).

11 O	12	13
21	22 X	23
31	32	33

X = Machine's move
O = Second player's move

FIGURE 9-20

There is no way the machine can get three in a row, so Rule 2 does not apply, and we go on to consider Rule 3. The second player does not have two in a row, so Rule 3 does not apply either. Rule 4 does apply, since the machine can get two in a row by moving at any one of the cells 12, 21, 32, 23, 13, or 31. (Moving to 33 would not count as getting two in a row, since the second player already has a move in that diagonal.) In order to choose among these possible moves, we must consider Rule 5, which says that a corner should be tried first. Thus, the machine should move at either 31 or 13. It does not matter which of these is selected as long as the machine has some way of choosing one or the other. Suppose it takes 13. The second player would then be forced to move at 31 as shown in Figure 9-21.

```
   11  |   12  |   13
    O   |       |    X
 _____ | _____ | _____
   21  |   22  |   23
       |    X   |
 _____ | _____ | _____
   31  |   32  |   33
    O   |       |
```

FIGURE 9-21

Now, the decision process starts again for the machine's next move. Rule 2 does not apply, because the machine cannot get three in a row, but Rule 3 applies, since the second player has two in a row in the first column. So, the machine should move at 21. If the second player now moves at cell 23, the game will result in a draw. Otherwise, the machine will win on its next move. In either case, the machine should print out a message announcing that the game is over.

The complete strategy for the machine is represented in the flowchart of Figure 9-22. Of course, this is just a general strategy. In order to program the solution in FORTRAN, we shall need a more specific procedure.

The first thing we need is some way of representing the board and moves. To do this, we shall use a 3 × 3 integer array called M. We shall set:

M(I, J) = 0 if no move has been made in cell IJ;
M(I, J) = 1 if the machine has moved in cell IJ;
M(I, J) = -1 if the second player has moved in cell IJ.

242

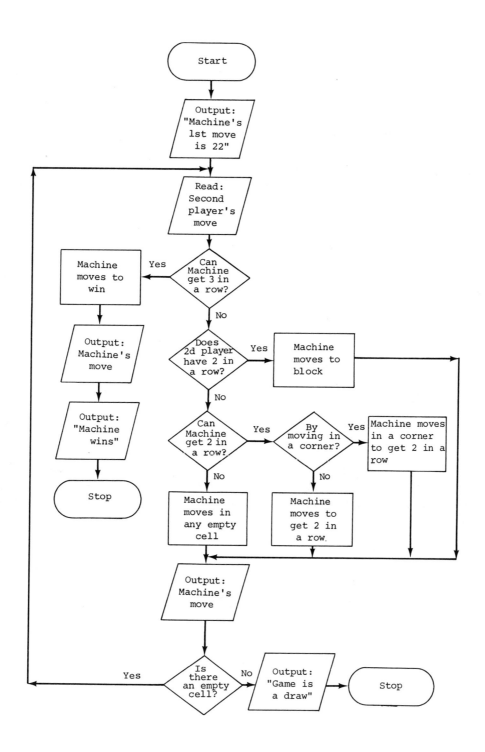

FIGURE 9-22

243

The first step in the program will be to initialize the array
M. Then the machine will make its first move, and the second player's first move will be read. First, to make sure the second player
is not cheating, we shall test to see if he has moved in an empty
cell. If not, we shall give him a chance to try again. When he
makes a valid move, the move will be recorded by assigning -1 to
the proper element of the array M.

Now, we shall be using three arrays besides M in the program.
These arrays will give the sums of the rows, columns, and diagonals
of the array M. NROW gives the sum of the rows, so

$$NROW(1) = M(1, 1) + M(1, 2) + M(1, 3)$$
$$NROW(2) = M(2, 1) + M(2, 2) + M(2, 3)$$
$$NROW(3) = M(3, 1) + M(3, 2) + M(3, 3)$$

Likewise, NCOL gives the sums of the columns, so

$$NCOL(1) = M(1, 1) + M(2, 1) + M(3, 1)$$
$$NCOL(2) = M(1, 2) + M(2, 2) + M(3, 2)$$
$$NCOL(3) = M(1, 3) + M(2, 3) + M(3, 3)$$

NDIAG gives the sums of the diagonals, so

$$NDIAG(1) = M(1, 1) + M(2, 2) + M(3, 3)$$
$$NDIAG(2) = M(1, 3) + M(2, 2) + M(3, 1)$$

These arrays will be used in determining the machine's move.
For instance, if NROW(1) = 2, we shall know that the machine can
win by playing in row 1, since the machine must already have two
moves in row 1. But we shall come to that in a moment. What
concerns us now is that after each move by the second player, we
have to recompute the values of these arrays.

The flowchart corresponding to this first part of the program
is shown in Figure 9-23. The FORTRAN statements are as follows:

```
        DIMENSION M(3, 3), NROW(3), NCOL(3), NDIAG(3)
        LOGICAL Z
        COMMON N, I, J, ND
        DO 10 I = 1, 3
        DO 10 J = 1, 3
   10   M(I, J) = 0
        I = 2
        J = 2
        NMOVE = 1
   20   M(I, J) = 1
        WRITE (2, 25) I, J
   25   FORMAT (17H MACHINE MOVES AT ,1X, 2I1)
   30   WRITE (2, 35)
```

244

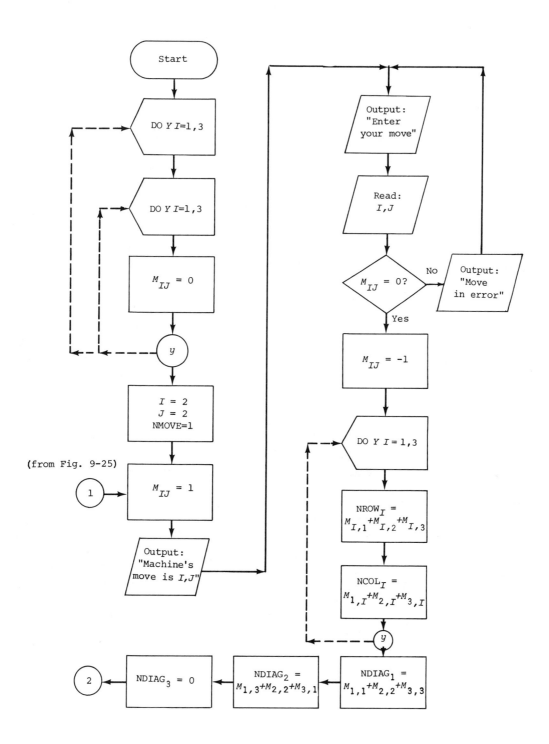

FIGURE 9-23

```
35   FORMAT (16H ENTER YOUR MOVE)
     READ (1, 40) I, J
40   FORMAT (2I1)
     IF (M(I, J) .EQ. 0) GO TO 50
     WRITE (2, 45)
45   FORMAT (17H MOVE NOT ALLOWED)
     GO TO 30
50   M(I, J) = -1
     DO 55 I = 1, 3
     NROW(I) = M(I, 1) + M(I, 2) + M(I, 3)
55   NCOL(I) = M(1, I) + M(2, I) + M(3, I)
     NDIAG(1) = M(1, 1) + M(2, 2) + M(3, I)
     NDIAG(2) = M(1, 3) + M(2, 2) + M(3, 1)
     NDIAG(3) = 0
```

The LOGICAL and COMMON are for use with later parts of the program. The variable NMOVE will also be used later on. The statement

```
          NDIAG(3) = 0
```

needs a little explanation. Actually, of course, there is no "third" diagonal on the board. It will turn out, however, that it is convenient to have a dummy element for the array NDIAG in order to make the testing sections shorter. We shall see shortly how this works.

Now, the first part of our strategy is to see if the machine can win. This is possible if the machine has two moves in a row. This will be the case if and only if some element NROW(I), NCOL(I), or NDIAG(I) is equal to 2. Now, in order to test for this, we shall consider each cell IJ on the board, and we test to see if the cell is empty, (M(I, J) = 0), and to see if the row, column, or diagonal containing that cell has a sum of 2. If this is the case, we shall move in the cell; otherwise, we shall go on to the next part of the strategy.

In order to carry out the testing involved, we shall have to repeatedly generate the pairs of subscripts for the array M. It will be convenient to have a subroutine to do this. The subroutine will be called CELL. It will share four variables in common with the main program:

N is an integer from 1 to 8. It will be used as an index of a DO loop in the main program.

I and J are integers from 1 to 3 which will be used as subscripts for the array M. I and J depend on N.

ND is a number from 1 to 3 which depends on N. It tells which diagonal the cell M(I, J) is in.

ND equals 1 if cell IJ is in the diagonal from 11 to 33.

ND equals 2 if cell IJ is in the diagonal from 13 to 31.

ND equals 3 if cell IJ is in no diagonal.

Given a number N, the values of I, J, and ND may be determined from the following table:

N	I	J	ND
1	1	1	1
2	1	3	2
3	3	3	1
4	3	1	2
5	1	2	3
6	2	3	3
7	3	2	3
8	2	1	3

The subroutine to generate these values is very straight-forward:

```
      SUBROUTINE CELL
      COMMON N, I, J, ND
      IF (N .NE. 1) GO TO 2
      I = 1
      J = 1
      ND = 1
      RETURN
    2 IF (N .NE. 2) GO TO 3
      I = 1
      J = 3
      ND = 2
      RETURN
    3 IF (N .NE. 3)  GO TO 4
      I = 3
      J = 3
      ND = 1
      RETURN
    4 IF (N .NE. 4) GO TO 5
      I = 3
```

```
              J = 1
              ND = 2
              RETURN
       5  IF (N .NE. 5) GO TO 6
              I = 1
              J = 2
              ND = 3
              RETURN
       6  IF (N .NE. 6) GO TO 7
              I = 2
              J = 3
              ND = 3
              RETURN
       7  IF (N .NE. 7) GO TO 8
              I = 3
              J = 2
              ND = 3
              RETURN
       8  IF (N .NE. 8) STOP
              I = 2
              J = 1
              ND = 3
              RETURN
              END
```

Now, getting back to the main program, consider the corner
cells 11, 13, 33, and 31. The machine can win by playing at one
of these cells if

1. The cell is empty (M(I, J) = 0);
2. Either the row, column, or diagonal containing
    the cell has a sum of 2.

For the cell 11, this condition can be expressed as

((NROW(1) .EQ. 2) .OR. (NCOL(1) .EQ. 2) .OR. (NDIAG(1) .EQ. 2)) .AND.
(M(1, 1) .EQ. 0))

Using the logical variable Z, we can break this down into four
parts:

```
    Z = NROW(1) .EQ. 2
    Z = Z .OR. NCOL(1) .EQ. 2
    Z = Z .OR. NDIAG(1) .EQ. 2
    Z = Z .AND. M(1, 1) .EQ. 0
```

Then Z will be .TRUE. if and only if the machine can win by playing
cell 11.

248

For the other three corner cells, the procedure is similar. Now, the coordinates of the four corner cells are returned by the subroutine CELL for the first four values of N, and we can perform the same test for all four corner cells by using the following DO loop.

```
      DO 75 N = 1, 4
      CALL CELL
      Z = NROW(I) .EQ. 2
      Z = Z .OR. NCOL(J) .EQ. 2
      Z = Z .OR. NDIAG(ND) .EQ. 2
      Z = Z .AND. M(I, J) .EQ. 0
      IF (Z) GO TO 100
   75 CONTINUE
```

At Statement 100, the machine will indicate that it has won. If the program "falls through" the DO loop, then we want to test to see if the machine can win by moving at one of the cells 12, 23, 32, or 21. The procedure for this is like the one above. The only difference is that these cells are not in any diagonal, so that part of the test is unnecessary. The coordinates of these cells are returned for the second four values of N by the subroutine CELL, and again we can use a DO loop.

```
      DO 80 N = 5, 8
      CALL CELL
      Z = NROW(I) .EQ. 2
      Z = Z .OR. NCOL(J) .EQ. 2
      Z = Z .AND. M(I, J) .EQ. 0
      IF (Z) GO TO 100
   80 CONTINUE
```

Actually, this DO loop can be combined with the previous loop to make the program a little shorter. This is done by using the dummy element NDIAG(3) which was set equal to zero earlier in the program. When ND = 3, the statement Z = Z .OR. NDIAG(ND) .EQ. 2 will leave the value of Z unchanged. In other words, we can let N run from 1 to 8 in the first DO loop and just omit the second DO loop.

If the machine cannot get three in a row, the program will fall through this DO loop and branch to Statement 105, where we begin the next part of the strategy. If the machine can get three in a row, the program will branch to Statement 100, where the machine will indicate its move and stop. The flowchart for this part of the program is given in Figure 9-24. The FORTRAN statements are as follows:

```
      DO 75 N = 1, 8
      CALL CELL
```

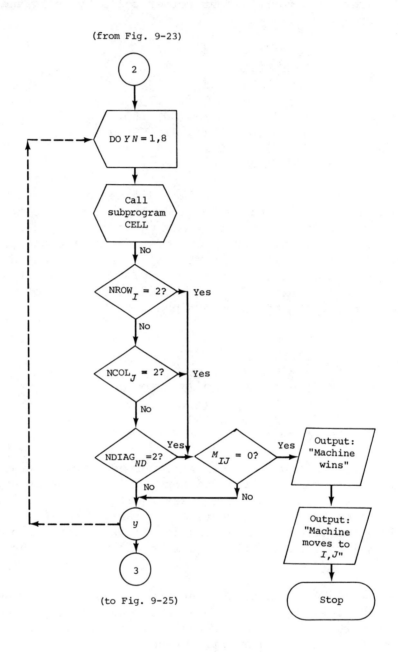

FIGURE 9-24. Machine wins if possible

250

```
       Z = NROW(I) .EQ. 2
       Z = Z .OR. NCOL(J) .EQ. 2
       Z = Z .OR. NDIAG(ND) .EQ. 2
       Z = Z .AND. M(I, J) .EQ. 0
       IF (Z) GO TO 100
   75  CONTINUE
       GO TO 105
  100  WRITE (2, 25) I, J
       WRITE (2, 101)
  101  FORMAT (13H MACHINE WINS)
       STOP
```

The next part of the strategy is to block the second player
if he has two in a row. This will be the case if the sum of a
row, column, or diagonal is -2. To test for this condition, we
use a procedure much like the one used to test for a machine win.
For each cell, we test to see if the cell is empty and if the
sum of the row, column, or diagonal containing the cell is -2.
If so, the machine will move in the cell. Referring to Figure
9-22, however, we see that we must remember to test to see if
the game is a draw. An easy way to do this is to observe that
since there are nine cells on the board, the game will be a draw
if the machine has not won on its fifth move. We can test easily
for this by initializing a variable NMOVE to 1 after the machine's
first move, and then adding 1 to NMOVE each time the machine moves.
If NMOVE equals 5 and the machine has not won, the game is a draw.

The flowchart for this part of the program is given in
Figure 9-25. The FORTRAN statements are:

```
  105  DO 110 N = 1, 8
       CALL CELL
       Z = NROW(I) .EQ. -2
       Z = Z .OR. NCOL(J) .EQ. -2
       Z = Z .AND. M(I, J) .EQ. 0
       IF (Z) GO TO 200
  110  CONTINUE
  200  NMOVE = NMOVE + 1
       IF (NMOVE .LT. 5) GO TO 20
       WRITE (2, 25) I, J
       WRITE (2, 205)
  205  FORMAT (15H GAME IS A DRAW)
       STOP
```

Notice that it is not necessary to check whether or not the
second player has two in a row diagonally, since the machine has
a move in the center.

If the second player does not have two in a row, the machine
will try to get two in a row. Thus, the machine will move in a
row, column, or diagonal whose sum is 1, and where there is an

251

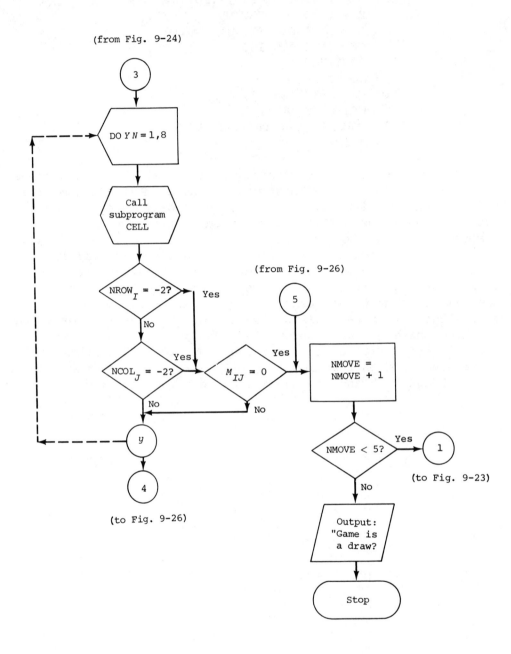

FIGURE 9-25. *Machine moves to block if necessary*

empty cell. This, again, is done by considering each cell in turn by calling the subroutine CELL, and determining whether or not the machine should move there. Recall that Rule 5 says that the machine should first try to move at a corner. Since CELL returns the coordinates of the corner cells for the first four values of N, we can just use a DO loop to do this.

Finally, if it is not possible to get two in a row, the machine should move in any vacant cell.

The flowchart for this last part of the program is shown in Figure 9-26. The complete tic-tac-toe program is:

```
C         PROGRAM TO PLAY TIC-TAC-TOE
C         USES SUBROUTINE CELL
          DIMENSION M(3, 3), NROW(3), NCOL(3), NDIAG(3)
          LOGICAL Z
          COMMON N, I, J, ND
          DO 10 I = 1, 3
          DO 10 J = 1, 3
   10     M(I, J) = 0
          I = 2
          J = 2
          NMOVE = 1
   20     M(I, J) = 1
          WRITE (2, 25) I, J
   25     FORMAT (17H MACHINE MOVES AT, 1X, 2I1)
   30     WRITE (2, 35)
   35     FORMAT (16H ENTER YOUR MOVE)
          READ (1, 40) I, J
   40     FORMAT (2I1)
          IF (M(I, J) .EQ. 0) GO TO 50
          WRITE (2, 45)
   45     FORMAT (17H MOVE NOT ALLOWED)
          GO TO 30
   50     M(I, J) = -1
          DO 55 I = 1, 3
          NROW(I) = M(I, 1) + M(I, 2) + M(I, 3)
   55     NCOL(I) = M(1, I) + M(2, I) + M(3, I)
          NDIAG(1) = M(1, 1) + M(2, 2) + M(3, 3)
          NDIAG(2) = M(3, 1) + M(2, 2) + M(1, 3)
          NDIAG(3) = 0
C         MACHINE MOVES TO GET THREE
C         IN A ROW IF POSSIBLE
          DO 75 N = 1, 8
          CALL CELL
          Z = NROW(I) .EQ. 2
          Z = Z .OR. NCOL(J) .EQ. 2
          Z = Z .OR. NDIAG(ND) .EQ. 2
          Z = Z .AND. M(I, J) .EQ. 0
```

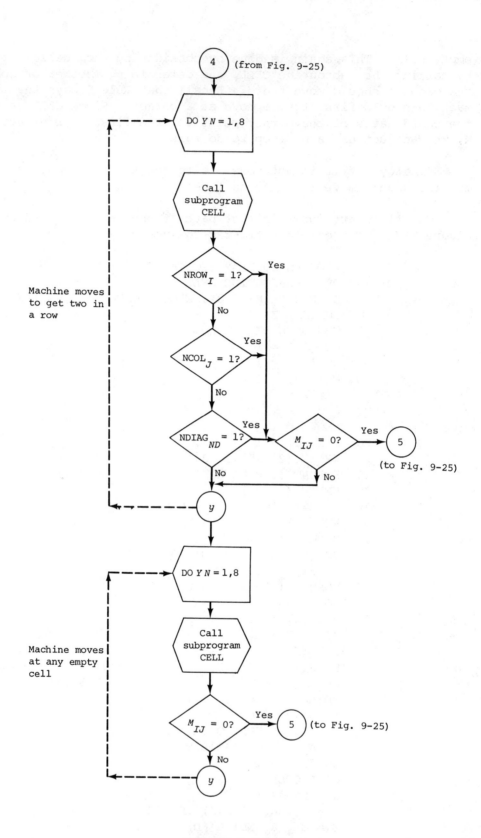

FIGURE 9-26

254

```
        IF (Z) GO TO 100
 75     CONTINUE
        GO TO 105
100     WRITE (2, 25) I, J
        WRITE (2, 101)
101     FORMAT (13H MACHINE WINS)
        STOP
C       IF SECOND PLAYER HAS TWO IN A ROW, BLOCK
105     DO 110 N = 1, 8
        CALL CELL
        Z = NROW(I) .EQ. -2
        Z = Z .OR. NCOL(J) .EQ. -2
        Z = Z .AND. M(I, J) .EQ. 0
        IF (Z) GO TO 200
110     CONTINUE
C       MACHINE MOVES TO GET TWO IN A ROW IF POSSIBLE
        DO 120 N = 1, 8
        CALL CELL
        Z = NROW(I) .EQ. 1
        Z = Z .OR NCOL(I) .EQ. 1
        Z = Z .OR. NDIAG(ND) .EQ. 1
        Z = Z .AND. M(I, J) .EQ. 0
        IF (Z) GO TO 200
120     CONTINUE
C       MACHINE MOVES IN ANY VACANT CELL
        DO 130 N = 1, 8
        CALL CELL
        Z = M(I, J) .EQ. 0
        IF (Z) GO TO 200
130     CONTINUE
        STOP
C       TEST TO SEE IF GAME IS A DRAW
200     NMOVE = NMOVE + 1
        IF (NMOVE .LT. 5) GO TO 20
        WRITE (2, 25) I, J
        WRITE (2, 205)
205     FORMAT (15H GAME IS A DRAW)
        STOP
        END
```

What is the value of each of the following logical expressions?

1. .TRUE. .AND. .TRUE.
2. .FALSE. .AND. .FALSE.
3. .FALSE. .AND. .TRUE.
4. .FALSE. .OR. .TRUE.
5. .FALSE. .OR. .FALSE.
6. (.TRUE. .AND. .FALSE.) .OR. .FALSE.
7. .TRUE. .AND. (.FALSE. .OR. .FALSE.)
8. (.NOT. .FALSE.) .AND. .TRUE.
9. (.NOT. .FALSE.) .OR. .FALSE.
10. .NOT. (.FALSE. .OR. .FALSE.)

When the value of P is .TRUE., Q is .FALSE., and R is .TRUE., what is the value of the logical variable S in each of the following?

11. S = P .OR. .NOT. Q
12. S = P .AND. R
13. S = .NOT. (P .OR. R)
14. S = .NOT. P .OR. .NOT. Q
15. S = .NOT. (P .AND. Q)

Construct truth tables for the following expressions:

16. P .AND. .NOT. Q
17. .NOT. (P .OR. Q)
18. .NOT. P .AND. .NOT. Q
19. P .OR. Q .AND. R
20. P .OR. .NOT. (Q .AND. R)

For what values of the variables below are the logical expressions .TRUE.?

21. P .OR. .NOT. Q
22. .NOT. (P .AND. Q)
23. .NOT. (.NOT. P .OR. .NOT. Q)
24. P .AND. Q .AND. .NOT. R
25. .NOT. .NOT. P

What is the value of each of the following relational expressions?

26. 1 .GE. 0
27. 5 .LT. 10
28. 2.1 .GE. 2.1
29. 1 .NE. 2
30. 6.0 .EQ. 7.0
31. 10.2 .GT. 10.2

Find values of A, B, and C for which the following expressions are .TRUE. .

32. A .GT. B .OR. B .GT. C
33. A .LE. B .OR. B .LE. C
34. A .GE. B .AND. B .LT. C
35. .NOT. (A .LT. B .AND. B .LT. C)
36. A .EQ. B .OR. A .EQ. C .OR. B .EQ. C

Write a single logical IF statement for each of the following decision flowcharts:

37.

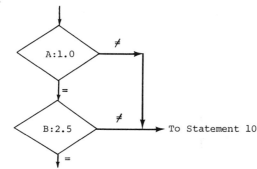

38.

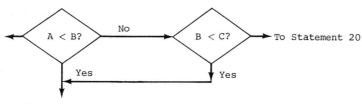

257

39.

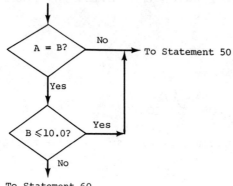

40.

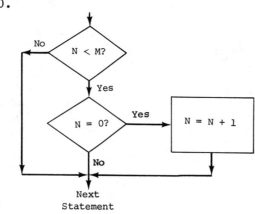

41.

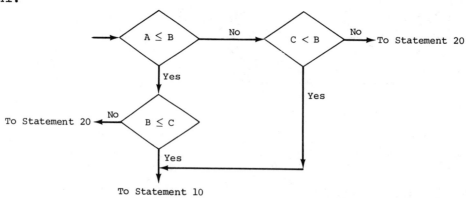

258

Write flowcharts to represent each of the decision statements in Problems 42-46.

42. IF (A .LT. 9.0 .AND. A .GT. 0.0) B = 2.0 * A
43. IF (N .EQ. 1 .OR. N .EQ. 3 .OR. N .EQ. 5) M = N
44. IF (MOLL/J * J .EQ. MOLL) LAB = 0
45. IF (P .EQ. 1.0 .OR. Q .EQ. P) GO TO 10
46. IF (R .LE. 0.0 .OR. G .GT. 100.0) R = 50.0

47. Modify Example 3 of this chapter (the macaroni and potatoes example) to find the minimum cost during the search. Before the outside loop, set CMIN = a large value, NPBEST = 0, and MBEST = 0. Then, near the WRITE statement, set C = 2.00 * FLOAT(NP) + 1.15 * FLOAT(M). Then if C < CMIN, set CMIN = C, NPBEST = NP, and MBEST = M.

Chapter 10

ALPHANUMERIC DATA AND THE DATA STATEMENT

THE A SPECIFICATION

In the preceding chapters, we have been careful to use only numbers for all of our FORTRAN arithmetic as well as input data. Output headings were made by using the Hollerith specification. Often our input will not be only in the form of numbers. For example, we might have the results of a mathematics examination punched on cards with the student's name in columns 1-20, his identification number in columns 21-26, and his score in columns 27-30. All that we need for any manipulations are the ID number and the score. However, in this example, we would also like to read in the name of the student and be able to list it in the output. FORTRAN provides a method for doing this with the *A specification*.

Characters used in this specification are known as *alphanumeric*, which comes from a combination of the words alphabetic and numeric. However, any FORTRAN character, such as +, -, /, or * can be input and output under the A format. The general form of this format is

$$mAn$$

where *n* in the field length and *m* is a repeat factor. This varies with the computer and may be as much as ten characters in word length. However, in all of our examples, we shall assume that an alphanumeric variable can have a maximum of only four characters.

Suppose we want to read a card that has the characters JOHN DOE in columns 1-8. To do so, we can consider it as two words, JOHN and DOE. We assign variable names just as we did in using numerical variables. Thus, the statement

```
        READ (1, 100) N, M
100   FORMAT (A4, A4)
```

would read in JOHN for M and DOE for N. Also,

```
        WRITE (2, 101) N, M
101   FORMAT (10X, A4, A4)
```

would print out the same characters, after skipping ten spaces.

Several alternate forms of input that accomplish the same steps are:

```
        READ (1, 10) A, B, C, D, E, F, G, H
   10   FORMAT (8A1)
        READ (1, 11) H, I, J
   11   FORMAT (A3, A3, A2)
        READ (1, 12) A, B, C, D
   12   FORMAT (A2, A2, A2, A2)
```

If a great deal of data is to be input under alphanumeric form, one can use alphanumeric arrays. For example, suppose a data card is punched as follows:

Columns

1-5	ID number of a student
6-8	Score on English final exam
9-11	Score on mathematics final exam
12-14	Score on chemistry final exam
15	Letter grade in English
16	Letter grade in mathematics
17	Letter grade in chemistry
18-77	Student's name and address
78-80	Blank: Can be used to stop input data

A typical card might be

12345092085087ABBJOHN DOE   123 MAIN ST   CHICAGO IL   60105

The following FORTRAN statements can be used to input the data:

```
        DIMENSION NAME (15)
        READ (1,2) ID, IENG, IMATH,ICHEM, IE, IM, IC,
   1      (NAME(I), I = 1, 15), LAST
   2  FORMAT (I5, 3I3, 3A1, 15A4, I3)
```

There is no special type declaration statement associated with alphanumeric data to indicate that the variables are different from numerical ones.

Example 1

A deck of data cards contains the following information:

Columns

1-24	Name of an individual
25-48	Address
49-72	City and State
73-74	Blank
75-79	Zip Code
80	Blank

261

The cards are to be read into the computer and address labels printed. This can be done by manually setting up the printer with special paper. The blank labels can contain up to six lines of printing and are ten lines apart vertically. Also, they are positioned on the left side of the printer and each line can contain thirty characters. To stop the program, a card is inserted at the end of the data deck with a 1 punched in column 80. The program to do this is given below for any amount of data cards.

```
      DIMENSION NAME (6), ADDRS (6), TOWN (6)
  1   READ (1, 100) (NAME (I), I = 1, 6), (ADDRS (I), I = 1, 6),
    1     (TOWN (I), I = 1, 6), IZIP, ITEST

100   FORMAT (18A4, 2X, I5, I1)
      IF (ITEST) 200, 201, 200
201   WRITE (2, 101) (NAME (I), I = 1, 6), (ADDRS (I), I = 1, 6),
    1     (TOWN (I), I = 1, 6), IZIP
101   FORMAT (4X, ///, 6A4, /, 4X, 6A4, /, 4X, 6A4, 2X, I5,
          ///////////)
      GO TO 1
200   STOP
      END
```

For most applications one uses the same format for both input and output as was done in the above example.

The following rules are to be followed for the more general cases of input and output using the A format. As sample input data, let us assume that each data card read in has the alphabet punched in the first twenty-six columns.

> *RULE 1:* If the READ statement has a format specification of A1, A2, or A3, the variable is read and stored with 3, 2, or 1 blanks to the right, respectively.

```
          READ (1, 100) NAME 1
    100   FORMAT (A1)
          READ (1, 101) NAME 2
    101   FORMAT (A2)
          READ (1, 102) NAME 3
    102   FORMAT (A3)
          READ (1, 103) NAME 4
    103   FORMAT (A4)
```

These statements will result in NAME 1 being stored as Abbb, NAME 2 being ABbb, NAME 3 is ABCb, and NAME 4 is ABCD.

262

> *RULE 2:* If the READ statement has a format specification
> of A5 or larger, the computer ignores the first
> columns and takes the last four characters for
> the variable.

Using the same data as above,

```
        READ (1, 50) A
   50   FORMAT (A6)
```

results in the variable A being stored as CDEF.

> *RULE 3:* If the WRITE statement has a format specification
> A1, A2, or A3, the computer outputs the first 1,
> 2, or 3 characters. When compared to Rule 1, this
> is what we would expect.

The statements

```
        READ (1, 20) N
   20   FORMAT (A4)
        WRITE (1, 21) N
   21   FORMAT (A3)
```

will output ABC. The statements

```
        READ (1, 22) M
   22   FORMAT (A2)
        WRITE (1, 23) M
   23   FORMAT (A4)
```

will output ABbb.

> *RULE 4:* If the WRITE statement has a format specification
> of A5 or larger, the left column(s) is(are) blank
> and four characters are printed.

The statements

```
        READ (1, 40) INAME
   40   FORMAT (5X, A2)
        WRITE (2, 30) INAME
   30   FORMAT (A10)
```

will output INAME as bbbbbbFGbb.

THE R SPECIFICATION

Another way of defining alphanumeric data is with the
R specification. The general form of this format is

$$mRn$$

where n is the field length and m is a repeat factor. This is nearly identical to the A specification, except that now the input data is stored with blanks on the left.

The rules for the A format can be rewritten to give the rules for using the R format as follows. Again assume the sample data are a deck of cards with the alphabet punched in the first twenty-six columns.

RULE 1: If the READ statement has a format specification R1, R2, or R3, the variable is read with 3, 2, or 1 blanks to the left, respectively.

The statements

```
        READ (1, 200) NAME
200  FORMAT (R1)
```

result in NAME being stored as bbbA.

RULE 2: If the READ statement has a format specification of R5 or larger, the computer ignores the first column and takes the next four characters. Notice that this is identical to Rule 2 for the A format.

The statements

```
        READ (1, 201) X
201  FORMAT (R5)
```

result in X being stored as BCDE.

RULE 3: If the WRITE statement has a format specification of R1, R2, or R3, the computer outputs the last 1, 2, or 3 characters.

The statements

```
        READ (2, 202) Y
202  FORMAT (R4)
        WRITE (2, 203) Y
203  FORMAT (1X, R2)
```

results in the output bCD. The statements

```
        READ (2, 204) W
204  FORMAT (R1)
```

264

```
        WRITE (2, 205) W
205   FORMAT (R4)
```

will output bbbA.

> *RULE 4:* If the WRITE statement has a format specification
> of R5 (or larger), the left column(s) is (are)
> blank and the word is output in the next four
> spaces, according to Rule 3.

The statements

```
        READ (2, 204) B
204   FORMAT (5X, R2)
        WRITE (2, 205) B
205   FORMAT (R10)
```

result in the output bbbbbbbbFG.

It is possible to use alphanumeric variables in IF statements. For example, if A and B are both alphanumeric, the
statement

```
IF (A .EQ. B) GO TO 100
```

will transfer control to statement number 100 if A and B are
identical. There are some restrictions in using statements
such as the one above. These are as follows.

> *RESTRICTION 1:* The modes of the variables should not be
> mixed. Thus, for A and I both alphanumeric
>
> ```
> IF (A .EQ. I) GO TO 100
> ```
>
> is not acceptable and may result in an error
> message or, even worse, depending on the
> system, be executed but give an erroneous
> answer.

> *RESTRICTION 2:* Alphanumeric variables can be compared only
> with other alphanumeric variables. Thus,
> for A an alphanumeric variable and B a
> floating-point variable, the statements
>
> ```
> IF (A .EQ. 9) GO TO 10
> IF (A .LE. B) STOP
> ```
>
> are incorrect.

Example 2

A data card contains alphanumeric data punched in columns 1-80. These data consist of only the twenty-six letters of the alphabet and blanks between words. Let us write a program to count the number of times that the letter E occurs and then the corresponding percentage. To compute this percentage, we shall need to count every character except blanks.

To solve this, we can read in the eighty possible characters as an array having eighty elements. Since we are going to compare each of these variables with the letter E, it is necessary to specify E as an alphanumeric variable. One way to do this is to use another READ statement. (Alternate ways are given in the next sections of this chapter.) This variable is called TEST. In addition, we must define a variable to be equal to a blank space. The flowchart shown in Figure 10-1 illustrates the logic used in the solution. The program corresponding to this flowchart is:

```
      DIMENSION ARRAY (80)
      READ (1, 100) TEST, BLANK
100   FORMAT (2A1)
      READ (1, 101) (ARRAY(I), I = 1, 80)
101   FORMAT (80A1)
      AMT = 80.0
      NUMB = 0
      DO 1 I = 1, 80
      IF (ARRAY(I) .EQ. TEST) NUMB = NUMB + 1
      IF (ARRAY(I) .EQ. TEST) GO TO 1
      IF (ARRAY(I) .EQ. BLANK) AMT = AMT - 1.0
  1   CONTINUE
      XN = NUMB
      PCT = XN/AMT * 100.0
      WRITE (2, 103) TEST, NUMB, PCT
103   FORMAT (1H1 //// 20X, 16HTEST LETTER WAS,
     1A1, 26H NUMBER OF THIS LETTER IS, I2,
     215H PERCENTAGE IS, F5.2)
      STOP
      END
```

Example 3

It is possible to generalize Example 1 and determine the number of times each letter of the alphabet occurs for any number of data cards. From this, one can determine the relative frequency of occurrence of each letter.

To solve this, let us assume that only the twenty-six letters of the alphabet, blanks, periods, and commas make up the data.

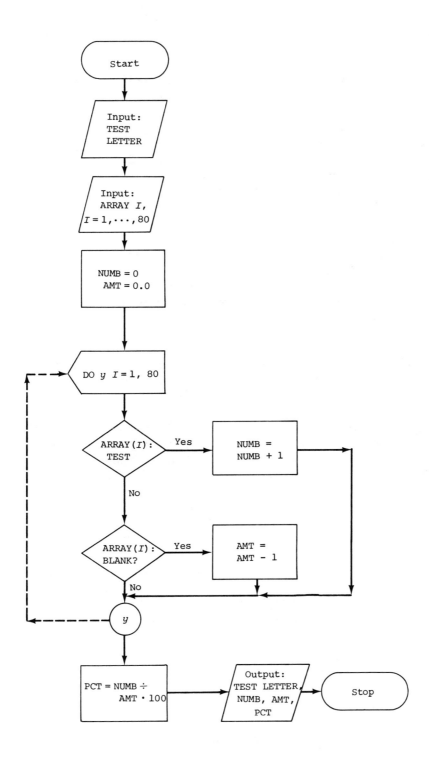

FIGURE 10-1

The data are punched in columns 1-72 and a card with a 1 punched in column 73 is placed at the end of the data to assist in terminating execution of the program.

The characters on the data cards are read in and stored in the array ARRAY. The letters of the alphabet are also read in as the single-dimensioned array ALPHA. Each letter is counted and stored in an array COUNT, where COUNT (1) tabulates the number of times the letter A appears, COUNT (2) the number of times the letter B appears, etc. Twenty-six frequencies are determined by dividing the total number of times each letter appears by the total of all letters.

The DIMENSION statement is written

DIMENSION ARRAY (72), ALPHA (26), COUNT (26), FREQ (26)

We first read in a data card and use an IF statement below it to determine if a 1 was punched in column 73. If not, we increment the counter for the total amount of characters by 72. Later, each time a character is encountered that is not a letter but a blank, comma, or period, this counter is decreased by 1.

The actual counting of the letters is done by using two DO loops. The outer is done 72 times, once for each character on the data card. The inner loop, corresponding to the actual search, is done a maximum of 26 times. As soon as the search is successful, either the counter corresponding to the letter is incremented or the total number of characters is decreased by 1. Then control transfers from the inner loop to the outer loop. This transfer of control must be done using another logical IF statement.

A portion of the DO loop to illustrate this point can be written:

```
                DO 20 I = 1, 72
                DO 21 J = 1, 26
                IF (ARRAY(I) .EQ. BLANK) AMT = AMT - 1.0
                IF (ARRAY(I) .EQ. BLANK) GO TO 20
                  .
                  .
                  .
                IF (ARRAY(I) .EQ. ALPHA(J)) GO TO 20
             21 CONTINUE
             20 CONTINUE
```

Suppose the first character on the data card was a blank. Then the first two IF statements decrease the amount of characters by 1 and transfer control out of the inner loop. The complete program is now given. The first six of the IF statements have been combined to make two statements.

```
       DIMENSION ARRAY (72), ALPHA (26), COUNT (26), FREQ (26)
       READ (1, 1) BLANK, DOT, COMMA
    1  FORMAT (3A1)
       READ (1, 2) (ALPHA(I), I = 1, 26)
    2  FORMAT (26A1)
       AMT = 0.0
       DO 10 I = 1, 26
   10  COUNT(I) = 0.0
   70  READ (1, 3) (ARRAY(I), I = 1, 72), ITEST
    3  FORMAT (72A1, I1)
       IF (ITEST .EQ. 1) GO TO 50
       AMT = AMT + 72.0
       DO 20 I = 1, 72
       DO 21 J = 1, 26
       IF (ARRAY(I) .EQ. BLANK .OR. ARRAY(I) .EQ. DOT .OR. ARRAY(I)
      1 .EQ. COMMA) AMT = AMT - 1.0
       IF (ARRAY(I) .EQ. BLANK .OR. ARRAY(I) .EQ. DOT .OR. ARRAY(I)
      1 .EQ. COMMA) GO TO 20
       IF (ARRAY(I) .EQ. ALPHA(J)) COUNT(J) = COUNT(J) + 1.0
       IF (ARRAY(I) .EQ. ALPHA(J)) GO TO 20
   21  CONTINUE
   20  CONTINUE
       GO TO 70
   50  DO 60 I = 1, 26
   60  FREQ(I) = COUNT(I)/AMT
       WRITE (2, 100) AMT
  100  FORMAT (1H1, ////, 10X, 31H THE TOTAL NUMBER OF LETTERS IS,
      1 F5.0, //, 10X, 40HBELOW ARE THE FREQUENCIES OF EACH LETTER,/)
       WRITE (2, 101) (ALPHA(I), COUNT(I), FREQ(I), I = 1, 26)
  101  FORMAT (///, 12X, 6H LETTER, 11X, 5H FREQ.,
      1 8X, 10HREL. FREQ. 1,
      2 (15X, A1, 5X, F10.0, 5X, F10.4))
       STOP
       END
```

The program can easily be generalized to handle characters
such as numbers or parentheses that might be part of the data.
This is done by adding appropriate IF statements in the DO loop
and defining proper alphanumeric variables for each character.

THE DATA *STATEMENT*

There is another way to assign alphanumeric values to
variables which does not involve the READ statement. This is by
using the DATA declaration statement. One general form is:

$$\text{DATA } var_1, var_2, \cdots, var_n/a_1, a_2, \cdots, a_n/, var_m, var_{m+1},$$

$$\cdots, var_r/b_1, b_2, \cdots, b_r, \cdots/$$

When this statement occurs in the program, the variable var_1 is initially given the value a_1, variable var_2 is a_2, and so on. Thus,

DATA A, B, C/1.0, 3.0, 5.0/

sets A = 1.0, B = 3.0, and C = 5.0. The variables may be subscripted, but only with integer constants. To use a DATA statement to initialize variables as alphanumeric values, we use a Hollerith specification. Again, let us assume that the size of the alphanumeric variable is limited to a maximum of four characters. Then

DATA A, B, I, J/3HABC, 2HAB, 4HXYZW, 1Hb/

will set A = ABCb
          B = ABbb
          I = XYZW
          J = bbbb.

For subscripted variables, either of the following two forms may be used:

DIMENSION A(4)
DATA A(1), A(2), A(3), A(4)/1H+, 1H-, 1H=, 1H*/

or

DIMENSION A(4)
DATA A/1H+, 1H-, 1H=, 1H*/

Both will define an array A consisting of four variables such that

A(1) is a + sign, A(2) is a - sign, A(3) an =, and A(4) an *.

The DATA statement is nonexecutable and must appear before any executable statement. It is placed after declaration statements, such as the DIMENSION statement.

It is important to remember that the DATA statement, being nonexecutable, initializes values once and only once. If the variable is used in the program and its value changed by an executable statement, it takes on this new value. Thus, the statements

```
  DATA X/0.0/
  WRITE (2, 1)X
1 FORMAT (1X, F3.1)
  X = X + 1.0
  WRITE (2, 1)X
```

270

will result in two different values of X to be printed, namely, 0.0 and 1.0. This should not cause the programmer any problem since the equals sign in the arithmetic statement acts to define a new value for a variable. Where one must be careful is when the DATA statement is used in a subprogram. There its value is *not* initialized every time the subprogram is called. Each time the subroutine TEST, as given below, is called, the value of N is the previous value (N + 1) and not 0.

```
SUBROUTINE TEST
DATA N/0/
    .
    .
    .
N = N + 1
RETURN
END
```

A useful feature of the DATA statement is that it may include repetition factors. A repetition factor is a DATA statement and an integer constant followed by an asterisk. This will cause the following constants to be repeated. For example,

$$3 * 1.0$$

would mean three factors of 1.0. Thus, the statement

```
DATA A, B, C/3 * 1.0/
```

would set A, B, and C to an initial value of 1.0, just like the statement

```
DATA A, B, C/1.0, 1.0, 1.0/
```

As another example, suppose we want to initialize A, B, and C to equal 0.0, and we also want to initialize I, J, K, and L to equal 1. This can be done with the statement

```
DATA A, B, C/3 * 0.0/, I, J, K, L/4 * 1/
```

The variables in the DATA statement may be array names. When this is the case, it is the same as writing out all the elements in the array. For example, the statements

```
DIMENSION X(10)
DATA X/10 * 0.0/
```

would set each of the variables X(1), X(2), ···, X(10) initially equal to 0.0. The X in the DATA statement specifies the whole

271

array X, that is, all ten variables. The repetition factor 10 denotes ten factors of the constant 0.0.

As another example, suppose MAT is declared as an integer array by the statement

DIMENSION MAT (3, 2)

Then, the statement

DATA MAT/6 * 5/

would give all six of the elements of the array MAT an initial value of 5.

The implied DO loop form used in a READ or WRITE statement may also be used in a DATA statement. For example, the statement

DATA (X(1, I), I = 2, 7)/6 * 0.0/

would set each of the variables X(1, 2), X(1, 3), X(1, 4), $\cdots$, X(1, 7) equal to 0.0 at the start of the program.

The statement

DATA (X(I), I = 1, 21, 2)/11 * 1.0/

would initialize X(1), X(3), X(5), $\cdots$, X(21) to equal 1.0.

A final feature of the DATA statement is that the constants may be grouped by parentheses, each preceded by a repetition factor. Thus, 2 * (1.0, 2.0) would mean the same thing in a DATA statement as 1.0, 2.0, 1.0, 2.0. The whole group is repeated. This is similar to repeated groups in a FORMAT statement. The statement

DATA (X(I), I = 1, 10)/5 * (0.0, 1.0)/

would initialize the elements X(1), X(3), $\cdots$, X(9) equal to 0.0, while initializing X(2), X(4), $\cdots$, X(10) equal to 1.0.

Any type of constant can be used in a DATA statement. The constants must be of the correct type for the corresponding type for the associated variable. The statements

```
        DIMENSION X(2), NAME(3)
        LOGICAL L, M
        DATA L, M/.TRUE., .FALSE./,
     1  X/1.0, 2.0/,
     2  NAME/4HPROB, 4HLEMb, 1H2/
```

272

would serve to initialize the logical constants L and M as well as the arrays X and NAME.

Example 4

Alphanumeric characters can be used in printing out contoured plots. Often this is a very convenient and illuminating way of presenting data. For example, the array might represent barometric pressure values, pollen counts, or temperature values. Suppose the data are stored in a 50 by 50 array, called ARRAY. While it may be desired to also have the 2,500 elements listed, the array will be much easier to view if presented as a plot. Let us assume that the values of the data are known to be between 0.0 and 50.0.

Let us now write a program to draw the contours. A contour interval of 10.0 is chosen. Thus, we shall have five different characters plotted. We can now examine every value of the array ARRAY and define a new array, called PLOT, such that each element of PLOT is equal to one of the five characters. However, the characters will be easier to view if we print a few blanks between each of them. These blanks will then actually be the contours. Our contour scheme is:

$$
\text{Plotted character is} \begin{cases}
\text{A for} & 0.0 \le \text{array value} \le 07.0 \\
\text{. for} & 10.0 \le \text{array value} \le 17.0 \\
\text{B for} & 20.0 \le \text{array value} \le 27.0 \\
\text{/ for} & 30.0 \le \text{array value} \le 37.0 \\
\text{D for} & 40.0 \le \text{array value} \le 47.0 \\
\text{and a blank otherwise.}
\end{cases}
$$

The necessary FORTRAN statements are

```
      DIMENSION ARRAY (50, 50), PLOT (50, 50), CHAR(6)
C     THE DIMENSION STATEMENT IS TO BE PLACED AT THE START
C     OF THE PROGRAM.  LIKEWISE, THE DATA STATEMENT
      DATA CHAR/1HA, 1H., 1HB, 1H/, 1HD, 1H /
        .
        .
        .
      DO 500 I = 1, 50
      DO 500 J = 1, 50
      IF (ARRAY(I, J) .LE. 7.0) PLOT(I, J) = CHAR(1)
      IF (ARRAY(I, J) .LE. 7.0) GO TO 500
      IF (ARRAY(I, J) .LE. 17.0 .AND. ARRAY(I, J) .GE. 10.0)
      PLOT(I, J) = CHAR(2)
      IF (ARRAY(I, J) .LE. 17.0 .AND. ARRAY(I, J) .GE. 10.0)
      GO TO 500
      IF (ARRAY(I, J) .LE. 27.0 .AND. ARRAY(I, J) .GE. 20.0)
      PLOT(I, J) = CHAR(3)
      IF (ARRAY(I, J) .LE. 27.0 .AND. ARRAY(I, J) .GE. 20.0
      GO TO 500
```

```
        IF (ARRAY(I, J) .LE. 37.0 .AND. ARRAY(I, J) .GE. 30.0)
        PLOT(I, J) = CHAR(4)
        IF (ARRAY(I, J) .LE. 37.0 .AND. ARRAY(I, J) .GE. 30.0)
        GO TO 500
        IF (ARRAY(I, J) .LE. 47.0 .AND. ARRAY(I, J) .GE. 40.0)
        PLOT(I, J) = CHAR(5)
        IF (ARRAY(I, J) .LE. 47.0 .AND. ARRAY(I, J) .GE. 40.0)
        GO TO 500
        PLOT(I, J) = CHAR(6)
  500   CONTINUE
        WRITE (2, 501) ((PLOT(I, J), J = 1, 50), I = 1, 50)
  501   FORMAT (1H1, //////////, (40X, 50A1))
        STOP
        END
```

The logic used in this program can be compared with the program on page 220.

ALTERNATE TO THE DATA *STATEMENT*[1]

Another method to specify alphanumeric values is to use the Hollerith specification in an arithmetic expression. This is done as follows:

```
              A = 4HABCD
              BLANK = 1H A
```

The alphanumeric variable A is now stored as ABCD and the variable BLANK is stored as a blank.[2] For systems that allow this statement, one can also use the Hollerith specification in IF statements. To illustrate this, suppose we have an array ARRAY consisting of 1,000 alphanumeric variables. We wish to determine how many of these are the character 9. FORTRAN statements that will do this are:

```
              NUMBER = 0
              DO 1 I = 1, 1000
              IF (ARRAY(I) .EQ. 1H9) NUMBER = NUMBER + 1
            1 CONTINUE
```

---

[1]This method will not work on all systems.

[2]The letter A is a dummy, necessary since the computer cannot read the blank after the H as a symbol in this case.

EXERCISES

1. A deck of data cards contains names and addresses punched as follows:

   Columns

1-25	Name
26-50	Street
51-75	Town and State
76-80	Zip code

   Write the FORTRAN that will read in the cards and then output the people with zip codes starting with the three digits 600. To stop the program, have a card with 99999 punched in the last five columns. The output should be in stardard address form.

2. For the data in Problem 1, output all the names and addresses according to the numerical order of the zip codes. For this, assume a maximum of 1,000 data cards.

3. The results of a 25-question true-false history examination are punched on cards as follows:

   Columns

1-25	Student's name
26-50	Either a 2, 1, or 0 in each column, where a 2 means the student answered "true," a 1 for "false," and a 0 if the student did not answer.

   The first data card contains the answer code punched in the first 25 columns. The grading system is given by

   SCORE = number of correct answers × 4 minus
   number of incorrect answers × 5.

   Thus, it is theoretically possible for a student to obtain a negative score. Rather than have this happen, the lowest score possible will be a zero. Write a program to input the cards, calculate a score for each student, and output his name and score.

4. Letter grades for the exam in Problem 3 are:

Range	Grade
100-85	A
84-70	B
69-55	C
54-40	D
39-0	F

Add the necessary statements to the program in this exercise
to:

    a. calculate a letter grade for each student.
    b. output the grades in descending order.

5. Suppose state license plates for cars are given by six
   characters, the first three being letters and the last
   three numbers. These are punched on cards in the first
   six columns. In column 80 a 1 is punched if the license
   belongs to a stolen car; otherwise, it is blank. Write
   a program to input the deck and list every stolen license
   plate number. To stop the program, use a card with a 9
   punched in column 80 at the end of the data deck.

6. Using the same data deck as in Problem 1, write a program
   to list only those names and addresses of people from the
   city of New York.

7. a. Write a program that will read a three-digit number and
   print out the number in words. For example, the number
   123 would be output as

   ONE HUNDRED AND TWENTY THREE

   b. When some companies print their payroll checks, the
   amount is written out together with the dollar amount.
   Write a program that first reads the following data
   from a card:

   Columns

1-29	Name of employee
30	Dollar sign
31-37	Employee's wage

   Then, have the computer print out the message:

   PAY TO THE ORDER OF: (employee's name)
   (amount, written out) $ (wage)

8. The international Morse code for the alphabet is

A	·—	H	····	O	———	V	···—
B	—···	I	··	P	·——·	W	·——
C	—·—·	J	·———	Q	——·—	X	—··—
D	—··	K	—·—	R	·—·	Y	—·——
E	·	L	·—··	S	···	Z	——··
F	··—·	M	——	T	—		
G	——·	N	—·	U	··—		

276

The dots and dashes can be punched on data cards as periods and minus signs. Write a program to read a number of cards on which are punched a message in Morse code and determine what the message is. Each code letter is punched in a field length of four spaces. The letter A is .-bb, E is .bbb, and so on. Thus, each data card can contain a maximum of 20 letters. Whenever four blanks are encountered in a data field, this is to be interpreted as a blank between words.

This problem can be solved by writing a long series of logical IF statements. For example, if the 80 characters are read into a single-dimensional array ARRAY, an IF statement for the letter A might be:

IF (ARRAY(I) .EQ. DOT .AND. ARRAY(I + l) .EQ. DASH .AND. ARRAY(I + 2) .EQ. BLANK) CODE(J) = ALPHA(l)

where DOT is the period, DASH is a minus sign, CODE is an array that will be filled with letters, and ALPHA is an array that contains the alphabet.

Rather than do this search by using the alphabet in proper order from A to Z, a more efficient way would be to search using the letters arranged in order of their expected relative frequencies of occurrence. This is

ETOANIRSHDLCFUMPYWGBVKXJQZ

9. Most computers list the actual time (usually in seconds) a program took to run as part of the output. In addition, there generally is a special subroutine such as CALL SECOND(t), CALL TIME, etc., so that the actual time can be found to run a particular portion of the program. Should this option be available, run the program given for Example 4 on pages 273-74 both as is and with IF statements similar to those used in the program on page 220. Determine which program runs faster.

Chapter 11

DOUBLE PRECISION AND COMPLEX VARIABLES

There are still two types of variables used in FORTRAN that we have not yet covered. These are double precision and complex variables. These types are not used as frequently as regular floating-point or integer variables, but they can be very useful for certain specific applications.

DOUBLE PRECISION NUMBERS

Remember that in a computer we must represent all numbers with a finite number of digits. A number like the square root of 2 (1.41424···) requires an infinite number of decimal digits for its exact representation, and so it cannot be represented on a computer; we have to approximate it with a finite number of decimal digits. If the computer can handle five significant digits, then $\sqrt{2}$ would be represented as 1.4142. Thus, in all floating-point computer arithmetic there is an inherent error caused by the limited number of digits which a computer word can store. Much of the time this error can be ignored. In some instances, however, more accuracy is needed than is available in floating-point arithmetic. For such cases we can use double precision arithmetic.

A double precision constant or variable is stored in two storage locations. This has the effect of doubling the number of significant digits, as compared to a regular floating-point number. If the computer used can store eight decimal digits for a floating-point variable, it will be able to store sixteen decimal digits for a double precision variable.

A double precision constant has a form that is very similar to the form of a floating-point number written in exponential form. An example of a double precision constant is 6.2D+4. This means 6.2×10^4. That is, it represents the same number as the FORTRAN floating-point constant 6.2E+4. The difference is that the double precision constant 6.2D+4 would be stored in two storage locations, and so it would be represented in the computer by twice as many digits as 6.2E+4. The rules for forming a double precision constant are given below.

$$\underset{a}{\underbrace{6.2}} \; \underset{b}{\underbrace{D}} \; \underset{c}{\underbrace{+}} \; \underset{d}{\underbrace{04}}$$

RULE *a*: The first part of the number is a regular fixed-point or floating-point constant. It can be

278

written with or without the decimal point,
but we can include more digits.

RULE b: Next, we put the letter D.

RULE c: Here we place a plus or minus sign. If no sign
appears, the computer assumes that it is a plus
sign. Thus 6.2D4 is the same as 6.2D+4.

RULE d: The last part is the exponent. Just as for the
E form, this number is an integer that gives the
power of ten to which the decimal part of the
number is to be raised. Thus 6.2D4 represents
$6.2 \times 10^4 = 62,000.0$. 6.2D-4 represents $6.2 \times 10^{-4} =$
0.00062.

Some examples of double precision constants are given in the
table below.

Double Precision Constant	*Meaning*
.07D-1	.007
7D+2	700.0
7.00D2	700.0
8D-3	0.008
-55D0	-55.0
-55D	-55.0

Variables in FORTRAN can also be declared as double precision.
A double precision variable is like a regular floating-point variable except that it is stored by the computer in two storage locations (just as is a double precision constant). In order to tell
the computer that a variable is to be used as a double precision
variable, a special declaration statement must be used. This
statement has the form

DOUBLE PRECISION $name_1$, $name_2$, $\cdots$, $name_n$

where each of the names ia a FORTRAN variable name. This statement is similar to the LOGICAL statement we used in the previous
chapter. Each of the variables named in the list will be treated
as a double precision variable throughout the program. The DOUBLE
PRECISION statement should come at the beginning of the program.
For example, if we want to use the variables I, MINE, X, and R as
double precision variables in a program, then the program should
include the statement

DOUBLE PRECISION I, MINE, X, R

279

Although I and MINE would normally be integer variables, they would be treated as double precision because the DOUBLE PRECISION declaration statement overrides the usual rules for naming variables. This statement applies to the whole main program. We could not use the variable I as a regular integer variable later in the program, since it has already been declared as double precision.

The DOUBLE PRECISION statement can also be used to give dimension information about the variables named. For example, suppose we want an array Z with 100 elements to be a double precision array (i.e., each Z(I) is a double precision variable). We could specify this with the two statements

```
DOUBLE PRECISION Z
DIMENSION Z(100)
```

But it is easier to combine them into the single statement

```
DOUBLE PRECISION Z(100)
```

This statement does the same thing. In general, any variable name in the list of the DOUBLE PRECISION statement may be dimensioned.

DOUBLE PRECISION ARITHMETIC

Arithmetic using double precision numbers is performed differently by the computer than floating-point arithmetic. Each number is stored in two storage locations to give twice the accuracy provided by regular floating-point arithmetic. The only difference in FORTRAN, however, is that double precision constants and variables are used. If X is a double precision variable, then

```
2.0D0 * (X - 1.0D0)/X
```

is a double precision arithmetic expression.

Double precision constants and variables may be combined in arithmetic expressions with regular floating-point constants and variables. In this case, the result is a double precision number. For example, suppose X is a double precision variable. Then the expression

```
2.0D0 * X + 1.0D0
```

is a double precision expression. Both the constants and variables are double precision in this case. Suppose now that we had the expression

```
2.0 * X + 1.0
```

In this case, X is a double precision variable, and 2.0 and 1.0 are regular floating-point constants. This sort of expression is allowed in FORTRAN. When this expression is evaluated, the constant 2.0 is automatically converted to the double precision constant 2.0D0, and this is multiplied by X to give the double precision result. The constant 1.0 is then converted to the double precision constant 1.0D0, and this is added to the previous result to give another double precision number. In general, if X is a double precision expression and Y is a regular floating-point expression, then

```
X + Y        Y + X
X - Y        Y - X
X * Y        Y * X
X / Y        Y / X
X ** Y       Y ** X
```

are all valid double precision expressions. In each case, the floating-point portion of the expression is converted to double precision and then the indicated operation is performed, giving a double precision result. The following are some examples of valid double precision expressions. (X is assumed to be a double precision variable.)

```
X + 1.9D-2
X + 1.9E-2
X + .019
2.0D0 * X
2.0 * X
X ** 2 + 1.0
X/2.0 + .999999999D2
```

The assignment statement has the same form for use with double precision expressions as it ordinarily does. If X is a double precision variable and E is any double precision expression, then the statement

```
X = E
```

will simply take the double precision value of E and store it in the double precision variable X. We may ask what happens if only one of the parts of this statement is double precision. The answer to this question is given by the following rules.

RULE 1: If X is a double precision variable and E is a regular floating-point or integer expression, then the statement X = E will evaluate E as usual, convert the final result to double precision form, and store it in X.

281

RULE 2: If X is a regular floating-point variable and E is a double precision expression, then E is evaluated in double precision form and the result is truncated and stored in X. If X is an integer variable, only the integer part of E is stored.

As an example of the first rule, suppose that the computer we are working with can store eight decimal digits for a single precision variable. If X is a double precision variable, it can then store sixteen digits. Then the statement

X = .99999999

would convert the constant .99999999 to double precision and store it in X as .9999999900000000. As an example of the second rule, the statement

X = .9999999999999999D0

would convert the double precision constant to single precision and store it in X as .99999999.

The exact degree of accuracy will depend on the computer used. But just for an example, suppose we have a computer that uses eight decimal digits in a single precision variable. Let us perform the calculation

X = 4.0 - 4.0 * .99999999

When we multiply 4.0 by .99999999, the exact answer is 3.99999996. This number has nine digits, however, so the last digit would be truncated, not rounded, and the number would be stored as .39999999 × 10. When we subtract this from 4.0, the result is $0.0000001 = .1 \times 10^{-6}$. Now, if we perform the same calculation using double precision numbers, the last place is not truncated, and we have 4.0 - 3.99999996, which is $.4 \times 10^{-7}$. Thus, we see that the statement

X = 4.0 - 4.0 * .99999999

will assign to X the value $.1 \times 10^{-6}$, while the statement

X = 4.0D0 - 4.0D0 * .99999999D0

will assign to X the value $.4 \times 10^{-7}$. While these results are very close in absolute value, the first result is more than twice as large as the second. In some computations, such a difference can be very important, and this is where double precision arithmetic is useful in FORTRAN.[1]

---

[1] See G. E. Forsyth, "Pitfalls in Computation, or Why a Math Book Isn't Enough," *Amer. Math. Mon.*, LXXVII, No. 9 (1970), 931-59, for a study of how roundoff error affects computation.

INPUT AND OUTPUT OF DOUBLE PRECISION NUMBERS

When we want to input or output the value of some double precision variable, we must use a special format field description.
This field descriptor has the form

Dn.m

where *n* and *m* are unsigned integer constants. The number *n* gives
the size of the field and *m* tells how many decimal places are to
be used. The D field is used exactly like the E field for regular
floating-point numbers. The only difference is that the D field
must be used with double precision variables.

As an example of how the D field is used for input, suppose
we read the following data from a card:

111D-122.22D233333

using the statements

DOUBLE PRECISION X, Y, Z
READ (1, 7) X, Y, Z
7   FORMAT (D6.1, D7.1, D5.4)

The first field is the D6.1. Since the field width is 6, the
characters read for X are 111D-1. The 1 in D6.1 means that there
is one assumed decimal place in the input data, so the number is
stored in X as 11.1D-1. The second field is 22.22D2. Since it
is written with a decimal point, the 1 in D7.1 has no effect, and
the number is stored in Y as 22.22D2. The last field is 33333,
read with a D5.4 description. The 4 in D5.4 means to assume four
decimal places, so Z receives the value 3.3333D0.

Used for output, the D*n*.*m* field is just like the E*n*.*m* field
except that the number written must be double precision. Specifically, a field written with a D*n*.*m* format will contain the following characters:

1. (*n* - *m* - 6) blank spaces
2. A minus sign or another blank space
3. *m* decimal digits
4. The letter D
5. A plus or minus sign for the exponent
6. A two-digit exponent

For example, if X = 777.66 is a double precision number, then the
statements

WRITE (2, 1) X
1   FORMAT (D13.5)

will print the characters

bb-.77766D+02

(where the b's stand for blank spaces).

Note that n must always be greater than or equal to $m + 6$ to allow room to print the decimal point, the minus sign, and the exponent.

DOUBLE PRECISION FUNCTIONS

When using a function subprogram in FORTRAN, the parameters and the function itself must be of a certain type. For instance, the function ABS(X) will give the absolute value of a number X, but X must be a floating-point number. If we want to find the absolute value of an integer variable, we must use the function IABS(N). It is incorrect to use the function ABS(X) to find the absolute value of an integer variable because ABS assumes that the argument of the function is a floating-point number. Similarly, we must use double precision functions when we want the result or the parameters to be double precision numbers. The table below gives a partial list of double precision variables supplied by FORTRAN. In each case, the variables are assumed to be double precision, and the value of the function itself will be double precision.

FUNCTION	*DEFINITION*
DABS(X)	Absolute value of x
DMAX1(X1, $\cdots$, XN)	Maximum value of $x_1, \cdots, x_n$
DMIN1(X1, $\cdots$, XN)	Minimum value of $x_1, \cdots, x_n$
DEXP(X)	Exponential function, e^x
DLOG(X)	Natural logarithm, $\log_e x$
DLOG10(X)	Common logarithm, $\log_{10} x$
DSIN(X)	Trigonometric sine, $\sin x$
DCOS(X)	Trigonometric cosine, $\cos x$
DSQRT(X)	Square root of x
DATAN(X)	Arctangent of x

Each of these functions is used just like its counterpart for single precision numbers. The only difference is that both the variable and the values of the function are double precision. For example, if X and Y are double precision variables, we can set Y equal to the sine of X with the statement

Y = DSIN(X)

If we wanted to define a double precision function of our own, we could do so by using the statement

DOUBLE PRECISION FUNCTION name $(X_1, X_2, \cdots, X_n)$

This statement works in the same way that the ordinary FUNCTION statement does. The difference is that the final value of the function named will be a double precision number. For example, we could use the following statements to define a double precision function ZZZ to find the absolute value of an integer variable:

```
        DOUBLE PRECISION FUNCTION ZZZ(N)
        IF (N) 20, 10, 10
10      ZZZ = N
        RETURN
20      ZZZ = -N
        RETURN
        END
```

or, more simply,

```
        DOUBLE PRECISION FUNCTION ZZZ(N)
        ZZZ = IABS(N)
        RETURN
        END
```

When we used this function in an expression, ZZZ would be treated just like a double precision variable. Therefore, one should declare it as double precision in the main program. Note that N itself is an integer variable. The DOUBLE PRECISION FUNCTION statement means that the *function* is double precision; the arguments may be any type.

Example 1

As pointed out earlier, we can use the FORTRAN-supplied function DLOG(X) to find the double precision natural logarithm of the double precision number X. For this example, however, we shall write a double precision function subprogram of our own to do this.

The formula we shall use is

$$\log_e x = 2\left(\frac{x-1}{x+1} + \frac{1}{3}\left(\frac{x-1}{x+1}\right)^3 + \frac{1}{5}\left(\frac{x-1}{x+1}\right)^5 + \cdots\right)$$

where $e = 2.71828\cdots$

This formula holds for all positive values of X. The difficulty is that for large values of x, the series converges very slowly, so we have to use a large number of terms to approximate the true logarithm of x with any degree of accuracy. This difficulty is easily overcome, however, if we recall the formula:

285

$$\log_e (ye^n) = \log_e y + \log_e e^n = \log_e y + n$$

If x is greater than 1, we divide x by some power of e so that $x = ye^n$ with $1/e < y < 1$. For y in this range, $(y - 1)/(y + 1)$ will lie between $-.426$ and 0. The formula converges quite rapidly in this range. Furthermore, since $(y - 1)/(y + 1)$ is negative, if we compute m terms of the series, the error will be less than the absolute value of the $(m{+}1)$st term. Having found $\log_e y$ by the formula, we can compute $\log_e x = \log_e y + n$. Similarly, if x is less than $1/e$, we multiply x by some power of e so that $x = y/e^n$ with $1/e < y < 1$. Then $\log_e x = \log_e y - n$.

The first step in our subroutine, which we shall call BLOG, is to find the correct power of e to multiply or divide x by. This procedure is shown in the flowchart of Figure 11-1. Notice that if x is an exact multiple of e, y will be 1, so $\log_e x = \log_e 1 + n = 0 + n = n$, and there is no need to carry out the rest of the calculation.

The procedure used in computing the formula for $\log_e y$ is shown in Figure 11-2. Setting $y = (x - 1)/(x + 1)$ and BLOG $= y$, we compute the next term TERM $= y^3/3$, and add TERM to BLOG. If TERM is less than $.5 \times 10^{-10}$ in absolute value, then BLOG will be accurate to 10 decimal places and we compute BLOG $= 2.0 *$ BLOG $+$ AN. Otherwise, we compute another term and repeat the process.

The FORTRAN program for this job uses double precision for the variables X, Y, E, TERM, and YSQ as well as for BLOG itself. The complete program follows:

```
        DOUBLE PRECISION FUNCTION BLOG(X)
C       BLOG(X) = NATURAL LOGARITHM OF X WHERE X IS DOUBLE
C       PRECISION.  BLOG HAS 10 PLACE ACCURACY.
        DOUBLE PRECISION X, Y, E, TERM, YSQ
        E = 2.718281828459045D0
        EINV = 1.0/E
        IF (X .GT. 0.0) GO TO 10
        WRITE (2, 5)
    5   FORMAT (18H NEGATIVE ARGUMENT)
        BLOG = 0.0
        RETURN
   10   AN = 0.0
        IF (X - 1.0) 30, 15, 20
   15   BLOG = AN
        RETURN
C       X IS GREATER THAN 1.  DIVIDE BY E UNTIL X IS
C       LESS THAN 1.
   20   X = X/E
        AN = AN + 1.0
        IF (X .GT. 1.0) GO TO 20
        GO TO 50
```

286

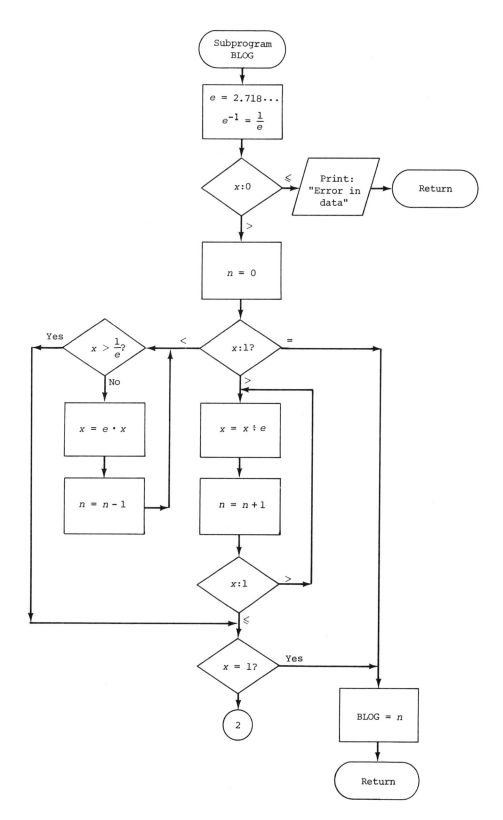

FIGURE 11-1

287

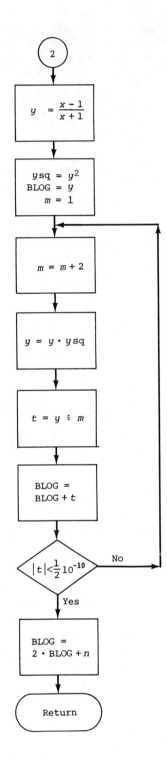

FIGURE 11-2

```
C        X IS LESS THAN 1.  MULTIPLY BY E UNTIL X IS
C        GREATER THAN 1/E.
   30    IF (X .GT. EINV) GO TO 50
         X = E * X
         AN = AN - 1.0
         GO TO 30
   50    IF (X .EQ. 1.0) GO TO 15
C        X IS BETWEEN 1/E AND 1.  BLOG = LOG X + AN.
C        LET Y = (X - 1)/(X + 1).
C        THEN Y IS BETWEEN -.426 AND 0.0.
C        LOG X = 2(Y + Y ** 3/3 + Y ** 5/5 + ...)
         Y = (X - 1.0)/(X + 1.0)
         YSQ = Y * Y
         BLOG = Y
         AM = 1.0
   60    AM = AM + 2.0
         Y = Y * YSQ
         TERM = Y/AM
         BLOG = BLOG + TERM
         IF (DABS(TERM) .GE. 0.5D-10) GO TO 60
         BLOG = 2.0 * BLOG + AN
         RETURN
         END
```

COMPLEX NUMBERS

A complex number in algebra is a number of the form $a + bi$, where a and b are real[2] numbers and $i = \sqrt{-1}$ is the base of the so-called imaginary numbers. Complex constants and variables can be used in FORTRAN too, and they have a special arithmetic of their own.

A complex constant in FORTRAN has the form

$$(a, b)$$

where a and b are FORTRAN floating-point constants. This number is interpreted as meaning the same thing as $a + bi$. Some examples of valid FORTRAN complex constants are given below:

FORTRAN Constant	Meaning	FORTRAN Constant	Meaning
(1.0, 1.0)	$1 + i$	(0.0, 0.0)	0.0
(0.0, 1.0)	$0 + i = i$	(6.2, .2E3)	$6.2 + 20.0i$
(5.0, 0.0)	5.0		

---

[2] The word "real" as used here and in the rest of this chapter has the mathematical meaning in referring to complex numbers. In computer terminology a *real* constant (or variable) is the same as a *floating-point* constant (or variable).

We may form arithmetic expressions using complex constants and the operators +, -, *, and /. For complex numbers, these operators have special meanings which are defined below.

$$(a, b) + (c, d) = (a + c, b + d)$$
$$(a, b) - (c, d) = (a - c, b - d)$$
$$(a, b) * (c, d) = (ac - bd, ad + bc)$$
$$(a, b) / (c, d) = ((ac + bd)/(c^2 + d^2), (-ad + bc)/(c^2 + d^2))$$

As examples of complex multiplication in FORTRAN, we see that

$$(0.0, 1.0) * (0.0, 1.0) = (-1.0, 0.0)$$

by the above definitions. This just expresses the fact that $i^2 = -1$. As another case, for any real constants a, c, and d,

$$(a, 0.0) * (c, d) = (ac, ad)$$

which expresses the algebraic fact that $a(b + ci) = ab + aci$. Using the above definition of complex division, we find that for any real constants c and d,

$$(1.0, 0.0)/(c, d) = (c/(c^2 + d^2), -d/(c^2 + d^2))$$

and when we use the above rule for multiplication, we find that

$$(c, d) * (c/(c^2 + d^2), -d/(c^2 + d^2)) = (1.0, 0.0)$$

as it should.

The exponential operator ** is not generally defined for complex numbers except in the case where the exponent is an integer. Thus,

$$(a, b) ** 4$$

would mean the same thing as

$$(a, b) * (a, b) * (a, b) * (a, b)$$

It is not permissible to raise a complex number to a floating-point or a complex exponent using the ** operator. However, we can use the complex exponential function to raise a complex number to a power which is a *rational* number with reasonably small denominator, as we shall explain later.

Variables may also be defined as complex variables in FORTRAN. This is done using the COMPLEX statement. This is a declaration statement similar to the DOUBLE PRECISION statement. The form is

$$\text{COMPLEX name}_1, \text{ name}_2, \text{ name}_3, \cdots, \text{ name}_N$$

where name_1, name_2, name_3, $\cdots$, name_N are FORTRAN variable names. This statement will cause the variables named to be treated as complex variables throughout the program and the values will use two storage locations. When a variable is defined as complex, it may assume complex values and be used in arithmetic expressions involving complex arithmetic. For example, the statements

```
COMPLEX Z
Z = (1.0, 1.0)
Z = Z * Z
```

would first assign the complex variable Z the value (1.0, 1.0), and then multiply this value by itself to give Z the value (1.0, 1.0) * (1.0, 1.0) = (0.0, 2.0). Any of the variables named in the COMPLEX statement may be dimensioned. The statement

```
COMPLEX WXY(5)
```

would set up an array of five elements, each occupying two storage locations. Each WXY(I) would then be treated as a complex variable. Like the LOGICAL and DOUBLE PRECISION statements, the COMPLEX statement should come at the beginning of the program, before the first executable statement, and before DATA and statement functions.

When the assignment statement Z = E is used with complex numbers, both the variable Z and the expression E *must* be complex. Thus, it would be incorrect to have the statement

```
Z = (1.0, 0.0)
```

unless Z were defined as complex in a statement COMPLEX Z. Also, if Z is a complex variable, it is incorrect to have the statement

```
Z = 1.0
```

since 1.0 is not a complex expression. We would have to rewrite this as

```
Z = (1.0, 0.0)
```

It is permissible to use floating-point constants and variables in a complex expression. For instance, if Z is a complex variable, then the expression

```
(2.0, 0.0) * Z + (1.0, 0.0)
```

could be written as

291

                    2.0 * Z + 1.0

since (2.0, 0.0) and (1.0, 0.0) mean the same thing, algebraically,
as 2.0 and 1.0. In general, if X is a real variable or constant
and Y is a complex variable or constant, then all of the following are valid FORTRAN expressions.

                X + Y   Y + X
                X - Y   Y - X
                X * Y   Y * X
                X / Y   Y / X

In each case, X is first converted to complex form, and then the
operation is performed. The result is a complex number. All of
the above expressions would be invalid in FORTRAN, however, if X
were an integer constant or variable. For example, it is incorrect to have the expression

                2 * Z + 1

where Z is a complex variable.

    Following are some examples of valid complex arithmetic
expressions:

                COMPLEX X, Z
                X * Z + (1.0, 0.0)
                X * Z + 1.0
                X ** 2
                X/(Z + 2.0)
                (0.0, 1.0) * (X + Z)/2.0

MIXED-MODE ARITHMETIC

    Some FORTRAN compilers allow a completely general mixed-
mode arithmetic. That is, any combination of variables may be
used together in an expression, no matter what their types. This
means we could add a complex variable to a double precision variable. In this case, the result would be a complex number. This
calculation would be carried out in three steps:

    1. First, the double precision number is converted to
        single precision by truncation.
    2. Next, the result of (1) is converted to complex by
        adding an imaginary part of 0.
    3. Finally, the two complex numbers are added.

Thus, the FORTRAN statements:

                            292

```
COMPLEX Z
Z = (1.0, 2.0) + 3.0D-1
```

would assign the value (1.3, 2.0) to Z.

The same procedure is used when multiplying a complex number by a double precision number, except, of course, in step 3, the two complex numbers are multiplied instead of added. The statements

```
COMPLEX Z
Z = (0.0, 1.0) * 2.0D
```

would assign the value (0.0, 2.0) to Z.

Statements involving complex and real numbers or complex and integer numbers are handled in a similar manner. For instance, if a complex number is added to an integer number, the integer number will be converted to floating-point, given an imaginary part of zero, then added to the complex number. Thus, the value of (0.0, 1.0) + 2 is (2.0, 1.0).

The mode of any mixed-mode operation can be determined from the following table.

	Complex	Double	Real	Integer
Complex	Complex	Complex	Complex	Complex
Double	Complex	Double	Double	Double
Real	Complex	Double	Real	Real
Integer	Complex	Double	Real	Integer

This table gives the type of the result of any arithmetic operation +, -, *, /, **. As an example, suppose that C is complex, D is double precision, R is real, and I is an integer variable. Suppose they have the following values:

```
C = (1.0, 2.0)
D = 3.1D0
R = 2.0
I = 4
```

Then the expression (C + D) * I/R would be evaluated as follows:

```
((1.0, 2.0) + 3.1) * 4/2.0
((1.0, 2.0) + (3.1, 0.0)) * 4/2.0
(4.1, 2.0) * (4.0, 0.0)/2.0
(16.4, 8.0)/(2.0, 0.0)
(8.2, 4.0)
```

INPUT AND OUTPUT OF COMPLEX NUMBERS

A complex number corresponds to a pair of real numbers.
The FORTRAN representation of the complex number 1 + 2i is
(1.0, 2.0), which is a pair of FORTRAN floating-point numbers.
There is no separate field description in FORTRAN to use for
printing complex numbers. Instead, we use two F- or E-type
field descriptors, one for each part of the complex number.
For example, suppose Z is a complex variable. To print its
value, we could use the statements

```
        WRITE (2, 11) Z
   11   FORMAT (2F12.4)
```

The field description in the FORMAT statement consists of two
F12.4 fields. The first of these would be used to print the
real part of Z, and the second would be used to print the
imaginary part. If Z = (32.4, -5.0), the resulting output
would be bbbbb32.4000bbbbb-5.0000. If we used the FORMAT statement

```
   11   FORMAT (F6.1, E8.1)
```

then the real part of Z would be printed with an F6.1 format
while the imaginary part of Z would be printed with an E8.1
format. The output in this case would be bb32.4b-.5E+01.

To read the value of a complex number, we simply put an
F or an E field for each part of the number. When a complex
variable name appears in the list of a READ statement, the next
two fields of the FORMAT statement will be used to read it. The
first field will be used to read the real part, and the second
field will be used to read the imaginary part of the number.
For example, if a program contained the statements

```
        COMPLEX X, Y
        READ (2, 9) X, Y
   9    FORMAT (F5.1, F4.1, F5.1, F4.1)
```

then the real part of X would be read with the F5.1 field, and
the imaginary part of X would be read with the F4.1 field. If
an input card contained the data

```
000100020 23.1 0.0
```

then the resulting values for X and Y would be

```
X = (1.0, 2.0)
Y = (23.1, 0.0)
```

COMPLEX FUNCTIONS

Several function subprograms are provided by FORTRAN, which are often useful for programs involving complex variables. For instance, it is frequently necessary to find the square root of a complex number. This can*not* be done, however, by using the function SQRT; that function is only for finding the square root of a real variable. When we write Y = SQRT(X), FORTRAN expects that X is a real variable, and if X were a complex variable, the results would be unpredictable. For complex numbers, we have the special function CSQRT. This function takes a complex argument and returns a complex value. If Y is a complex variable in FORTRAN, then the statement

```
Y = CSQRT((-1.0, 0.0))
```

would assign to Y the complex value (0.0, 1.0).

The trigonometric and exponential functions as well have their counterparts for complex variables. These are given in the table below. The arguments of each function must be of complex type, and the value returned will also be complex.

Function	Description
CSQRT(X)	Square root of x
CEXP(X)	Exponential function, e^x
CLOG(X)	Natural logarithm, $\log_e x$
CSIN(X)	Trigonometric sine, $\sin x$
CCOS(X)	Trigonometric cosine, $\cos x$
CONJG(X)	Conjugate of x. The conjugate of (a, b) is $(a, -b)$.

Some other useful FORTRAN functions take complex variables and return real function values. These are given below.

Function	Description
REAL(X)	Real part of complex number: REAL((A, B)) = A
AIMAG(X)	Imaginary part of complex number: AIMAG((A, B)) = B
CABS(X)	Modulus of complex number: $CABS((A, B)) = \sqrt{A^2 + B^2}$

One final function takes two real arguments and returns a complex number.

Function	Description
CMPLX(X, Y)	Expresses the two real numbers X and Y as the complex number X + Yi

Some examples of these functions are given below.

Example	Value
REAL((3.1, 4.0))	3.1
AIMAG((3.1,4.0))	4.0
CABS((3.0, 4.0))	5.0
CMPLX(3.0, 4.0)	(3.0, 4.0)

To define a complex-valued function of our own, we use the statement

$$\text{COMPLEX FUNCTION name}(x_1, x_2, \cdots, x_n)$$

This statement works just like the DOUBLE PRECISION FUNCTION statement, except that the value of the function named will be complex. For example, the following is a function subroutine to compute the reciprocal of a complex number.

```
COMPLEX FUNCTION REC(Z)
COMPLEX Z
REC = (1.0, 0.0)/Z
RETURN
END
```

The COMPLEX statement specifies that the variable Z is a complex variable. The COMPLEX FUNCTION statement specifies that the function itself will take a complex value. The statements

```
COMPLEX X, Y, REC
X = (0.0, 1.0)
Y = REC(X)
```

would then set Y equal to (0.0, -1.0), which is 1.0/(0.0, 1.0).

Example 2

For positive real numbers, we can find the positive nth root using the exponential operator **. For instance, to find the fifth root of X, we can use the statement

```
Y = X ** (1.0/5.0)
```

296

For complex numbers, the situation is more complicated. In general, there are n nth roots of a complex number. If $z = a + bi$ is a complex number, and n is any positive integer, the n nth roots of z are the complex numbers w_1, w_2, $\cdots$, w_n given by

$$w_k = |z|^{1/n}\left(\cos\left(\frac{\theta + 2\pi k}{n}\right) + i\sin\left(\frac{\theta + 2\pi k}{n}\right)\right)$$

where $k = 1, 2, \cdots, n$,
$\quad\theta = \text{Tan}^{-1}(b/a)$,
$\quad|z| = \sqrt{a^2 + b^2}$.

In this example, we want to write a subroutine ROOT(N, Z, W), where N is a positive integer, Z is a complex variable, and W is a complex array of N elements, which will set W(K) equal to the Kth Nth root of Z as defined by the above formula.

The subroutine will use several of the functions discussed in the previous section. The first thing we must do is to find θ. To do this, we shall use the function ATAN, which gives the arctangent of a number expressed in radians. We use the statements

```
X = REAL(Z)
Y = AIMAG(Z)
THETA = ATAN2(Y, X)
```

$|Z|$ can be computed with the function CABS as

```
AA = CABS(Z) ** (1.0/AN)
```

where AN is equal to N in floating-point form. When we have computed the quantities

$$X = \cos\frac{\theta + 2\pi k}{n}$$

and

$$Y = \sin\frac{\theta + 2\pi k}{n}$$

we can use the function CMPLX to express these as a complex number X + NYI. W(K) can then be computed with the statement

```
W(K) = CMPLX(AA * X, AA * Y)
```

The complete FORTRAN subroutine is:

```
      SUBROUTINE ROOT(N, Z, W)
C     THIS SUBROUTINE STORES THE N NTH ROOTS OF THE
C     COMPLEX NUMBER Z IN THE COMPLEX ARRAY W.
      COMPLEX Z, W(N)
      AN = N
      PI = 3.14159
      X = REAL(Z)
      Y = AIMAG(Z)
      IF (X .EQ. 0.0) THETA = PI/2.0
      IF (X .NE. 0.0) THETA = ATAN(Y/Z)
      AA = CABS(Z) ** (1.0/AN)
      THETA = THETA/AN
      PHI = 2.0 * PI/AN
      DO 10 K = 1, N
      THETA = THETA + PHI
      X = COS(THETA)
      Y = SIN(THETA)
   10 W(K) = CMPLX(AA * X, AA * Y)
      RETURN
      END
```

EXERCISES

1. Which of the following are valid FORTRAN double precision constants?

   a. .99   f. 100.0
   b. 9.5D3   g. .01D4
   c. 7.2E1   h. .9999999
   d. 6.0D   i. 0D
   e. 7D0   j. 0.0D

2. A certain computer stores five digits in a memory location and truncates any digits beyond this. What is the result of the computation

   12345 * 67890 ?

   What is the exact value? How could using double precision variables make the result more accurate?

3. Write a double precision function ROOT to find the square root of a double precision variable. Do this two ways, one using the exponential operator ** and one without it.

4. Which of the following are valid FORTRAN complex constants?

4.—*continued*

a.	(1.0, 1.0)	f.	(0, 0)
b.	(0.0, 0.0)	g.	(12.0E2, 0.0)
c.	(0.0)	h.	(1.4E-2, -1.4E2)
d.	(5, 2)	i.	(7.0, 1.1)
e.	(5.0, 2.0)	j.	(X, 1.0)

5. Perform the indicated operations, using complex arithmetic.

a.	(1.0, 2.0) + (3.0, 4.0)	d.	(0.0, -1.0) ** 2
b.	(1 0, 1.0)/(0.0, 1.0)	e.	(10.0, 0.0)/(0.0, 10.0)
c.	(0.0, 2.0) * (0.0, 2.0)		

6. Evaluate the following functions.

a.	REAL((4.0, 2.0))	d.	CMPLX(1.0, 0.0)
b.	AIMAG((1.0, 0.0))	e.	CONJG((1.0, 5.0))
c.	CABS((5.0, 12.0))		

7. If $Y = A(1) + A(2) * Z + A(3) * Z ** 2 + \cdots + A(N) * Z ** (N - 1)$, where A(I) and Z are complex, write a complex function subroutine Y(N, A, Z) to compute this expression.

8. If Z and W are complex numbers, write a function subroutine NSIGN, which will set

$$NSIGN = \begin{cases} 1 & \text{if } Z = W \\ -1 & \text{if } Z = CONJG(W) \\ 0 & \text{otherwise} \end{cases}$$

9. A complex number (x, y) can be expressed in polar coordinates as (r, A), where $r^2 = x^2 + y^2$ and $A = \text{Tan}^{-1}(y/x)$. Write a complex function POLE(Z) which will express the complex number Z as a complex number in polar coordinate form.

10. If W1 and W2 are complex numbers in polar coordinate form (r_1, A_1) and (r_2, A_2), then W1 * W2 in polar coordinate form is $(r_1 r_2, A_1 + A_2)$. Write a complex function subroutine PROD(W1, W2) which will set PROD equal to the polar coordinate form of the product of W1 and W2, where W1 and W2 are in polar coordinate form.

Chapter 12

MAGNETIC TAPE AND DISK STORAGE

TAPE AND DISK STORAGE

Up until now in our discussion of input and output operations, we have been assuming that the input was coming from a card reader and the output was to be printed on a printer. Actually, there are several other devices that are more commonly used to store large volumes of information. The most common are magnetic tape and disk units. In this chapter, we shall see how to use these in a FORTRAN program.

A magnetic tape can be used by a computer to store data in much the same way that the magnetic tape used by a tape recorder stores sound signals. The surface of the tape is coated with a substance which can hold a magnetic charge. In the case of the audio tape recorder, sound signals are transformed into variations in a magnetic field, and these variations are recorded on the tape as it moves past the recording head. Once magnetized, the tape can be played back, and the variations in magnetism can be transformed into sound waves to produce the original sound. The tape drives used by a computer are bigger and more complicated than the average tape recorder, but they use the same principle.

Instead of storing sound waves, however, a computer tape stores numeric and alphabetic data. Any information that can be printed on a printer could just as well be written on a tape. We would not be able to read it directly, of course, but the tape could be saved, and then at some future time the information could be read back into the computer to be used by another program.

Data are stored on tape by using magnetized pulses. These pulses represent either one of two digits, a zero (0) or a one (1), and are known as *bits*. These bits correspond to the columns on a punch card. Instead of punching holes in the columns as on a card, the tape unit magnetizes the bits on the tape. A tape unit typically writes (or reads) 800 columns of such bits in a single inch of tape. So, a reel containing 100 feet of tape can store a very large amount of information very compactly.

In addition to being considerably more compact, information on a tape can be processed much faster than information punched on cards. Also, tapes are reusable. After we are through with the data on a tape, we can write new data on the same tape; we may even want to do this many times in a single program. As we go along, we shall see how these properties can make tape storage very advantageous for some applications.

To be used by a computer, a reel of tape is mounted on a tape drive. This is done by the operator before the beginning of the program. The tape is positioned at the load point, which is a mark on the tape to indicate where the information on the tape begins. A FORTRAN program, then, can either read information which has already been written on the tape, or it can write new information on the tape. Each READ or WRITE operation will advance the position of the tape a little. We rarely have to worry about coming to the end of the tape, since a reel can store a very large amount of data. At the conclusion of the program, the tape is rewound (either by the program or by the operator) and it is then dismounted by the operator to be saved for later use.

The data on a tape cannot be seen as can the data on a punch card. Actually, there is no difference in the way we write FORTRAN between reading data from a card and reading formatted data from a tape. The method of recording the data is different, but the programming is virtually the same. The complicated process of decoding the magnetic tape into numeric data for use by a program is taken care of automatically, just as it is for reading cards. The only thing that is important to the programmer is that when he knows *how* the data has been written on the tape, he will be able to read it in his program.

A disk unit operates on the same principle as a tape unit, except that the data are recorded on a magnetic disk. This disk is something like a phonograph record covered with magnetic material. The disk revolves at high speed, and data are read or written by movable arms which are free to move over the surface of the disk. Some systems use a drum instead of a disk, but the idea is the same.

There is no "beginning" to a disk as there is to a tape. When we write information on the disk, the computer will pick out some location on the disk (which it keeps track of automatically), and then it will start writing information at that point of the disk surface. The next time we write on the disk, the recording arm may move to another area of the disk before it starts to write. On a third WRITE operation, still another area of the disk may be used. Obviously, it is a complicated process to keep track of all the areas on the disk where information has been written. Fortunately for us, however, this is done automatically by the computer, and we do not have to worry about it at all in FORTRAN. After we have finished writing information on a disk, we can reposition the reading arm at its original point, and begin to read the information just as it was written. As an example, suppose that unit number 7 is a disk

301

unit. In a FORTRAN program, we might want to write the values of three variables A, B, and C on this unit, using the statements

```
WRITE (7, 99) A
WRITE (7, 99) B
WRITE (7, 99) C
```

where 99 is some FORMAT statement. We have no idea where these numbers are actually written on the disk. The computer knows, but we do not. However, as we shall see, we can reposition the read arm of the disk at the starting point, wherever that may be, by using the FORTRAN statement

```
REWIND 7
```

We can then read the data back into the computer by using the statements

```
READ (7, 99) A
READ (7, 99) B
READ (7, 99) C
```

As with tape storage, the complicated process of reading and writing the data is done for us automatically by the computer. The only thing we need to be concerned with in FORTRAN is that once we know how the data have been written on the disk, we can always read them back in by using the same FORMAT statement.

Thus, in FORTRAN, we can think of a disk unit as functioning just like a tape unit. Actually, we can think of a disk unit as functioning just like several tape units. In the above example, we assumed that the number 7 corresponded to a disk unit. In the same program, we might use the numbers 8 and 9 to correspond to the same disk unit. However, since different numbers are used, the computer would keep track of the information separately, just as though three different disk units were being used.

The question of what type of device is most suitable for a job depends on the nature of the information to be stored. Cards may be easily prepared on a keypunch, but reading cards is slower than reading tapes. Also, tape storage is much more compact than card storage. When dealing with large amounts of data, where it would be impractical to save all the information on cards, a common practice is to punch the data on cards, and then to have a program transfer these data to tape. Since a disk unit can take the place of many tape units, disk storage is well suited to many applications where it is necessary to store large amounts of information only for the duration of a program. Later in this chapter, we shall see examples of how each type of unit may be used in a specific application.

302

FORTRAN does not explicitly distinguish among the different input-output devices. Data are thought of as being organized into files, and it makes little difference, as far as FORTRAN is concerned, whether the file is a tape file, a disk file, or a card or print file.

A file is an area used by a program as input or output. An example of an input file is a deck of cards to be read. Printed output from a program is an example of an output file. A tape on a tape drive may be used either as an input or an output file. As mentioned before, a disk unit can accommodate many files. This emphasizes the difference between files and input-output devices. Even though the same device is used for many files, each file may be thought of as a separate body of data, just as though each one were written on a different device. The "unit number" in the READ or WRITE is different for each file.

Files are made up of "records." A record is the smallest element of a file which can be read or written by a single operation in FORTRAN. For a card reader, each card is a record. As we know, each READ statement in FORTRAN will start reading at the beginning of a new card. For a printer, a record consists of one print line, since each WRITE statement will start at the beginning of a new line.

On a tape, the information is written sequentially, so while we do not talk about reading the next card or writing the next line, we can think about it that way. A record on a tape or disk file is just a group of characters that is read or written together. When we talk about reading the next record from a tape, this is just like saying reading the next card. While for cards we are limited by the fact that each card has 80 columns, on a tape or disk file we can make records any size we want. If we write out 500 characters using a single WRITE statement, this will result in a record 500 characters long. When reading such a record, we would have to read it with a single READ statement, since the next READ statement would automatically start reading at the beginning of the next record (just as for reading cards).

In previous chapters, we have been assuming that all the input was coming from a card file, and all the output was to be printed. We shall now see examples of programs that use several input and output files.

Consider the problem of ordering items for a large store. First, we would need to know what items were carried by the store. This information might be kept in a tape file. Each record in the file would contain an identification number for some item,

the name of the item, the amount to be stocked, the price per
unit, and so forth. Next, we would need to know how much of each
item is actually on hand. This would be determined by taking
inventory and then punching a card for each item, giving the item
number and the amount on hand. Both of these files would be used
as input to the program, which would then compute the amount of
each item to be ordered and the price. This information might be
written on a tape to be used in other programs. The program
might also make a printed copy of the output. Thus, in this program, we have two input files and two output files.

It is sometimes convenient to be able to diagram the files
used by a program. We can use flowchart symbols for this. The
symbol for each type of file is shown in Figure 12-1.

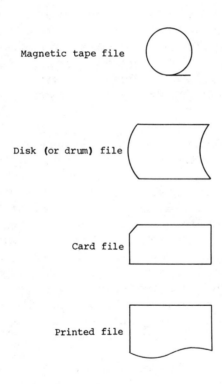

Magnetic tape file

Disk (or drum) file

Card file

Printed file

FIGURE 12-1

Using a rectangular box to represent the program, we can make a
diagram of the files used by a program which looks something
like a flowchart. A diagram for the example above regarding the
store inventory would be like the one shown in Figure 12-2.

304

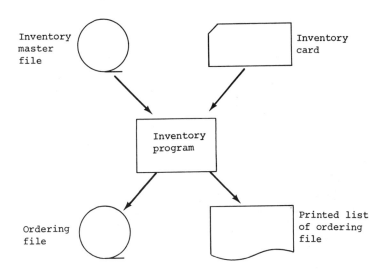

Inventory master file

Inventory card

Inventory program

Ordering file

Printed list of ordering file

FIGURE 12-2

This type of diagram can be especially useful in keeping track of files which are used in several programs. For instance, the master inventory file shown in Figure 12-2 might have come from another program which created it by making changes to an old master file to tell what new products were to be carried by the store, or what old products discontinued. The whole process could be represented as shown in Figure 12-3.

THE READ *AND* WRITE *STATEMENTS*
FOR TAPE AND DISK FILES

The READ and WRITE statements in FORTRAN are the same for tape or disk files as they are for card and print files. The form of the WRITE statement is

WRITE (*n*, *f*) list

where   *n* is an integer constant or a simple integer variable which denotes the "unit number" designating the file;

f is the number of a FORMAT statement;

list is the list of variables to be written.

305

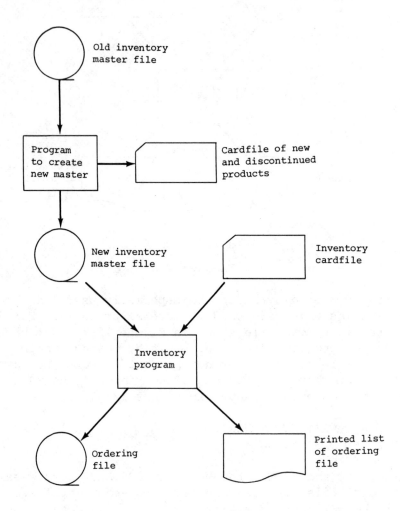

Old inventory
master file

Program
to create
new master

Cardfile of new
and discontinued
products

New inventory
master file

Inventory
cardfile

Inventory
program

Ordering
file

Printed list
of ordering
file

FIGURE 12-3

What *n* actually is will depend on the particular computer used. On some systems, the programmer can assign any number he wants to any device by using control cards in front of the FORTRAN program. For this chapter, we shall assume that the computer in question has two tape drives and a disk unit, and that the numbers are as follow:

3   designates a tape file;

4   designates another tape file;

5, 6, 7, and any higher numbers correspond to disk
     files on the disk unit.

The form of the READ statement is

                    READ (*n, f*) list

where *n*, *f*, and list are as above.

   Each WRITE statement will begin writing a new record, and
each READ statement will begin reading at the beginning of a new
record. Suppose that A, B, C, D, E, and F are variables having
the values 1.0, 2.0, 3.0, 4.0, 5.0, and 6.0. If we write on a
tape, using the statements

                 WRITE (3, 50) A
            50   FORMAT (F4.2)
                 WRITE (3, 51) B, C, D
            51   FORMAT (3F4.2)
                 WRITE (3, 52) E, F
            52   FORMAT (2F4.2)

then the resulting output may be thought of as looking like
Figure 12-4.

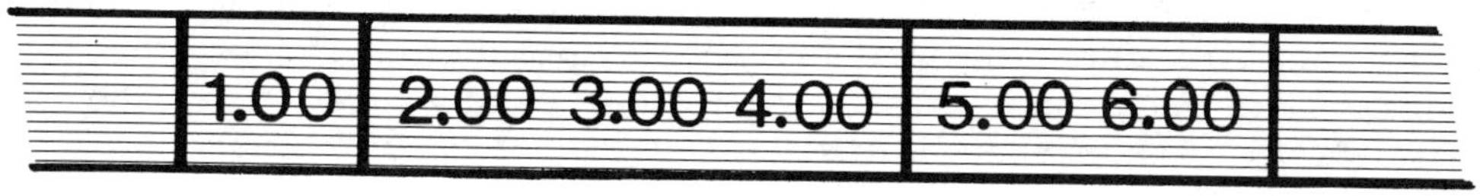

FIGURE 12-4

Each block in this figure represents one record on the tape.
Of course, the tape does not really look like this. The numbers
are represented by magnetized bits, and the end-of-record marks
would also be special magnetized patterns on the tape. But we
can think of it in this way. Now, suppose the tape is rewound,
and suppose we read it with the statements

                 READ (3, 50) X
                 READ (3, 50) Y
                 READ (3, 50) Z
            50   FORMAT (F4.2)

The value read for X will be 1.0. The value read for Y will be 2.0.

But the value read for Z will be 5.0, not 3.0. The reason for this is that the second READ statement reads all of the second record, but the second record consists of 12 characters, and only the first four are assigned to a variable, so the last part is lost. The third READ statement starts reading at the beginning of the third record, which begins with the characters 5.00.

We can process more than one record at a time with a single READ or WRITE statement by using the slash (/) in a FORMAT statement. For instance, the statements

```
        WRITE (3, 99) (A(I), I = 1, 15)
    99  FORMAT (5(3F10.0/))
```

would create the next five records on a tape, each record consisting of three F10.0 fields. The slash means to begin a new record on the tape just like beginning a new print line, as we did in Chapter 7. In a READ statement, the slash means to start reading at the beginning of the next record. Thus, to read the tape segment shown in Figure 12-4, we could use the statements

```
        READ (3, 100) A, B, C, D, E, F
    100 FORMAT (F4.2 / 3F4.2 / 2F4.2)
```

and this would read all three records.

For reading or writing on a disk file, the statements are the same as for reading or writing on a tape. As we have seen, there is really no difference between these statements and those used for reading cards or writing on the printer. The only difference is that the records are groups of characters on the tape or disk, rather than individual cards or print lines and may be longer.

TAPE HANDLING STATEMENTS

Every file has a beginning. For a card file, it is the first card in the deck. For a printed file, it is the first line printed. On a tape file, there will be a mark before the first record to indicate the beginning of the file. We can reposition a file at its beginning by using the REWIND statement. This statement has the form

        REWIND *n*

where *n* is an integer constant or a simple integer variable giving the number of the unit containing the file. This statement simply repositions file *n* at its starting point. If *n* is a tape file, the tape will be physically rewound on the tape drive to

308

the beginning of the first record. For a disk file, this statement will position the read arms at the initial point of the file. If file *n* is already at the beginning, or if the statement is not applicable (as for a card file), the REWIND statement will do nothing. It is a good idea to rewind all tape and disk files at the beginning of a program to make sure that they are positioned at the beginning before they are used the first time.

As an example of this statement, suppose that A is an array, and we have written 100 records on a tape or disk file with the statements

          WRITE (JOE, 57) (A(I), I = 1, 100)
       57 FORMAT (100(F12.3/))

Then the statement

          REWIND JOE

will position this file at its beginning, and we can then read the values and store them in an array B with the statement

          READ (JOE, 57) (B(I), I = 1, 100)

To indicate that the end of a file has been reached, we can create a special mark on the file called an end-of-file mark. This is done with the ENDFILE statement, which has the form

          ENDFILE *n*

where *n* is again the file number. This statement will simply write a mark on the file which the computer will recognize as an indication that there is nothing more to be read on the file. When an end-of-file mark is encountered on a read operation, the computer will take note of the fact, and any further attempt to read the file will either result in an execution error or serve to terminate the program, depending on the computer.

We can test for an end-of-file mark by using a special function. This logical function has the form[1]

          EOF (*n*)

where *n* is the file number. This function will return a value .TRUE. if an end-of-file mark was encountered on file *n* on the

---

[1]The form of this function may vary somewhat on different computer systems.

last read operation, and a value of .FALSE. otherwise. Since
the value returned is a logical value, we can use a logical IF
statement to test for an end-of-file *n*. Usually, each time we
read a tape or disk file, we follow the READ statement with an
IF statement such as

IF (EOF(K)) GO TO 99

This will cause the program to go to Statement 99 if an end-of-
file mark was read on file K. If no such mark was read, the
next statement will be performed. Suppose we have written 100
records on a tape, using the statements

```
          WRITE (3, 77) (A(I), I = 1, 100)
       77 FORMAT (100(F10.3/))
          ENDFILE 3
```

The ENDFILE statement will write an end-of-file mark after the
last record written. Now, we could go back and add up all these
values written by using the statements

```
          SUM = 0.0
          REWIND 3
       10 READ (3, 78) X
       78 FORMAT (F10.3)
          IF (EOF(3)) GO TO 79
          SUM = SUM + X
          GO TO 10
       79 REWIND 3
          STOP
```

Each READ statement will read one record. For the first 100
times the READ statement is performed, the function EOF(3) will
be .FALSE., so the number read will be added to the sum. On the
101st time, however, the READ statement will read an end-of-
file mark. In this case, the FORMAT statement will have no
meaning, and X will have an undefined value. But the function
EOF(3) will be .TRUE., so the program will branch to Statement 79,
where the input tape is rewound.

Example 1

A certain company keeps a tape file of employees. Each
record on the tape consists of 44 characters giving the following data.

Characters	*Data*
1-5	Employee number
6-30	Name

Characters	*Data*
31-35	Pay rate—a five-digit number with an assumed decimal point before the last two digits
36-44	Social security number

There is an end-of-file mark after the last record. Now, every employee is to get a 5 percent pay raise. The problem is to read the old tape and to create a new tape with the new pay rates.

The files used in this program are shown in Figure 12-5. The numbers 3 and 4 indicate the numbers we shall call the files by in the FORTRAN program.

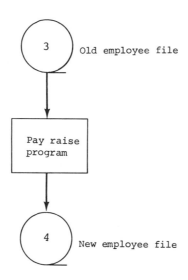

FIGURE 12-5

The solution to this problem is quite simple. We just read a record from the old file, compute the new pay rate, and write a record on the new file. We continue this procedure until an end-of-file is encountered on the old file, at which time we write an end-of-file on the new file, rewind both files, and stop. The flowchart for this program is shown in Figure 12-6. Notice that we rewind both files at the beginning of the program. This is always a good idea, as it insures that the files are positioned at their starting points. If the files are already at their starting points (as they should be), the REWIND statements cause no action.

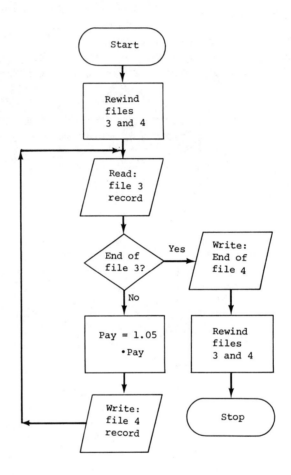

FIGURE 12-6

In the FORTRAN program for this job, we use an array NAME to hold the name. We shall assume here that the computer can store 10 characters in a word. So, the array NAME will have three elements that will contain the first 10 characters, the second 10 characters, and the last 5 characters of the 25-character name on the employee record. The program is:

```
DIMENSION NAME (3)
REWIND 3
REWIND 4
```

```
   5   READ (3, 10) NUM, NAME, PAY, NSS
  10   FORMAT (I5, 2A10, A5, F5.0, I9)
       IF (EOF(3)) GO TO 99
       PAY = 1.05 * PAY
       WRITE (4, 10) NUM, NAME, PAY, NSS
       GO TO 5
  99   ENDFILE 4
       REWIND 3
       REWIND 4
       STOP
       END
```

In FORMAT Statement 10, we have specified that the pay is
read with an F5.0 format. The reason for this is so that when
we write the pay again we shall not write a decimal point, since
we do not want one to appear explicitly. For instance, if the
pay is written 02510, this means 25.10. But we are going to
read it as 2510.0. The new pay rate will be computed as 3765.0,
but when we write it with the F5.0 format, it will be written
as 03765, as we want it to be.

Example 2

In the above example, we assumed that everyone received the
same raise. Now let's consider the general problem of how to
update the employee file. There are three things we might want
to do to an employee's record on the tape. First, we might want
to change some of the information, as we did above. In addition
to this, some employees will leave the company for various reasons, so we will want to be able to delete certain records from
the tape. Finally, we shall need to be able to add records to
the tape for new employees. In order to tell what changes are
to be made to the tape file, we shall use a card file. Each
card will correspond to one record on the tape, and will have
the following format.

Columns	Data
1-5	Employee number
6-30	Name
31-35	Pay rate
36-44	Social security number
45-79	Blank
80	Operation code—either "1" or blank.

The operation code in column 80 tells what is to be done with the
record. If column 80 contains a 1, the card is a deletion, so
the record on the tape with the same employee number as the card
will not be written on the new tape file. If column 80 is blank,
the card is an insertion or a correction card. If there is a

record on the tape with the same employee number as on the card, then the information on this tape record will be replaced with the information on the card record on the new tape file. If there is no record on the tape with the same employee number as the card, a record will be created on the new tape from the information on the card. The three files used in the program are shown in Figure 12-7.

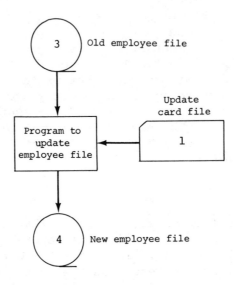

FIGURE 12-7

In order to program this problem, we must assume that the input files are sorted on the employee number. In other words, we assume that the cards the tape records are sorted so that each record read will have a greater employee number than the previous record. With this assumption, the main idea of the program will be to compare the employee number on the card to the employee number of the tape and determine the appropriate action to be taken based on this comparison. Suppose, then, that we have read in a tape record and a card record. There are four possible things that might be the case:

1. The employee number on the card is greater than the employee number on the tape. In this case, we are not ready yet to do anything with the card. The record on the tape will go onto the new tape just as it is, so we write a new tape record, and again compare the employee numbers.

2. The employee number on the tape is greater than the employee number on the card. Since the tape is sorted, and we have suddenly come to a number higher than the one on the card, the record on the card must be an addition to the tape. So we write a new tape record from the information on the card, then we read another card and go back to the comparison.

3. The card and tape numbers are equal, and column 80 on the card contains a 1. In this case, the record on the tape is to be deleted from the new tape. To do this, we simply read another card and tape record, and go back to the comparison.

4. The card and tape numbers are equal, and column 80 of the card does not contain a 1. In this case, the card is a correction for the tape record, so we write a record on the new tape using the information on the card, then we read another card and tape record and go back to the comparison.

This procedure is shown in the flowchart in Figure 12-8. In this flowchart, NUM1 and NUM3 are the employee numbers for files 1 and 3. NOP is the operation code (column 80) on the card. In the flowchart, we have statements such as "Record 4 = Record 1" as a shorthand way of saying that the information to be written on the file 4 record comes from the information read from file 1. In the FORTRAN program, we will read information from file 1 into variables NUM1, NAME1, PAY1, and NSS1. The variables NUM3, NAME3, PAY3, and NSS3 are the corresponding items read from file 3. To write a record on file 4 from the information on file 1, we would just use the statement

WRITE (4, 11) NUM1, NAME1, PAY1, NSS1

This sort of procedure occurs time and again in programs dealing with several files which have to be matched. In order to visualize the method, suppose that the numbers on the input files are as follows:

NUM1 (Card File)	Operation Code (Column 80)	NUM 3 (Tape File)
3		1
5		2
6	1	4
10	1	5
11		6
		8
		9
		10
		11

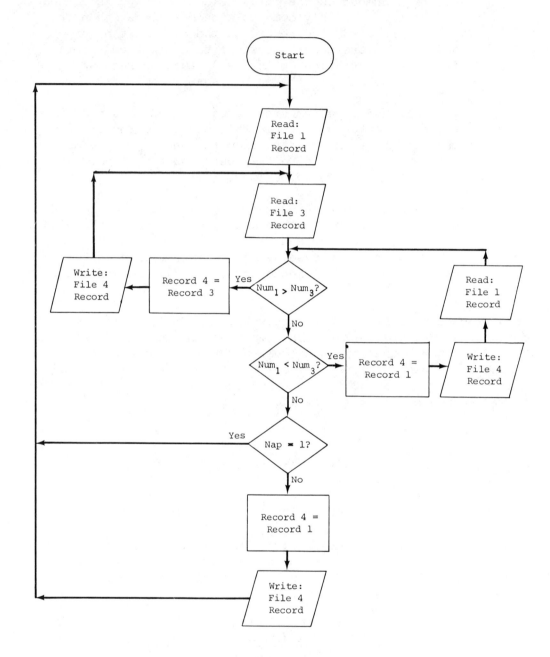

FIGURE 12-8

316

On the first comparison, the tape number is lower, so a new
tape record is written from the old tape record, and another
old tape record is read. The same thing happens on the second comparison. On the third comparison, however, the card
number is lower, so the card is an addition to the tape. A
new tape record is written from the card, and another card is
read before the next comparison. The student should convince
himself that the new tape would have the records numbered

$$1, 2, 3, 4, 5, 8, 9, 11.$$

Records 6 and 10 are deleted from the tape. Records 5 and 11
are corrected on the new tape.

We have omitted one thing from the flowchart shown in
Figure 12-8. We have not considered the action to be taken
after the end is reached on one of the input files. After
we read the last tape record, there still might be come cards
left to indicate additions to the new tape. In this case, we
would read each remaining card and create a corresponding record
on the new tape. Also, we might have tape records left to be
read after the last card is processed. In this case, we would
read each remaining tape record and write an identical record
on the new tape. When the end is reached on both files, we
shall write an end-of-file mark on the new tape, then rewind
the tapes. The complete flowchart for this example is shown in
Figure 12-9 and Figure 12-10.

The FORTRAN program for this example is as follows:

```
C         PROGRAM TO UPDATE EMPLOYEE FILE
          DIMENSION NAME1(3), NAME3(3)
          REWIND 3
          REWIND 4
     5    READ (1, 6) NUM1, NAME1, PAY1, NSS1, NOP
     6    FORMAT(I5, 2A10, A5, F5.0, I9, 26X, I1)
          IF (EOF(1)) GO TO 99
    10    READ (3, 11) NUM3, NAME3, PAY3, NSS3
    11    FORMAT(I5, 2A10, A5, F5.0, I9)
          IF (EOF(3)) GO TO 100
    15    IF (NUM1 .LE. NUM3) GO TO 20
C         NUM1 IS GREATER THAN NUM3, SO CARD IS NOT PROCESSED YET.
C         WRITE FILE 4 RECORD FROM FILE 3.
          WRITE (4, 11) NUM3, NAME3, PAY3, NSS3
          GO TO 10
    20    IF (NUM1 .GE. NUM3) GO TO 25
C         NUM1 IS LESS THAN NUM3, SO CARD IS AN ADDITION.
C         WRITE FILE 4 RECORD FROM FILE 1.
          WRITE (4, 11) NUM1, NAME1, PAY1, NSS1
          READ (1, 6) NUM1, NAME1, PAY1, NSS1, NOP
```

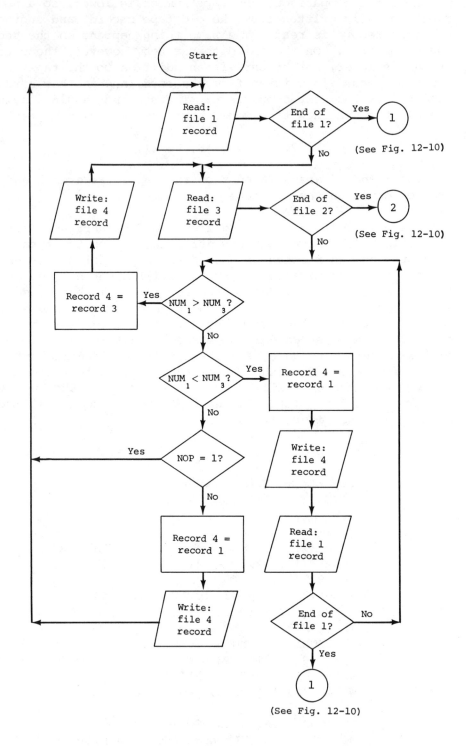

FIGURE 12-9

318

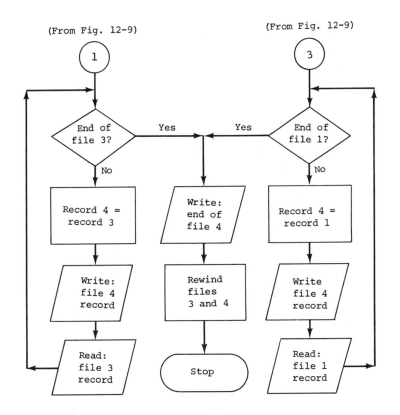

FIGURE 12-10

```
        IF (EOF(1)) GO TO 99
        GO TO 15
C       NUM1 EQUALS NUM3, SO CARD IS EITHER A CORRECTION
C       OR REPLACEMENT.
     25 IF (NOP .EQ. 1) GO TO 5
C       IF NOP IS 1, RECORD IS DELETED
        WRITE (4, 11) NUM1, NAME1, PAY1, NSS1
        GO TO 5
C       END OF FILE 1 REACHED
     99 IF (EOF(3)) GO TO 200
        WRITE (4, 11) NUM3, NAME3, PAY3, NSS3
        READ (3, 11) NUM3, NAME3, PAY3, NSS3
        GO TO 99
C       END OF FILE 3 REACHED
    100 IF (EOF(1)) GO TO 200
```

319

```
              WRITE (4, 11) NUM1, NAME1, PAY1, NSS1
              READ (1, 6) NUM1, NAME1, PAY1, NSS1, NOP
              GO TO 100
      C       END OF BOTH INPUT FILES REACHED
         200  ENDFILE 4
              REWIND 3
              REWIND 4
              STOP
              END
```

Example 3

Let us now consider one aspect of the record-keeping in a library, e.g., mailing overdue book notices. We shall assume that we have two input files. The first of these is the name and address file. For each patron of the library, this file will give his library card number, his name, and his address. The other file used will be a file of books checked out. For each book checked out, this file gives the library card number of the person the book is loaned to, the author and title of the book, and the date due. The program will also read a card which gives today's date. The object of the program will then be to match the information on the two input files and to print a notice to each patron having overdue books, telling him what books are overdue and asking him to return them. The files used in the program are shown in Figure 12-11.

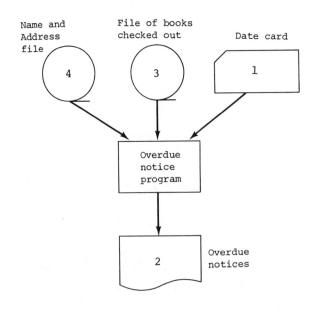

FIGURE 12-11

The format of these files is given below:

FILE OF BOOKS CHECKED OUT (File 3)	
Characters	Data
1-5	Library card number of person to whom loaned
6-15	Call number of book
16-25	Author's last name (or first 10 characters if name is too long)
26-45	Title of book (or first 20 characters if title is too long)
46-51	Date due (written in form MMDDYY—i.e., 022372 would mean February 23, 1972)

NAME AND ADDRESS FILE (File 4)	
Characters	Data
1-5	Library card number of patron
6-25	Patron's name
26-45	First line of address
46-65	Second line of address
66-85	Third line of address

DATE CARD (File 1)	
Columns	Data
1-6	Today's date (written in form MMDDYY)
7-80	Blank

We shall need to assume that both of the tape files are sorted on the library card number. Note that the file of books checked out may have several records for one library card number (as would be the case if one person has several books checked out). The only thing that matters is that these records are arranged by library card number. Thus, the order of some records on this file might be 1, 3, 3, 3, 6, 7, 7, 8, ···. On the name and address file, some numbers might not be used as library card numbers, but each patron will have a single number. So, the records on this file might be numbered 1, 2, 4, 7, 8, 11. ····.

321

Since the object of the program is to print overdue notices, it will be useful to decide how we want these notices to look before trying to write the program. In some situations, the simplest thing to do would be to use special paper for the output. Instead of the standard computer paper, a roll of specially printed forms could be loaded onto the printer, and we could write the output right on these. We will assume, however, that we are using standard paper, so our program will have to print all the headings. The output will have one page for every patron who has overdue books, so that each page could be mailed separately. A sample page is shown in Figure 12-12.

```
                                              7/ 9/77

    JOHN DOE
    411 OAK ST
    TUCSON, AZ
    85710

    DEAR SIR,
    THE FOLLOWING BOOKS ARE NOW OVERDUE.

    AUTHOR      TITLE                 DATE DUE
    YOLK        THE PRICE OF EGGS     7/ 7/77
    YOLK        EGGS AND THEIR PRICE  7/ 7/77
    YOLK        EGG PRICE ANALYSIS    7/ 7/77
    YOLK        COLLECTED WORKS       7/ 7/77

    PLEASE RETURN THESE PROMPTLY.
    A FINE OF FIVE CENTS PER DAY IS CHARGED.
                                   THANK YOU
```

FIGURE 12-12. Sample output from library program

The basic logic of the program is shown in the flowchart in Figure 12-13. We begin by reading a record from each file. We shall call the library card numbers of files 3 and 4 NUM3 and NUM4. If NUM4 is less than NUM3, then the person with number NUM4 has not checked out any books, so we go back and read another file 3 record. NUM4 should never be greater than NUM3, since this would mean that a book was checked out to someone not on the name and address file. In this case, we would stop after printing an error message. If NUM4 equals NUM3, we check to see if the book represented by the file 3 record is overdue. This is the case when the date due (which we shall call NDATD) is greater than the current date (which we shall call NDATE). If the book is overdue, we print the book title, author, and date due on an overdue notice. If not, we go back to read another file 3 record.

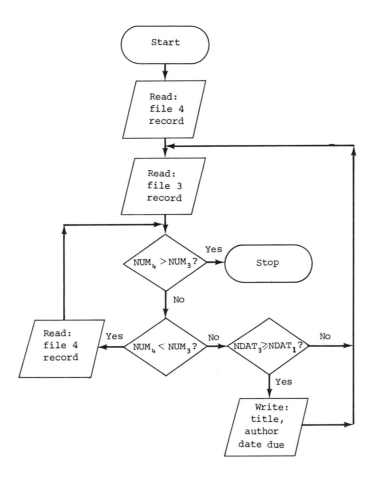

FIGURE 12-13

While Figure 12-13 gives the basic idea of the program, there are a few problems still to be worked out. For one thing, we must remember to test for an end-of-file on the input file, and if one is read, we rewind the input tapes and stop. A more difficult problem is the job of separating the output into pages with heading and closing messages on each page. In order to do this, we need to know when we change from one person to the next. This can be done by using a logical variable which we shall call FIRST. Every time we read a record from file 4, we shall set FIRST = .TRUE., and every time we print an overdue book title, we shall set FIRST = .FALSE. . This will give the variable FIRST

323

the value .TRUE. when we have just changed from one person to the next on the name and address tape. This enables us to determine when the heading should be printed. Before printing the title of an overdue book, we see if the value of FIRST is .TRUE. . If so, then the title is the first one to be printed for the person, so we first print the heading, giving the address, date, and so on. To determine when the closing message is to be printed, we can also use the variable FIRST. Each time a new record from file 4 is read, we are changing to a new person. Now, if an overdue notice was printed to the previous person, the variable FIRST would have the value .FALSE., so we would print the closing message at this time. If FIRST has the value .TRUE., then the previous person did not get an overdue notice, so we would not print the closing message before reading the next file 4 record. The complete flowchart for this example is shown in Figure 12-14. Notice from the flowchart that when the end of file 3 is reached, we must write the closing on the last overdue notice before stopping. The student should try going through this flowchart to see what would happen if the input were as follows.

NUM4	NUM3
1	2 (book not overdue)
2	2 (book overdue)
3	4 (book overdue)
4	4 (book not overdue)
5	4 (book overdue)

The only difficulty encountered in writing the FORTRAN program from the flowchart is in the input and output statements. We shall consider these individually. First of all, we assume that the computer used can store ten characters of alphabetic data in a word. Now, to read a record from the name and address file, we shall use an array NAME of two elements to store the name, and an array ADDR of six elements to store the address. The name is read with a 2A10 format, so the first ten characters of the name go in NAME(1), and the last ten characters go in NAME(2). The same format is used to read each line of the address, so the first line of the address is in ADDR(1) and ADDR(2), the second line in ADDR(3) and ADDR(4), and the third line in ADDR(5) and ADDR(6). The READ statement for file 4 would then be

```
        READ (4, 10) NUM4, NAME, ADDR
     10 FORMAT (I5, 8A10)
```

To read a record from the file of books checked out, we shall use the array TITLE to store the title. The date due for each book could be read as a six-digit integer. However, on

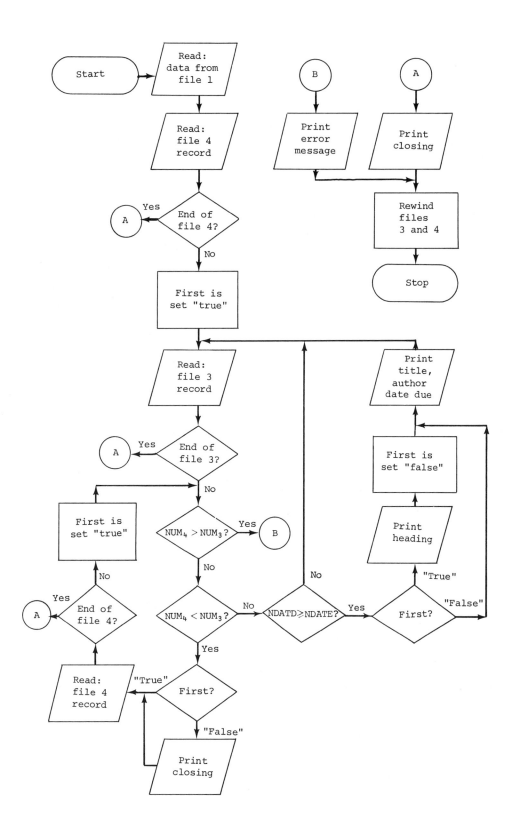

FIGURE 12-14

the overdue notice, we are going to want to print it in the form MM/DD/YY, rather than just as MMDDYY as it is written on the tape. To facilitate this, we can read the date due into an array MDATD. MDATD(1) will be a two-digit integer giving the month, MDATD(2) will give the day, and MDATD(3) will give the year. For the purpose of comparing the date due with the current date, we can convert the values in this array back into a single number with the formula

$$NDATD = 10000 * MDATD(3) + 100 * MDATD(1) + MDATD(2)$$

For example, if the date due is written as 113355, we would read it and store it as MDATD(1) = 11, MDATD(2) = 33, MDATD(3) = 55. The above formula would set NDATD equal to 551133. Notice that the two digits for the year come first. When dates are written like this, we can tell whether or not one date is later than another by simply subtracting them. This same procedure is used in reading the date card, so that the current date can be printed on each overdue notice. The READ statement for file 3 is

```
        READ (3, 20) NUM3, AUTH, TITLE, MDATD
     20 FORMAT (I5, 10X, 3A10, 3I2)
```

The first item for the heading of the overdue notice is the date. This is written with the statements

```
        WRITE (2, 50) MDATE
     50 FORMAT (1H1, 32X, I2, 1H/, I2, 1H/, I2)
```

The 1H1 field will cause the printer to skip to the top of the next page. The 1H/ fields will insert the slashes between the values of the array MDATE, so that the date will be written as MM/DD/YY. The name and address are written with the statements

```
        WRITE (2, 55) NAME, ADDR
     55 FORMAT (/4(1X, 2A10/))
```

The slash in the 4(1X, 2A10/) part will make the printer begin a new line after the name and each line of the address. The last part of the heading is printed with an H field to print

```
        DEAR SIR,
        THE FOLLOWING BOOKS ARE NOW OVERDUE.

        AUTHOR     TITLE                      DATE DUE
```

The only problem here is to get everything in the right column. The word "AUTHOR" starts in column 2 (remember that column 1 is only for carriage control). "TITLE" starts in column 13, and

326

"DATE" in column 34. This is so we can print the author, title, and date due with one space between them.

The output statement for each overdue book is

```
      WRITE (2, 80) TITLE, AUTH, MDATD
   80 FORMAT (1X, A10, 1X, 2A10, 1X, I2, 1H/, I2, 1H/, I2)
```

This leaves a space for carriage control and a space between each field. The date will be written MM/DD/YY, the slashes being provided by the 1H fields. The closing message is written with H fields, just as the heading was.

With the READ and WRITE statements done, the rest of the program is easily written from the flowchart. The complete program is:

```
C        PROGRAM TO PRINT OVERDUE BOOK NOTICES
         DIMENSION NAME(2), ADDR(6), TITLE(2), MDATE(3), MDATD(3)
         LOGICAL FIRST
         READ (1, 5) MDATE
    5    FORMAT (3I2)
C        CONVERT DATE TO COMPUTATIONAL VALUE
         NDATE = 10000 * MDATE(3) + 100 * MDATE(1) + MDATE(2)
         REWIND 3
         REWIND 4
C        READ NAME/ADDRESS RECORD
         READ (4, 10) NUM4, NAME, ADDR
   10    FORMAT (I5, 8A10)
         IF (EOF(4)) GO TO 99
         FIRST = .TRUE.
C        READ BOOK FILE RECORD
   15    READ (3, 20) NUM3, AUTH, TITLE, MDATD
   20    FORMAT (I5, 10X, 3A10, 3I2)
         IF (EOF(3)) GO TO 99
C        CONVERT DATE TO COMPUTATIONAL VALUE
         NDATD = 10000 * MDATD(3) + 100 * MDATD(1) + MDATD(2)
C        IF NUM4 IS GREATER THAN NUM3, FILE 3 RECORD HAS NO MATCH
C        ON FILE 4
   25    IF (NUM4 .LE. NUM3) GO TO 30
         WRITE (2, 26)
   26    FORMAT (17H UNMATCHED RECORD)
         GO TO 100
C        IF NUM4 IS LESS THAN NUM3, READ ANOTHER NAME/ADDRESS RECORD
C        IF THEY ARE EQUAL, SEE IF BOOK IS OVERDUE
   30    IF (NUM4 .LT. NUM3) GO TO 35
         GO TO 45
C        PRINT CLOSING IF FIRST IS .FALSE.
   35    IF (.NOT. FIRST) WRITE (2, 40)
   40    FORMAT (30H PLEASE RETURN THESE PROMPTLY./
```

```
      1 41H A FINE OF FIVE CENTS PER DAY IS CHARGED./
      2 31X, 10H THANK YOU)
C        READ NAME/ADDRESS RECORD.  SET FIRST = .TRUE.
         READ (4, 10) NUM4, NAME, ADDR
         IF (EOF(4)) GO TO 99
         FIRST = .TRUE.
         GO TO 25
C        IF BOOK IS OVERDUE, PRINT RECORD ON OVERDUE NOTICE
C        IF FIRST IS .TRUE., PRINT HEADING
   45    IF (.NOT. FIRST) GO TO 75
         WRITE (2, 50) MDATE
   50    FORMAT (1H1, 32X, I2, 1H/, I2, 1H/, I2)
         WRITE (2, 55) NAME, ADDR
   55    FORMAT (/4(1X, 2A10/))
         WRITE (2, 60)
   60    FORMAT (10H DEAR SIR,/37H THE FOLLOWING BOOKS ARE NOW OVERDUE.)
         WRITE (2, 65)
   65    FORMAT (/7H AUTHOR, 3X, 6H TITLE, 15X, 9H DATE DUE)
   75    WRITE (2, 80) AUTH; TITLE, MDATD
   80    FORMAT (1X, A10, 1X, 2A10, 1X, I2, 1H/, I2, 1H/, I2)
         GO TO 15
C        AT END OF INPUT, WRITE CLOSING AND REWIND FILES
   99    WRITE (2, 40)
  100    REWIND 3
         REWIND 4
         STOP
         END
```

THE UNFORMATTED READ AND WRITE STATEMENTS

When we read a card, what we are actually reading is a string
of characters. It is the FORMAT statement which tells the computer how these characters are to be interpreted. The computer
then stores the information read as the value of some variable.
Thus, when we read the characters 12.76 into the variable X, the
computer converts the *characters* 12.76 into the *value* 12.76, and
stores the value in the variable X. All this is done electronically, of course. As far as the computer is concerned, the value
of the variable X is just some electronic configuration of the
computer memory. In order for us to find out what the value of X
is, we must convert the value back to a string of characters and
print it out.

Suppose that we write the value of a variable X on a tape
with the statements

```
         WRITE (3, 3)X
       3 FORMAT (F12.4)
```

What happens is that the value of X is converted into a string of 12 characters and written on the tape. When we reread the tape, the 12 characters will be converted back to a value and assigned to a variable. There is a way, in FORTRAN, of eliminating this intermediate step of changing values into character strings and vice versa. This is done with the unformatted READ and WRITE statements.

The form of the unformatted WRITE statement is

WRITE (*n*) list

where *n* is an integer constant or variable that denotes the file, and list is the variable list. In other words, the unformatted WRITE statement has the same form as the WRITE statement we have been using, except that there is no FORMAT statement number.

What this statement does is to take each variable in the list and write its value on file *n*. The values are written in the internal code of the machine, just as they are stored. We would not use this type of WRITE statement to write data on the printer, because the data is output in internal machine code and we would not be able to read it. The thing that we must do with data written this way would be to read it back using an unformatted READ statement.

The unformatted READ statement has the form

READ (*n*) list

where *n* and list are as above. This statement is the reverse of the unformatted WRITE. Values from file *n* are read and assigned to the variables in the list. The values read must have been written with an unformatted WRITE statement and the list on READ must agree with the list on WRITE. It is not possible to write information with a formatted WRITE statement and read it with an unformatted READ statement.

Each execution of the unformatted WRITE statement will create exactly one record on the file. The length of the record is the number of variables written. For instance, the statement

WRITE (3) A, B, C, N, M

would write the values of the variables A, B, C, N, and M on file 3 to create a record five values long. Note that it does not make sense in this case to ask how many characters are in the record, since we are writing values instead of characters.

329

The unformatted READ statement will read exactly one record of file *n*. There should be the same number of variables in the list as there were in the list of the unformatted WRITE statement which created the record. If the record created by the above unformatted WRITE were read with the statement

    READ (3) D, E, F, I, J

this would result in these variables receiving the values of the variables written, just as though we had put

            D = A
            E = B
            F = C
            I = N
            J = M

A file created by unformatted WRITE statements is called an unformatted file. The records on such a file consist of values written in the machine's internal code, so we could not print such a file or read it in any format other than the machine's code. The only thing we would normally do with an unformatted file would be to rewind and read it again using unformatted READ statements.

The main thing to remember about the data on an unformatted file is that when it is read, it will be stored in the computer exactly as it was before it was written. Thus, the statements

            REWIND 7
            WRITE (7) X
            REWIND 7
            READ (7) Y

will have the same effect as the statement

            Y = X

The advantage of using an unformatted file for some applications is that since no conversion of values is needed to change the machine's internal representation into character strings, the input and output are faster. It is sometimes also more convenient if we don't care how the data "looks" on a tape or disk file, but only that it is stored there. We shall see this in Example 4.

Example 4

We have a tape file on which each record is a single decimal number written in an F12.4 format. This file is sorted in

330

descending order. We want to write a program to create an identical file, but with the numbers written in ascending order.

If the input file contained only a few numbers, the solution to this problem would be simple. We could just read the entire file and write it out in reverse order. Suppose, however, that the input file is very large, containing thousands of numbers, and there is not enough storage available in the computer to read them all in at the same time. What we would have to do in this case is to use intermediate files to store the numbers. We will call the input file, File 3. The output file will be called File 4. In addition to these, we will use two files for intermediate storage. Each of these files will be used both as an input and an output file; we shall call these File 5 and File 6. Since these files are used only for intermediate storage, and not saved at the end of the program, we shall assume that they are disk files. The files used by the program are shown in Figure 12-15.

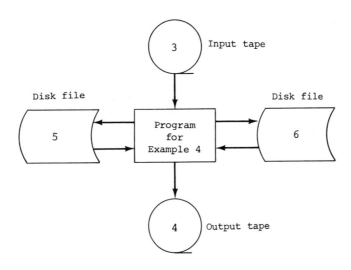

FIGURE 12-15

The basic procedure we shall use in this program can be understood by considering a specific example. Suppose that the input tape contains the values:

File 3: 12, 11, 10, 9, 8, 7, 6, 5, 4, 3, 2, 1

Now, we are assuming that we cannot read in the whole file at once, so we start by reading the first four values. We then write

331

these in reverse order on File 6. Now, we read in four more values from File 3, and we write them in reverse order on File 5. We then rewind File 6 and copy it onto File 5. Altogether, we have written eight numbers on File 5.

File 5: 5, 6, 7, 8, 9, 10, 11, 12

The next step is to read the last four numbers on File 3. Now, we rewind Files 5 and 6. Then the numbers from File 5 are read and copied onto File 6. File 6 now contains 12 values. The first four were just read from File 3, and the last eight were copied from File 5.

File 6: 1, 2, 3, 4, 5, 6, 7, 8, 9, 10, 11, 12

Since we have finished reading File 3, we are through. All that remains to be done is to copy File 6 onto the output tape, File 4.

If there were more numbers to be read on File 3, we would read another group, write it in reverse order on File 5, then copy File 6 onto File 5. We see that Files 5 and 6 keep interchanging roles in the program. First, File 5 is used as input and File 6 is used as output, then File 6 becomes the input file, with File 5 as the output file. It will be helpful to use integer variables to refer to these two files. Start with M = 5 and N = 6. The procedure just described can then be expressed as follows.

1. Read a group of numbers from the input tape (File 3).
2. Write them in reverse order on File N.
3. Copy File M onto File N.
4. Rewind Files M and N.
5. Interchange the values of M and N and go back to Step 1.

These steps are repeated until we have read all the numbers on the input tape. In the FORTRAN program, we shall read groups of 100 numbers from the input tape, and store them in an array called A. The procedure is illustrated in the flowchart in Figure 12-16. Notice from the flowchart that we write an end-of-file mark on File M at the very beginning of the program. Thus, on the first time through, the first read operation on File M will encounter an end-of-file mark, and nothing will be copied from File M to File N. Notice also that we must remember to write an end-of-file mark on File N after each step.

The disk files used in this program will not be saved after the end of the program, and so we are free to choose whatever format we like for these files. The easiest (and probably the most efficient) thing to do is to make them unformatted files, using unformatted READ and WRITE statements. Now, the input tape

332

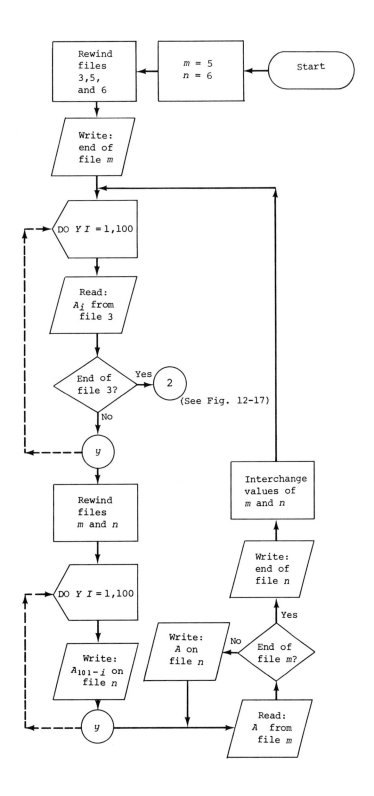

FIGURE 12-16

333

file is given to be a formatted file. To read this file, we shall use the statements

```
            READ (3, 15) A(I)
     15    FORMAT (F12.4)
```

However, when writing the values of the array A, we can use the statement

```
            WRITE (N)(A(101 - I), I = 1, 100)
```

First of all, since this is an unformatted WRITE statement, it will create a record on File N consisting of a string of values. The variable list in this case is an implied DO loop that causes the values of the array A to be written in reverse order. Thus, the first value written (corresponding to I = 1) is A(100), and the last value written (corresponding to I = 100) is A(1). When we copy File M onto File N, we will also use unformatted READ and WRITE statements. These would be

```
            READ (M) A
            WRITE (N) A
```

Remember that A is an array of dimension 100, so each of these statements is dealing with 100 variables, just as though they were written

```
            READ (M) (A(I), I = 1, 100)
            WRITE (N) (A(I), I = 1, 100)
```

   One problem we have not yet considered is what happens when we reach the end of the input tape. There may be fewer than 100 values to read on the last time through the program. This is handled easily, however. When we read an end-of-file mark on File 3, we branch out of the DO loop used to read the variables. The last value read from File 3 is then written on the output tape, File 4. Then the next-to-last value read from File 3 is written on the output tape, and so on for all the leftover values. After this, we copy the values on File M onto the output tape. This has to be done for 100 values at a time, since each record on File M consists of 100 values. The statements used are

```
            READ (M) A
            WRITE (4, 135) A
     135   FORMAT (100(F12.4/))
```

   After reaching the end of File M, we are finished, so we rewind the tape files and stop. The whole procedure to be followed after reaching the end of the input tape is given by the flowchart of Figure 12-17.

334

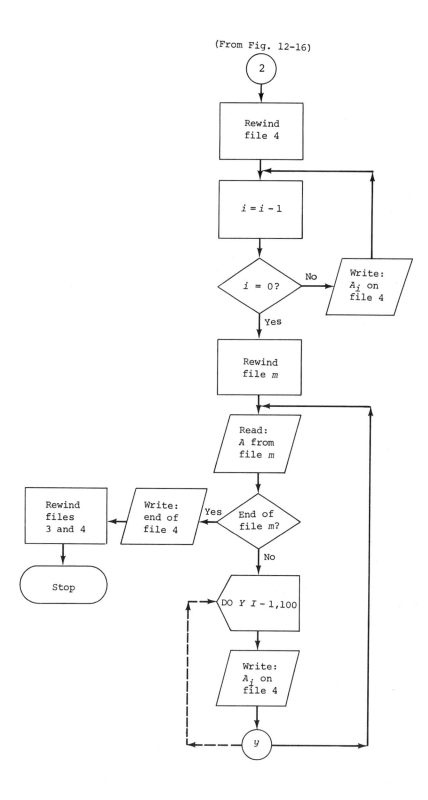

FIGURE 12-17

The complete FORTRAN program is:

```
        DIMENSION A(100)
C       M IS THE INPUT INTERMEDIATE FILE
C       N IS THE OUTPUT INTERMEDIATE FILE
        M = 5
        N = 6
        REWIND 3
        ENDFILE M
   10   DO 20 I = 1, 100
        READ (3, 15) A(I)
   15   FORMAT (F12.4)
        IF (EOF(3)) GO TO 100
   20   CONTINUE
C       IF ALL 100 VALUES HAVE BEEN READ, WRITE THEM
C       IN REVERSE ORDER ON FILE N
        REWIND N
        WRITE (N) (A(101 - I), I = 1, 100)
C       COPY FILE M ONTO FILE N
        REWIND M
   30   READ (M) A
        IF (EOF(M)) GO TO 40
        WRITE (N) A
        GO TO 30
C       WRITE END OF FILE ON N
C       INTERCHANGE VALUES OF M AND N
   40   ENDFILE N
        L = N
        N = M
        M = L
        GO TO 10
C       WRITE LEFTOVER VALUES ON FILE 4 IN REVERSE ORDER
  100   REWIND 4
  110   I = I - 1
        IF(I .EQ. 0) GO TO 120
        WRITE (4, 15) A(I)
        GO TO 110
C       COPY FILE M ONTO FILE 4
  120   REWIND M
  130   READ (M) A
        IF (EOF(M)) GO TO 200
        WRITE (4, 135) A
  135   FORMAT (100(F12.4/))
        GO TO 130
C       AT END OF FILE M, REWIND FILES AND STOP
  200   ENDFILE 4
        REWIND 4
        REWIND 3
        STOP
        END
```

Example 5

During registration at a certain school, three cards are prepared for each student: a name card, an address card, and a degree card. The format of each of these cards is given below.

NAME CARDS	
Columns	Item
1-5	Matric number
6-25	Last name
26-40	First name
41	Middle initial
42-79	Blank
80	"N"
ADDRESS CARDS	
Columns	Item
1-5	Matric number
6-25	First line of address
26-45	Second line of address
46-65	Third line of address
66-79	Blank
80	"A"
DEGREE CARDS	
Columns	Item
1-5	Matric number
6-10	Student's department
11-15	Degree sought
16-19	Graduation date
20-79	Blank
80	"D"

Each of these sets of cards is sorted on the matric number. We want to write a program that will create a master tape file for students by reading all three sets of cards and merging the information onto a tape file in the following format:

TAPE FILE	
Characters	Item
1-5	Matric number
6-25	Last name
26-40	First name
41	Middle initial
42-61	First line of address
62-81	Second line of address
82-101	Third line of address
102-106	Student's department
107-111	Degree sought
112-115	Graduation date

The basic idea of the program is to merge the three cards for each student. However, the input cards are in three different sets, so in order to merge them, we first have to read them in and create three separate files. These will be disk files 5, 6, and 7. In order to separate the three sets of cards, we shall put a blank card after each set of cards, then we shall arrange the sets as shown in Figure 12-18, with the name cards first, then the address cards, then the degree cards.

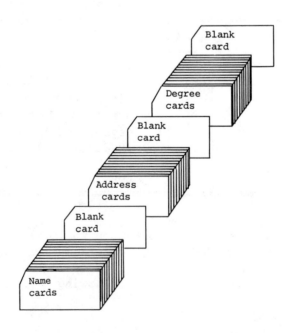

FIGURE 12-18

338

The first part of the program will be concerned merely
with copying the three decks of cards onto the three disk files.
After this is done, the program will rewind the disk files and
read them in again to merge them into the master file. The
files used by the program are shown in Figure 12-19.

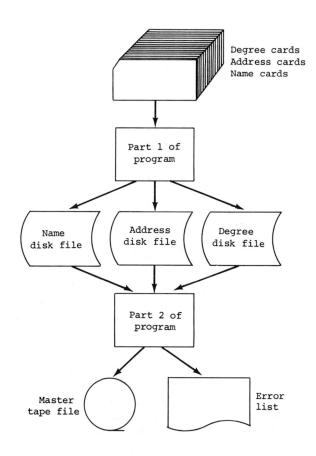

Degree cards
Address cards
Name cards

Part 1 of
program

Name
disk file

Address
disk file

Degree
disk file

Part 2 of
program

Master
tape file

Error
list

FIGURE 12-19

While in the process of creating the disk files, we shall
check the input cards to make sure that they are in the right
order. We can perform two checks on the cards. The first is to
see that column 80 contains an N, A, or D. When reading the name
cards, we shall read column 80 into a variable called N80. This
is read with an A1 format. If we set NN = 1HN, then the statement

339

will cause the program to go to 25 only if column 80 contains an N. If not, we shall print a message saying INPUT ERROR ON N CARDS, then stop, since there is no use continuing if the input data are wrong. The other thing we can do is to check that the cards are sorted as they should be. To do this, we use a variable called MPREV to represent the previous matric number read. If the matric number MAT is not greater than the previous matric number MPREV, the name cards are out of order, so we print a message saying N CARDS OUT OF SEQUENCE, and stop. Similar procedures are used when reading the address and degree cards. The flowchart for this part of the program is shown in Figure 12-20.

After the disk files 5, 6, and 7 are created, they are rewound for use in the second part of the program. The basic idea of this part of the program is to read one record from each disk file, and merge the three records into one record on the output tape. One thing we must consider, however, is the possibility that a student might be missing one or more cards. He might, for instance, have a name card, but no address or degree card. To account for this possibility, we shall test the matric numbers read to see if they are all the same. If one of them is less than the others, we shall print a message to indicate there is no match for the card with the lowest number, then we shall read another record from that file. No record will be written on the output tape for the student unless we have all three cards for him. The output from the program will consist of two files: the tape file, for students whose records are complete; and a printed file telling which students are missing cards.

To program this part of the job, we shall read the matric numbers from disk files 5, 6, and 7 into variables M5, M6, and M7, respectively. After each read operation, we shall set a variable called MAX equal to the maximum value of M5, M6, and M7. This can be done using the standard function MAX0 (see Chapter 8). If M5 is less than MAX, we shall know that either an address or a degree card is missing for the student with matric number M5. We print a message to this effect, then read another record from File 5. Similar tests are made to see if M6 or M7 is less than MAX. The flowchart for this part of the program is shown in Figure 12-21.

When an end is reached on one of the disk files, the other disk files should also be at the end. Suppose, however, that the last record on the name file has no matching address or degree record. We still want to print out the message saying that the name record is unmatched. So, when the end of any file is reached,

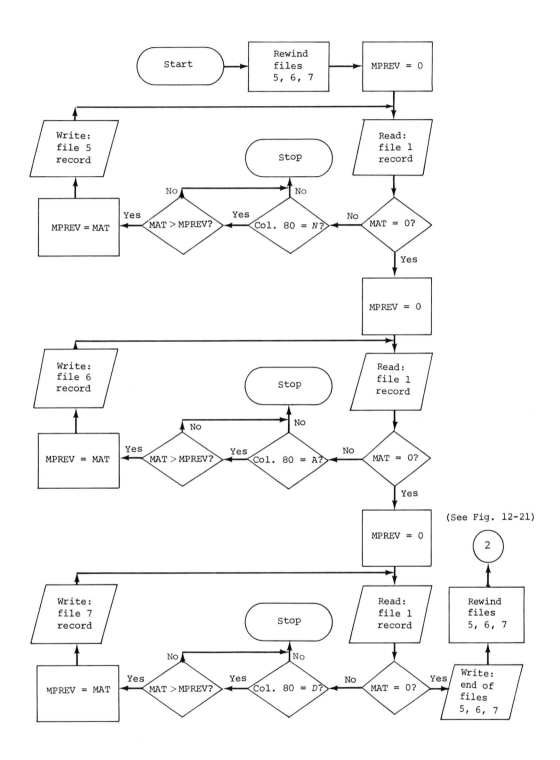

FIGURE 12-20

341

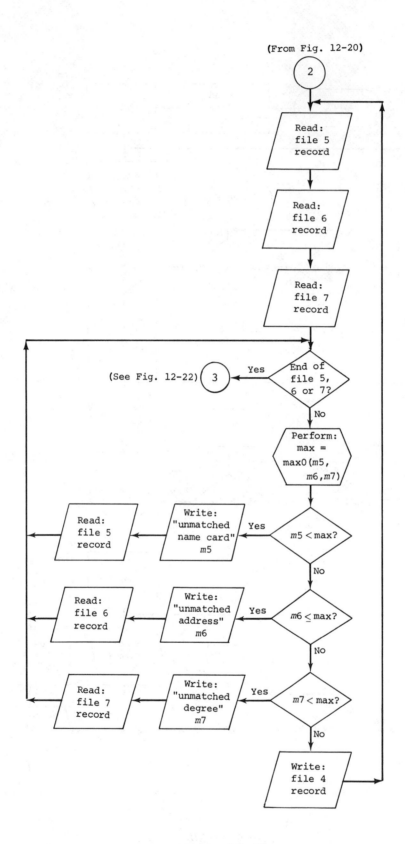

FIGURE 12-21

we test each of the other files to see if there are any records
left on them, and if there are, we print an error message for
each record left to indicate that it was unmatched. After this,
we can write an end-of-file mark on the output tape and rewind
it. This last part of the program is illustrated in the flowchart
of Figure 12-22.

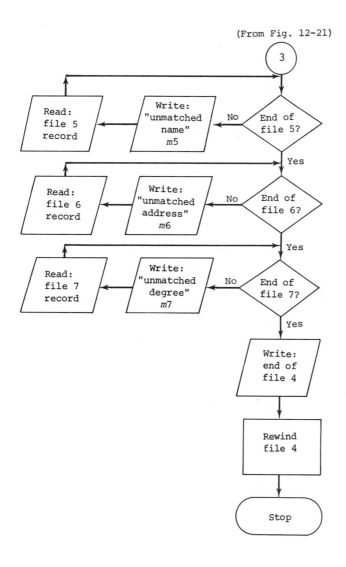

FIGURE 12-22

To read and write data on the three disk files used in the program, we can use the unformatted READ and WRITE statements. For example, a name card can be read with the statements

```
        READ (1, 15) MAT, NAME, N80
    15  FORMAT (I5, 3A10, A5, A1, 38X, A1)
```

where NAME is an array consisting of five elements. The first two elements contain the last name, the second two contain the first name, and the fifth contains the middle initial. To store the matric number and name on disk file 5, we can simply use the statement

```
        WRITE (5) MAT, NAME
```

This will write a record consisting of a string of six values: one for MAT, and five for the array NAME. These values will be reread in the second part of the program with the statement

```
        READ (5) M5, NAME
```

which will read the matric number into the variable M5, and the name back into the array NAME.

The complete FORTRAN program for this example is:

```
C        PROGRAM TO CREATE STUDENT MASTER TAPE
         DIMENSION NAME(5), ADDR(6), DEG(3)
         NA = 1HA
         NN = 1HN
         ND = 1HD
C        REWIND DISK FILES
         REWIND 5
         REWIND 6
         REWIND 7
         MPREV = 0
C        COPY NAME CARDS ONTO DISK FILE 5
    10   READ (1, 15) MAT, NAME, N80
    15   FORMAT (I5, 3A10, A5, A1, 38X, A1)
         IF (MAT .EQ. 0) GO TO 40
C        CHECK SEQUENCE AND COLUMN 80
         IF (N80 .EQ. NN) GO TO 25
         WRITE (2, 20)
    20   FORMAT (23H INPUT ERROR ON N CARDS)
         STOP
    25   IF (MAT .GT. MPREV) GO TO 35
         WRITE (2, 30)
    30   FORMAT (24H N CARDS OUT OF SEQUENCE)
         STOP
```

```
      35  WRITE (5) MAT, NAME
          GO TO 10
C         COPY ADDRESS CARDS TO DISK FILE 6
      40  MPREV = 0
      45  READ (1, 50) MAT, ADDR, N80
      50  FORMAT (I5, 6A10, 14X, A1)
          IF (MAT .EQ. 0) GO TO 75
C         CHECK SEQUENCE AND COLUMN 80
          IF (N80 .EQ. NA) GO TO 60
          WRITE (2, 55)
      55  FORMAT (23H INPUT ERROR ON A CARDS)
          STOP
      60  IF (MAT .GT. MPREV) GO TO 70
          WRITE (2, 65)
      65  FORMAT (24H A CARDS OUT OF SEQUENCE)
          STOP
      70  WRITE (6) MAT, ADDR
          GO TO 45
C         COPY D CARDS TO DISK FILE 7
      75  MPREV = 0
      80  READ (1, 85) MAT, DEG, N80
      85  FORMAT (I5, 2A5, A4, 60X, A1)
          IF (MAT .EQ. 0) GO TO 110
C         CHECK SEQUENCE AND COLUMN 80
          IF (N80 .EQ. ND) GO TO 95
          WRITE (2, 90)
      90  FORMAT (23H INPUT ERROR ON D CARDS)
          STOP
      95  IF (MAT .GT. MPREV) GO TO 105
          WRITE (2, 100)
     100  FORMAT (24H D CARDS OUT OF SEQUENCE)
          STOP
     105  WRITE (7) MAT, DEG
          GO TO 80
     110  ENDFILE 5
          ENDFILE 6
          ENDFILE 7
          REWIND 5
          REWIND 6
          REWIND 7
C         READ NAME, ADDRESS, AND DEGREE RECORD
     120  READ (5) M5, NAME
          READ (6) M6, ADDR
          READ (7) M7, DEG
     125  IF (EOF (5) .OR. EOF(6) .OR. EOF(7)) GO TO 900
          MAX = MAX0(M5, M6, M7)
C         IF M5 IS LESS THAN MAX, THERE IS A NAME CARD WITH
C         NO ADDRESS OR DEGREE CARD
          IF (M5 .EQ. MAX) GO TO 135
          WRITE (2, 130) M5
```

```
      130   FORMAT (17H UNMATCHED N CARD, I6)
            READ (5) M5, NAME
            GO TO 125
C           IF M6 IS LESS THAN MAX, THERE IS AN ADDRESS CARD
C           WITH NO NAME OR NO DEGREE CARD
      135   IF (M6 .EQ. MAX) GO TO 145
            WRITE (2, 140) M6
      140   FORMAT (17H UNMATCHED A CARD, I6)
            READ (6) M6, ADDR
            GO TO 125
C           IF M7 IS LESS THAN MAX, THERE IS A DEGREE CARD
C           WITH NO NAME OR NO ADDRESS CARD
      145   IF (M7 .EQ. MAX) GO TO 155
            WRITE (2, 150) M7
      150   FORMAT (17H UNMATCHED D CARD, I6)
            READ (7) M7, DEG
            GO TO 125
C           WRITE OUTPUT TAPE RECORD
      155   WRITE (4, 160) M5, NAME, ADDR, DEG
      160   FORMAT (I5, 3A10, A5, A1, 6A10, 2A5, A4)
            GO TO 120
C           AT END OF ANY INPUT FILE, ALL RECORDS LEFT
C           ON THE OTHER FILES ARE UNMATCHED
      900   IF (EOF(5)) GO TO 905
            WRITE (2, 130) M5
            READ (5) M5, NAME
            GO TO 900
      905   IF (EOF(6)) GO TO 910
            WRITE (2, 140) M6
            READ (6) M6, ADDR
            GO TO 905
      910   IF (EOF(7)) GO TO 915
            WRITE (2, 150) M7
            READ (7) M7, DEG
            GO TO 910
C           END OF JOB
      915   ENDFILE 4
            REWIND 4
            STOP
            END
```

1. In Example 2, what would happen if we had a deletion card for which there was no corresponding tape record? Include statements to detect this possibility and print an error message when it occurs.

2. In Example 2, what might happen if the correction cards were not in order? What might happen if the master tape were not sorted in the proper order? Include statements to detect these possibilities and print error messages if they occur.

3. In Example 2, it is necessary to punch a whole new card to change any part of an employee's tape record. One way to make this easier is to write the program so that any item that is blank on the correction card will be replaced by the corresponding item from the old master tape. This way, only the information that changes need be punched on the correction card; the other information is supplied automatically from the old tape. Write a flowchart and a program to do this.

4. Write a program to update the file of books checked out used in Example 3. Two kinds of input cards will be used, that is, one for books being checked out and one for books being returned. An input card for a book being checked out will have the format:

Columns	Data
1-5	Library card number of person to whom loaned
6-15	Call number of book
16-25	Author's last name
26-45	Title of book
46-51	Date due
52-80	Blank

An input card for a book being returned will have the format:

Columns	Data
1-5	Library card number of person to whom loaned
6-15	Call number of book
16-45	Blank
46-51	Date returned
52-79	Blank
80	"R"

4.—*continued*

Assume that the tape file of books checked out and the input cards are sorted on the library card number and the call number of the book.

5. Include statements in the program of Problem 4 to compute the total fines collected for books being returned. A fine of five cents per day is charged on each overdue book.

6. File 1 and File 2 are unformatted files giving weather observations on different days. Each record consists of the following values:

   Item 1   Date
   Item 2   Temperature
   Item 3   Barometric pressure
   Item 4   Wind velocity

   The files are sorted on the date. Write a program to merge these two files into an output tape called File 3, which is also sorted on the date.

7. Write a subroutine to compare two unformatted files, M and N, to make sure that they are identical. Assume that the records consist of L values. L, M, and N will be parameters in the subroutine list. If the files are identical, print a message to that effect. If some record on one file is different from the corresponding record on the other file, print an error message and stop.

Chapter 13

ADDITIONAL FORTRAN STATEMENTS

In this chapter, we shall cover some additional FORTRAN statements. Some versions of FORTRAN do not admit all of these statements; beginning students will probably not find too many occasions to use them. When they are available, however, they can be quite useful.

INTEGER *AND* REAL *STATEMENTS*

We have seen how the LOGICAL, COMPLEX, and DOUBLE PRECISION statements can be used to declare variable types. In the absence of such a statement, a variable is assumed to be either integer (fixed-point) or real (floating-point) type. FORTRAN determines whether a variable is integer or real by the first letter of the variable name. If we wish to depart from the usual naming convention for these types, we can use the INTEGER and REAL statements. The first of these has the form

INTEGER $name_1$, $name_2$, $\cdots$, $name_n$

All the variables named in the list will be treated as integer variables throughout the program. For instance, if a program contains the statement

INTEGER A, B, C

then the variables A, B, and C will be used as integer variables in the program, although they would normally be real variables. Similarly, the statement

REAL $name_1$, $name_2$, $\cdots$, $name_n$

would cause the variables named to be treated as real variables throughout the program, regardless of the usual naming conventions.

As with other type declaration statements, these statements, if used, must come at the beginning of the program. They may also give dimension information. For instance, the statement

REAL I(10, 5)

would cause I to be set up as a 10×5 real array in the program.

THE EQUIVALENCE *STATEMENT*

The EQUIVALENCE statement permits us to use two different names for the same variables in a program. This statement has the form

EQUIVALENCE (name$_1$, name$_2$, $\cdots$, name$_n$), ($\cdots$), ($\cdots$)

where each set of parentheses encloses a list of variable names. All the names enclosed in each set of parentheses will refer to a single variable in the program.

For example, the statement

EQUIVALENCE (A, B), (I, J)

would cause the names A and B to refer to the same variable. I would also refer to the same variable as J.

Array names cannot be equivalenced by this statement, but array elements can. If X is an array, the statement

EQUIVALENCE (X(1), FIRST)

would allow us to use the names X(1) and FIRST interchangeably in a program.

THE LABELED COMMON *STATEMENT*

This statement is just an extension of the regular COMMON statements. Instead of having just one block of common storage, we can have several such blocks, by using this form. The form is

COMMON /X_1/a_1/X_2/a_2 $\cdots$ /X_n/a_n

Here each *X* is the name of a common block, while each *a* is the list of variables to be placed in the common block. For example, suppose a main program uses two subroutines ALPHA and BETA. We want the variables I, J, and K to be stored in common storage between the main program and the subroutine BETA. To do this, we place I, J, and K in a common block called BLK1, and we place X in a common block called BLK2. The labeled common statement in the main program would be

COMMON/BLK1/I, J, K/BLK2/X

Then, in subroutine ALPHA, we would use the statement

COMMON/BLK1/I, J, K

For subroutine BETA, we would use the statement

COMMON/BLK2/X

This way, the two subroutines do not share any storage in common with each other, but each shares common storage with the main program.

THE COMPUTED GO TO *STATEMENTS*

The computed GO TO statements can be used to replace a series of IF statements. The form of the statement is

$$GO\ TO\ (k_1,\ k_2,\ \cdots,\ k_n),\ I$$

where k_1, k_2, $\cdots$, k_n are statement numbers and I is any integer variable name. When this statement is executed, if I = 1, the program will go to Statement k_1. If I = 2, the program will go to Statement k_2, and so on. If I is less than 1, control transfers to Statement k_1 and if I is greater than n, control transfers to Statement k_n. On some computer systems, the comma is optional. As an example, Figure 13-1 shows a flowchart for the statement

GO TO (5, 10, 5, 20), I

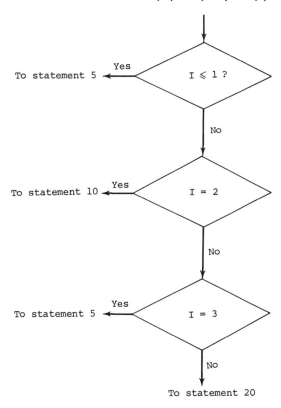

FIGURE 13-1

351

The statement

        GO TO (10, 11, 12, 25, 50), NOD

will make the program go to Statement 11 if NOD = 2. If NOD = 4,
it will act like the statement GO TO 25. For NOD = 7, the statement does the same as for NOD = 5; it will act like GO TO 50.

The following statements will write out one, two, and three
values, depending on whether N is 1, 2, or 3.

```
          GO TO (5, 10, 15), N
     5    WRITE (2, 105) X
          GO TO 100
    10    WRITE (2, 110) X, Y
          GO TO 100
    15    WRITE (2, 115) X, Y, Z
   100    CONTINUE
```

THE ASSIGNED GO TO STATEMENT

The assigned GO TO is a GO TO statement with a variable
statement number. The form of the statement is

        GO TO i, $(k_1, k_2, \cdots, k_n)$

where i is an integer variable, and $k_1, k_2, \cdots, k_n$ are statement
numbers. Before executing this statement, we must use an ASSIGN
statement to assign a statement number to the variable I. The
ASSIGN statement has the form

        ASSIGN k TO i

where k is the statement number and i is the integer variable.
The statement number which is assigned to i must be one of the
statement numbers $k_1, k_2, \cdots, k_n$ in the list of the assigned
GO TO. The statement

        GO TO i, $(k_1, k_2, \cdots k_n)$

will then cause the program to branch to the statement number.

For example, the statements

        ASSIGN 100 to IVY
        GO TO IVY, (10, 15, 100)

would cause the assigned GO TO statement to act just like the
statement GO TO 100. The other numbers 10 and 15 which appear
in the list are the other possible statement numbers which we

352

might want to branch to. Whenever we execute the statement

GO TO IVY, (10, 15, 100)

we must first execute one of the statements

ASSIGN 10 TO IVY
ASSIGN 15 TO IVY
ASSIGN 100 TO IVY

THE STOP *n* *AND* PAUSE *n* *STATEMENTS*

An alternate form of the STOP statement is the statement

STOP *n*

where *n* is an octal number of four or fewer digits. An octal number is a number in base 8. For the purpose of this statement, it is just a number that does not contain the digits 8 or 9. So, 1125 is correct but 93 is not, since it contains the digit 9.

The STOP *n* statement does exactly the same thing as a STOP statement. The only difference is that the number *n* will be displayed on the program listing when the STOP *n* statement is executed. If the program uses several STOP *n* statements with different values of *n*, this allows the programmer to determine where the program stopped. For instance, suppose we are dividing Y by X to give A. X should never be zero, but just in case, we might include the statement

IF (X .EQ. 0.0) STOP 3

If X were, in fact, equal to zero, the number 3 would be displayed in the output and we would be able to go back and find the trouble in the program.

The PAUSE and PAUSE *n* statements do almost the same thing as the STOP and STOP *n* statements. The difference is that the computer operator can restart the program manually. Suppose that in some program we want the computer operator to mount a magnetic tape on unit 3. We then want to read this tape. The program might include the statements

```
      WRITE (2, 25)
   25 FORMAT (13H MOUNT TAPE 3)
      PAUSE
      READ (3, 30) X
```

When the PAUSE statement is executed, the program will pause and wait for the operator to take some manual action. When the operator restarts the program, the next statement (the READ statement in this case) is performed.

READING INTO AN H FIELD

Normally, an H field in FORTRAN is used only for output. The statements

```
        WRITE (2, 5)
    5   FORMAT (8H HEADING)
```

would print the eight characters bHEADING. We may also read into an existing H field. When the field nH is used with a READ statement, the next n characters are read into the H field. For example, the statement

```
    5   FORMAT (20H                    )
```

sets up an H field consisting of 20 blanks. The statement

```
        READ (1, 5)
```

would read the next 20 characters from unit 1 into the existing H field in the FORMAT statement. Those characters would replace the blanks. For instance, if the program contains the statements

```
        READ (1, 10)
    10  FORMAT (5H12345)
        WRITE (2, 10)
```

then if their input card contains the characters ABCDE, these characters would replace the H field 12345. The WRITE statement would then write out the characters ABCDE, just as though the format statement had been written as FORMAT (5HABCDE).

EXTERNAL STATEMENT

In Chapter 8, the parameter list used to call a function or subroutine subprogram consisted only of variables. It is possible to include a function or subroutine name in this list by use of the EXTERNAL statement. The general form of this is

$$\text{EXTERNAL name}_1, \text{ name}_2, \cdots$$

where each name is the name of a subprogram. This is placed in the main program directly *before* the first statement which calls a function or a subroutine subprogram. For example,

Main Program	Subprogram
	SUBROUTINE TEST (A,B,C,D,E)
.	.
.	.
EXTERNAL SIN, COS	E = A(C) + B(D)
	.
	.
CALL TEST (SIN,COS,ALPHA,BETA,SUM)	RETURN
.	END
.	

The subroutine calculates the sine of angle alpha plus the cosine of angle beta. Alternately, the same operation could have been done without an EXTERNAL statement:

Main Program	Subprogram
	SUBROUTINE (X, Y, Z)
.	.
.	.
CALL TEST (SIN(A), COS(B), SUM)	Z = X + Y
.	RETURN
.	END

ENTRY *STATEMENT*

When a subprogram is called by either the main program or another subprogram, the first statement executed is the first executable one encountered. The ENTRY statement allows one to call a function or subroutine subprogram and begin execution at any desired entry point. This entry point is given a variable name, and the associated statement has the form

ENTRY name

where name specifies the entry point. It does not have an associated statement number and may appear anywhere within the subprogram.

For use with a subroutine subprogram, it has an associated CALL statement. For example,

```
     Main Program                          Subprogram

                                           SUBROUTINE ADD

                 .                                    .
                 .                                    .
     CALL ADD                              ENTRY HERE
                 .                                    .
                 .                                    .
     CALL HERE                             RETURN
                 .                         END
                 .

     END
```

The first time the subroutine ADD is called by CALL ADD,
execution begins with the first executable statement after the
SUBROUTINE ADD, but the next time it is entered by CALL HERE.
This time execution begins with the statement following the
ENTRY HERE statement.

The ENTRY statement can be used with dummy arguments.
The CALL statement and the corresponding ENTRY statement must
have the same number, order, and mode of these dummy arguments.

An example of this would be:

```
     Main Program                          Subprogram

                                           SUBROUTINE TEST(X,Y,Z,P,I,J)

                 .                                    .
                 .                                    .
     CALL ENTER1(SUM, DIFF, MAX)
                 .                         ENTRY ENTER1(X,Z,J)
                 .                                    .
     END                                             .

                                           RETURN
                                           END
```

The subroutine TEST is entered at ENTRY ENTER1(X,Z,J).

G FIELD DESCRIPTOR INPUT-OUTPUT

Another field descriptor that can be used for inputting or
outputting floating-point numbers is the G field descriptor.
This is actually not a separate field but acts to convert the
number to either the F or E field. Although not commonly used,
it can prove to be quite handy, especially when the programmer
is not certain of the magnitude of the numbers.

356

Used for input, the form is

$Gn.m$

and acts in a manner similar to the $Fn.m$ field specification.
Data are input, and stored exactly the same as if the F field
was used. The rules covered in Chapter 4 hold and will not be
repeated here. It is when used to output data that the G field
descriptor acts in a different manner.

The form for the output is

$Gn.m$

When used in a format statement, the data to be output will be
converted to either F field or E field. First, the conversion
to the F field is attempted. The conversion to F field is subject to certain rules that apply to both the specification
numbers n and m. The first is that the data are to be output
with four blanks in the field, right justified. This has the
effect of always reducing the actual field width as given by n
in $Gn.m$ to $n - 4$. For example, the 7 in G7.1 is converted to a
3 as in F3.1. The specification number m also is converted.
This is done, depending on the magnitude of the number. If the
magnitude, M, is $0.1 \leq M < 1$, the m in $Gn.m$ converts directly to
$Fn.m$; if the magnitude is $1 \leq M < 100$, the m converts to $m - 1$;
for magnitudes $100 \leq M < 1000$, the m converts to $m - 2$, and so
on. A few examples of these conversions are given below.

Magnitude M	Conversion to F Field	Example
$0.1 \leq M < 1$	$F(n-4).n,bbbb$	For: X = 0.12 under G10.3 outputs as b0.120bbbb
$1 \leq M < 10$	$F(n-4).n-1,bbbb$	X = 1.2345 under G10.3 outputs as bb1.23bbbb
$10 \leq M < 100$	$F(n-4).n-2,bbbb$	X = 12.345 under G10.3 outputs as bb12.3bbbb
$100 \leq M < 1000$	$F(n-4).(n-3),bbbb$	X = 123.456 under G10.3 outputs as bbb123bbbb
$\vdots$	$\vdots$	

If the above conversion cannot be done for any reason such
as the field being too small to contain the data (or, equivalently,
if the data are too large for the field), the data are output under
the E conversion. In this case, the data are output according to
the rules given in Chapter 4. Thus, unlike conversion to the F
field, four blanks are *not* inserted into the field.

Suppose, for example, TEST contains 12345.67.   The statements

                    WRITE (2, 50) TEST, TEST
            50   FORMAT (1X, G10.3/,1X, G10.4)

result in

                    bbb1.235E+04
                    b1.2345E+04

but

                    WRITE (2, 50) TEST
            50   FORMAT (1X, G12.6)

result in

                    bb12345.7bbbb

since conversion can occur.

THE P SCALE FACTOR

    It is possible to have the D, E, and F fields as well as the
G conversion field preceded by a scale factor. This scale factor,
n, is a fixed-point constant. It can be written with or without
a plus or minus sign, but it must be in the range $-8 \le n \le 8$.
This scale factor appears in the format statement followed by the
letter P and then the appropriate D, E, F, or G specification.
Samples of it as used in format statements are:

                    FORMAT (6PF8.2)
                    FORMAT (8PF20.4, 2PE10.3, 0PF10.2)
                    FORMAT (-3PE20.2, 1PG8.3)
                    FORMAT (-2PF6.1, E10.3, 0PF6.5)

    Input—F or G Field. When a scale factor is used with the F
field specification, it has a special definition. The scale
factor acts as follows.

$10^{-n} \cdot$ (actual external quantity) = (actual quantity stored)

    Example

Assume X punched on a card as 1234.56 in columns 1-10. Then

                    READ (1, 100) X
            100   FORMAT (1PF10.2)

stores X as 123.456 ($1234.56 \cdot 10^{-1}$).

358

```
           READ (1, 101) X
    102    FORMAT (0PF10.1)
```

stores X as 1234.56, the same as if the format statement had been

```
    FORMAT (F10.1)
```

When one uses a scale factor, either for input or output, the following is very important to remember: *Once a scale factor is encountered in a format statement, it holds for all subsequent field specifications.* Thus,

```
    FORMAT (F10.2, 1PF10.3, F12.6, I2)
```

is the same as

```
    FORMAT (F10.2, 1PF10.3, 1PF12.6, I2)
```

To write the above format and not have the F12.6 specification scaled, we must do the following

```
    FORMAT (F10.2, 1PF10.3, 0PF12.6, I2)
```

The scaling for the G conversion for input is the same as the F scaling.

E and D Fields—Input. Some computers will allow scale factors with D and E field specifications for input. In this case, they are ignored and the input data are stored under the E and D field specifications.

F Fields—Output. When a scale factor is used with the F field specification for output, the scaling is done as follows:

(actual output quantity) = (stored quantity) $\times 10^{+n}$

In the actual representation, the decimal point remains fixed and the number moves either right or left.

Example

For TEST stored as 1.2345, the statements

```
        WRITE (2, 20) X
        WRITE (2, 21) X
        WRITE (2, 22) X
        WRITE (2, 23) X
        WRITE (2, 24) X
    20  FORMAT (F10.2)
    21  FORMAT (1PF10.2)
```

359

```
22   FORMAT (2PF10.2)
23   FORMAT (3PF10.2)
24   FORMAT (-1PF10.2)
```

result in the output

```
   1.23
  12.35
 123.45
1234.50
    .12
```

E and D Fields—Output. In practice, scale factors are
used mostly with the E field for output. This is because,
unlike the F field, the number is not changed in value. As
used with the E field, a positive scale factor has the effect
of shifting the decimal in the output number to the right *n*
places and reducing the exponent by *n*. A negative scale factor
shifts the decimal to the left *n* places but raises the exponent
by *n*. The actual representation of the output keeps the decimal
point fixed and shifts the number to the left or right.

Example

For X stored as 123.45, the statements

```
       WRITE (2, 500) X
       WRITE (2, 501) X
       WRITE (2, 502) X
       WRITE (2, 503) X
  500  FORMAT (E10.2)
  501  FORMAT (1PE10.2)
  502  FORMAT (2PE10.2)
  503  FORMAT (-1PE10.2)
```

will result in X being output as

```
  1.23E+02
 12.35E+01
123.45E+00
   .12E+03
```

When the scale factor is used with the D field, the effect is the
same as with the E field.

G Field—Output. When used with the G field, the effect of
a scale factor will depend on the particular computer. In some,
the G output makes use of the scale factor only if E conversion
is made.

```
```

ANSWERS
and
INDEX

ANSWERS

1. When $I = 1$, Y is 12, but if I is 2, there is an infinite loop. One way to guard against this is to test $Y \geq 12$.

3.

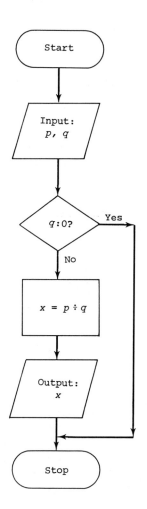

5.

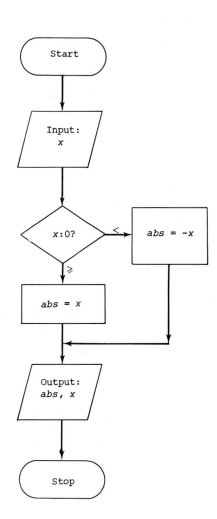

7.

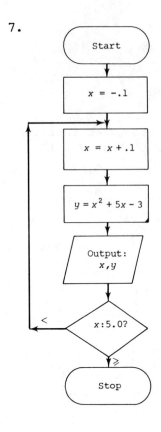

9.

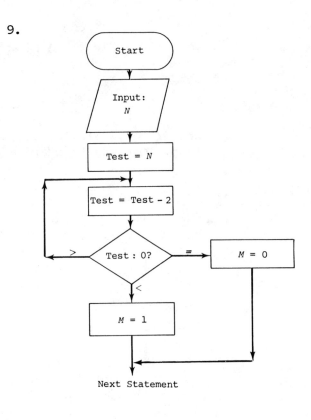

EXERCISES 1B

1.

3.

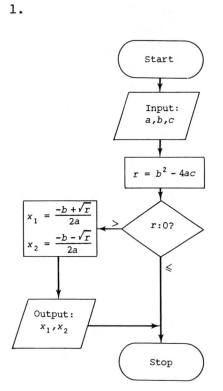

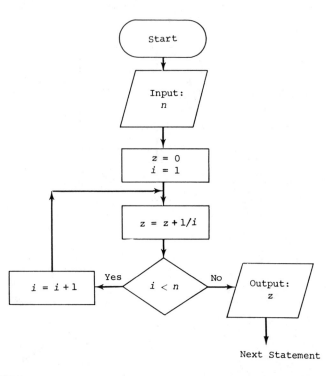

364

5.

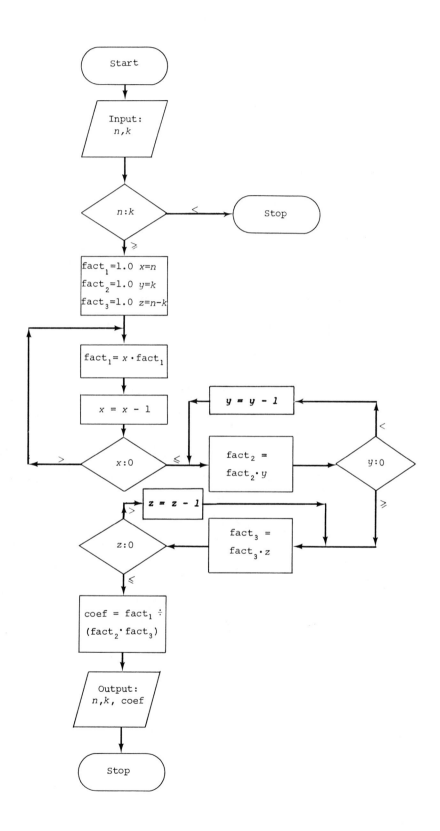

365

7.

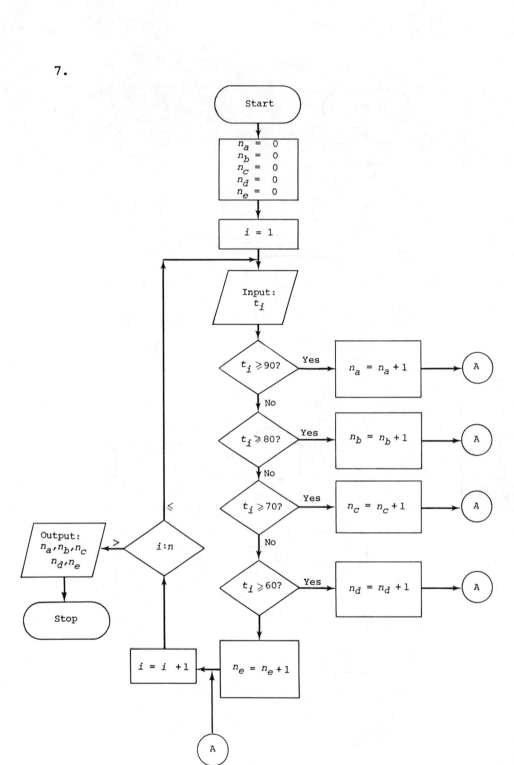

1.	6.2E00	3. 4.36E-05	5. 1.0E-09
7.	2.E02	9. 3.E08	11. .01
13.	1.0	15. 1010.0	17. .001
19.	1,000,000.	21. Valid fixed-point variable.	

23. Invalid: does not start with a letter.
25. Invalid: too many characters.
27. Valid floating-point variable.
29. Invalid: has a character other than letter or number.
31. Invalid: has a character other than letter or number.
33. Valid floating-point variable.
35. Valid fixed-point variable.
37. Valid floating-point variable.
39. Invalid: has a character other than letter or number.

41. $\dfrac{a^b}{c}$ 43. $\dfrac{ab}{c}$ 45. $a + \dfrac{b}{c}$ 47. $a^b c$ 49. $\dfrac{2^{2x}}{x^2}$

51. A = R ** 2   53. R = 1./(1./R1 + 1./R2 + 1./R3)
55. V = (X ** 2 + Y ** 2) ** .5   57. AINP = X1 * Y1 + X2 * Y2 + X3 * Y3
59. G = D/(B + C/(D + E/F))   61. Valid
63. Invalid: must have a variable on left side of equals sign.
65. Valid   67. Valid
69. Invalid: variable name contains too many characters.
71. Invalid: variable name contains a symbol.
73. Invalid: mixed-mode division. 75. Valid
77. Invalid: mixed-mode   79. Valid
81. -1.0   83. -7.0   85. .25   87. 20.0   89. 9.0
91. 0   93. 8   95. 0   97. 1   99. 6
101. N = N + 2   103. X = 4.0 * (W3 - W4) - (W1 - W2)
105. K4B = K4B + 6   107. TOP = C1 * D - B * C2
                           BOT = C1 * C4 - C2 * C3
                              X = TOP/BOT

109. R = A + B + C
     S = 1.0/A + 1.0/B + 1.0/C
     C = R/S

1. $c = \dfrac{x}{\sqrt{x^2 + y^2 + z^2}}$ 3. $a = b + \dfrac{c}{d + \dfrac{e}{f}}$

5. $a = 4.7\left(\dfrac{x_2 - x_1}{2}\right)^2 - 6\left(\dfrac{x_2 - x_1}{2}\right)$

7. S = -B + (B ** 2 - 4.0 * A * C) ** .5
   X = S/(2.0 * A)

9. FIRST = 4./3. * ((X - Y)/(Z - W)) ** E
    SECOND = ((A - B)/(C - D)) ** F
     THIRD = (P ** 2 * (R - S)) ** (1./3.)
         G = FIRST * SECOND/THIRD

EXERCISES 3A

1. IF (X - Y) 10, 20, 20
3. IF (B ** 2 - 4. * A * C) 99, 50, 100
5. IF ((4. * X + 7.) -10.) 10, 20, 30
7. IF (X - (Y - 3.0) ** 3) 1, 4, 5
9. IF (R - P/Q) 999, 1, 999

11.

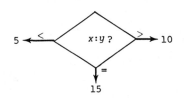

13.

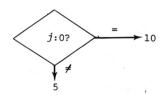

15.

17.

19.

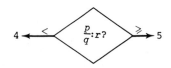

21. $x < 9$ transfer to 10; $x = 9$ transfer to 20, $x > 9$ transfer to 30
23. $x < -6$ transfer to 10; $x = -6$ transfer to 20, $x > -6$ transfer to 30
25. $x < 1$ transfer to 30; $x = 1$ transfer to 20, $x > 1$ transfer to 10
27. $x < 0$ transfer to 30; $x = 0$ transfer to 20;
     $0 < x < 2$ transfer to 10; $x = 2$ transfer to 20; $x > 2$ transfer to 30

29. $x = 0$ transfer to 20; transfer to 10 for any other value

31.   IF (M − N) 5, 20, 20   33.   IF (P/Q − (X + 1.0)) 1, 102, 2
     5 IF (M − 5) 30, 30, 40   1 IF (P/Q − (X − 1.0)) 100,100,101
                                          2 IF (P/Q − Y) 100,100,102

35.

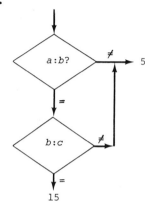

37.

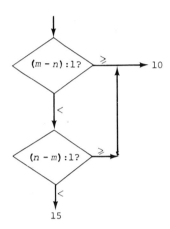

39.

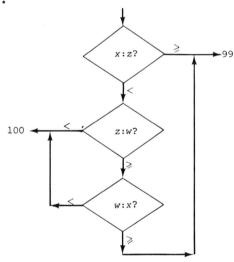

1. See Exercise 1A, Problem 9, for the flowchart.

```
       M = I - I/2 * 2
       IF (M) 5, 10, 5
   5   J = 1
       GO TO 15
  10   J = 0
  15   Next statement
```

3.

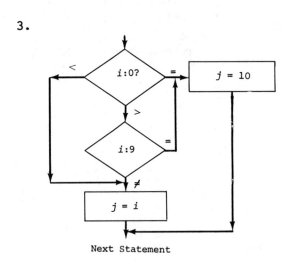

Next Statement

```
       IF (I) 1, 2, 3
   2   J = 10
       GO TO 100
   3   IF (I - 9) 1, 2, 1
   1   J = I
 100   Next statement
```

5.

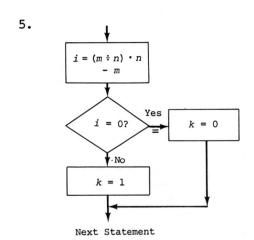

Next Statement

```
       I = (M/N) * N - M
       IF (I) 1, 2, 1
   2   K = 0
       GO TO 3
   1   K = 1
   3   Next statement
```

7. 10 (makes no difference)

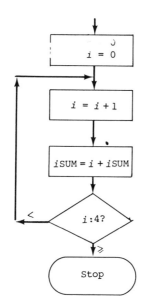
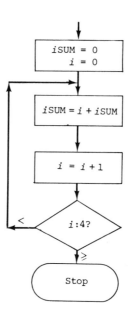

9.

```
C        SET EACH POLYNOMIAL EQUAL TO ZERO
C        THEN LATER WE CAN OUTPUT EVERY ONE
         P0 = 0
         P1 = 0
         P2 = 0
         P3 = 0
         P4 = 0
         P5 = 0
         IF (N) 1, 1, 2
   1     P0 = 1
         GO TO 99
   2     IF (N - 1) 3, 3, 4
   3     P1 = X
         GO TO 99
   4     IF (N - 2) 5, 5, 6
   5     P2 = 1./2.*(3.* X ** 2 - 1.0)
         GO TO 99
   6     IF (N - 3) 7, 7, 8
   7     P3 = 1./2.*(5.* X ** 3 - 3.)
         GO TO 99
   8     IF (N - 4) 9, 9, 10
   9     P4 = 1./8.*(35.* X ** 4 - 30.* X +3.)
         GO TO 99
  10     P5 = 1./8.*(63.* X ** 5 - 70.* X** 3 +15.* X)
  99     Next statement
```

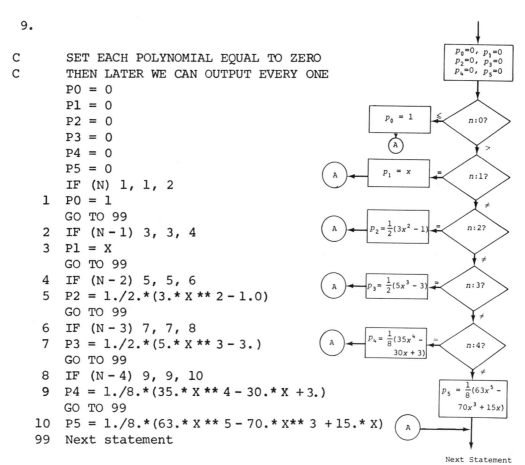

371

11.

```
C       ASSUME N INPUT
C       SEE FLOWCHART, PAGE 18, CHAPTER 1
C       FOR INPUT AND OUTPUT WE USE COMMENT CARDS
C       IN CHAPTER 4 WE LEARN THE FORTRAN TO DO THIS
        SUM = 0
        I = 0
    1   I = I + 1
C       INPUT X
        SUM = SUM + X
        IF (I - N) 1, 2, 2
    2   XN = N
        AV = SUM/XN
C       OUTPUT AV
        STOP
        END
```

13.

```
C       INPUT N, THE NUMBER OF CHECKS
        XN = N
        IF (N - 5) 2, 2, 3
    3   IF (N - 10) 4, 4, 5
    5   IF (N - 15) 6, 6, 7
    2   TC = XN * .10
C       OUTPUT TC, N
        STOP
    4   TC = .50 + (XN - 5.)*.09
C       OUTPUT TC, N
        STOP
    6   TC = .95 + (XN - 10.)*.08
C       OUTPUT TC, N
        STOP
    7   TC = 1.35 + (XN - 15.)*.07
C       OUTPUT TC, N
        STOP
        END
```

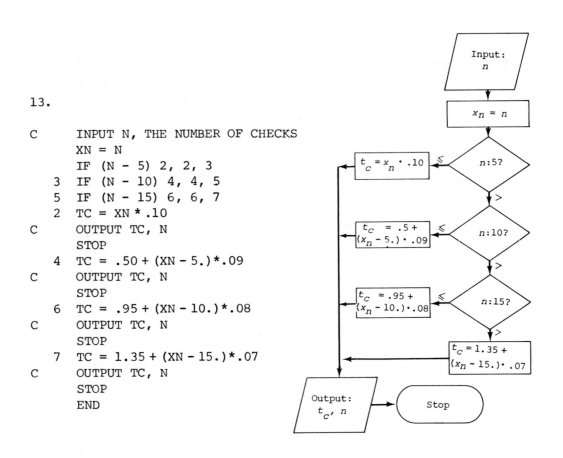

15.

```
      X = -2.0
      YMIN = -2.0 * X ** 2 + 4.0 * X - 2.0
      YMAX = YMIN
   6  X = X + .1
      Y = -2.0 * X ** 2 + 4.0 * X - 2.0
      IF (Y - YMAX) 3, 2, 2
   2  YMAX = Y
      GO TO 5
   3  IF (Y - YMIN) 4, 4, 5
   4  YMIN = Y
   5  IF (X - 2.0) 6, 7, 7
   7  Next statement
```

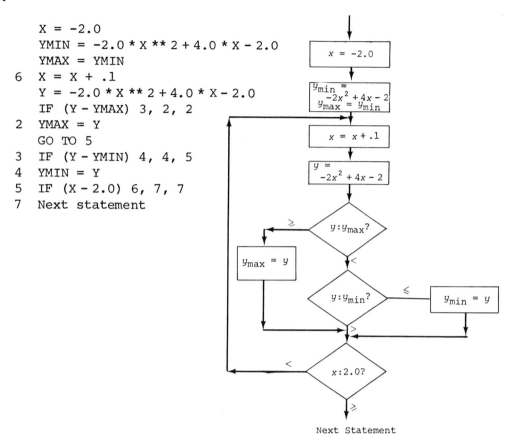

17.

```
C        INPUT A, B, C, D
C        LINES ARE SAME IF A = C AND B = D
C        LINES ARE PARALLEL IF A = C and B ≠ D
         IF (A - C) 1, 2, 1
   2     IF (B - D) 4, 3, 4
   4     N = -1
         GO TO 5
   3     N = 0
   5     X = 0.0
         Y = 0.0
         GO TO 99
   1     X = (D - B)/(A - C)
         Y = A * X + B
         N = 1
   99    Next statement
```

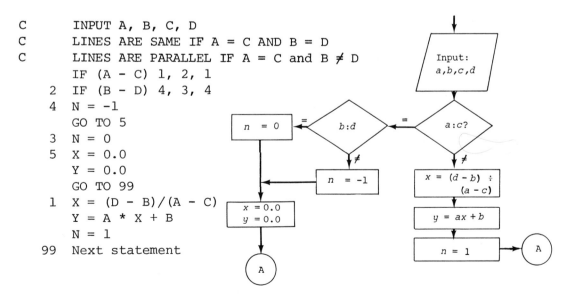

19.

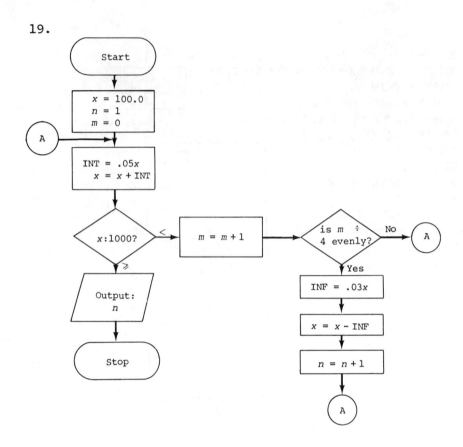

```
      X = 100, 0
      N = 1
      M = 0
  4   XINT = .05 * X
      X = X + XINT
      IF (X - 1000.) 1, 1, 2
  1   M = M + 1
      IF ((M/4) * 4 - M) 4, 3, 4
  3   XINF = .03 * X
      X = X = XINF
      N = N + 1
      GO TO 4
C     STATEMENT 2 IS TO OUTPUT N
      STOP
```

1. a. Should not have a comma after the READ statement.
    b. Valid   c. Improper field description
    d. Valid   e. Valid   for ZZZ

3.
```
     READ (5, 1) N
  1  FORMAT (I10)
     I = 1
     COUNT = 0.0
 50  READ (5, 2) GRADE
  2  FORMAT (F20.4)
     IF (GRADE - 90.0) 30, 20, 20
 20  COUNT = COUNT + 1.0
 30  I = I + 1
     IF (I - N) 50, 50, 60
 60  WRITE (6, 3) COUNT
  3  FORMAT (9H COUNT = , F10.0)
```

5.
```
     READ (5, 3) A, B
  3  FORMAT (2F10.0)
     IF (A - 1.0)  5, 10, 5
  5  IF (B - 1.0) 103, 102, 103
 10  IF (B - 1.0) 102, 101, 102
101  C = 1.0
     GO TO 100
102  C = 2.0
     GO TO 100
103  C = 3.0
100  WRITE (6,4) C
  4  FORMAT (5H C =, F10.0)
```

7.
```
      WRITE (6, 1000)
1000  FORMAT (6H TEST1, 7X, 6H TEST2, 6H TEST3, 7X, 11H FINAL AVG.)
      READ (5, 2000) T1, T2, T3
2000  FORMAT (F4.0, F4.0, F4.0)
      AVG = (.19 * T1 + .37 * T2 + .44 * T3)/3.0
      WRITE (6, 1001) T1, T2, T3, AVG
1001  FORMAT (2X, F4.0, 8X, F4.0, 8X, F4.0, 8X, F4.0)
      STOP
      END
```

```
1.          WRITE (6, 200)
      200   FORMAT (7X, 1HX, 9X, 1HY, 9X, 1HR, 9X, 9H POSITION)
       14   READ (5, 300) X, Y, R
      300   FORMAT (F10.2, F10.2, F10.2)
   C        ON LAST DATA CARD TYPE A ZERO FOR R
            IF (R) 1, 99, 1
        1   IF ((X ** 2 + Y ** 2) - R ** 2) 2, 3, 4
        2   M = 0
            GO TO 100
        3   M = 1
            GO TO 100
        4   M = 2
      100   WRITE (6, 400) X, Y, R, M
      400   FORMAT (F10.2, F10.2, F10.2, I3)
            GO TO 14
       99   STOP
            END


3. C        ASSUME PRINTER HAS 120 CHARACTERS PER LINE
            WRITE (2, 1)
        1   FORMAT (37X, 4H30 X)
        2   FORMAT (39X, 1H.)
            WRITE (2, 2)
            WRITE (2, 2)
            WRITE (2, 2)
            WRITE (2, 4)
        4   FORMAT (34X, 7HY   20 X)
            WRITE (2, 5)
        5   FORMAT (31X, 9H VALUES .)
            WRITE (2, 2)
            WRITE (2, 2)
            WRITE (2, 2)
            WRITE (2, 6)
        6   FORMAT (37X, 4H10   X)
            WRITE (2, 2)
            WRITE (2, 2)
            WRITE (2, 2)
            WRITE (2, 7)
        7   FORMAT (39X, 15H . . . . X . . ., 24H . X . . . . X . . . . X)
            WRITE (2, 8)
        8   FORMAT (39X, 1H0, 7X, 2H10, 8X, 2H20, 8X, 2H30, 8X, 2H40)
            STOP
            END
```

```
5.            WRITE (6, 200)
       200    FORMAT (33X, 40H RESULTS OF ENGLISH TEST (20 QUESTIONS).,
              12H A, /, 20X, 35H0 INDICATES AN ERROR FOR QUESTION Q,
              231H A 1 INDICATES A CORRECT ANSWER, ..., 5X,
              314HSTUDENT ID NO., 4X, 2HQ1, 3X, 2HQ2, 3X, 2HQ3, 3X, 2HQ4,
              43X, 2HQ5, 3X, 2HQ6, 3X, 2HQ7, 3X, 2HQ8, 3X, 2HQ9, 3X, 2HQ10,
              53HQ11, 3X, 3HQ12, 3X, 2HQ13, 3X, 3HQ14, 3X, 3HQ15, 3X, 2HQ16,
              63HQ17, 3X, 3HQ18, 3X, 3HQ19, 3X, 3HQ20, 4X, 5HSCORE,/)
       C  N1,N2,ETC. ARE THE CORRECT ANSWERS
              READ (5, 100) N1, N2, N3, N4, N5, N6, N7, N8, N9, N10,
              1N11, N12, N13, N14, N15, N16, N17, N18, N19, N20
       100    FORMAT (I1, I1, I1, I1, I1, I1, I1, I1, I1, I1, I1, I1,
              1I1, I1, I1, I1, I1, I1, I1, I1)
       101    FORMAT (I3, I1, I1, I1, I1, I1, I1, I1, I1, I1, I1, I1,
              1I1, I1, I1, I1, I1, I1, I1, I1, I1)
        30    READ (5, 101) ID, M1, M2, M3, M4, M5, M6, M7, M8, M9,
              1M10, M11, M12, M13, M14, M15, M16, M17, M18, M19, M20
       C  TEST TO SEE IF DONE.  LAST CARD HAS 000 FOR ID
              IF (ID - 0) 1, 2, 1
         1    ISCORE = 100
       C  NOW SET IQ1 = 1, IQ2 = 1, ..., IQ20 = 1

              IF (N1 - M1) 10, 11, 10
        10    ISCORE = ISCORE - 5
              IQ1 = 0
        11    IF (N2 - M2) 12, 13, 12
        12    ISCORE = ISCORE - 5
              IQ2 = 0
              etc.
                .
                .
                .
              WRITE (6, 201) ID, IQ1, IQ2, IQ3, IQ4, IQ5, IQ6, IQ7,
              1IQ8, IQ9, IQ10, IQ11, IQ12, IQ13, IQ14, IQ15, IQ16,
              2IQ17, IQ18, IQ19, LQ20, ISCORE
       201    FORMAT (19X, I3, 11X, I1, 4X, I1, 4X, I1, 4X, I1, 4X, I1,
              14X, I1, 4X, I1, 4X, I1, 5X, I1, 5X, I1, 5X, I1,
              25X, I1, 6X, I3)
              GO TO 30
         2    STOP
              END


7.            I = 0
        20    I = I + 1
              IF (I - 30) 1, 2, 3
         3    IF (I - 39) 2, 2, 1
         2    WRITE (6, 100)
       100    FORMAT (10X, 3H  X)
              GO TO 50
         1    IF ((I/3) * 3 - I) 4, 2, 4
         4    IF (I - 13) 5, 2, 5
```
377

7.—*continued*

```
   5   IF (I - 23) 6, 2, 6
   6   IF (I - 43) 7, 2, 7
   7   IF (I - 53) 8, 2, 8
   8   IF (I - 73) 9, 2, 9
   9   IF (I - 83) 10, 2, 10
  10   WRITE (6, 101) I
 101   FORMAT (10X, I3)
  50   IF (I - 100) 20, 25, 25
  25   STOP
       END
```

EXERCISES 5A

1. a. V   b. V   c. Y(5)   d. V   e. V
   f. V   g. V   h. V
   i. DIMENSION X(10), ZZ(1000), Y(4)   j. V   k. V
   l. V   m. V (GO TO 5 IS A VARIABLE NAME)   n. V
   o. B (IN, IOUT)   p. V

3.
```
       DIMENSION CBROOT(10)
       I = 1
       XI = I
       POWER = 1./3.
   1   CBROOT(I) = XI ** POWER
       WRITE (6, 10) I, CBROOT(I)
  10   FORMAT (10X, I2, 2X, F20.8)
       I = I + 1
       IF (I - 10) 1, 1, 2
   2   STOP
       END
```

5.
```
       DIMENSION SUM(5)
       READ (5, 100) N
 100   FORMAT (I3)
       I = 1
   1   SUM(I) = 0.0
       I = I + 1
       IF (I - 5) 1, 1, 2
   2   J = 1
   5   X = J
       I = 1
   3   SUM(I) = SUM(I) + X
       I = I + 1
       IF (I - 5) 3, 3, 4
   4   J = J + 1
       IF (J - N) 5, 5, 6
   6   Next statement
```

7.
```
       DIMENSION MATH(1000), IENGL(1000), IDIFF(1000)
       I = 0
       ICOUNT = 0
       READ (5, 100) N
 100   FORMAT (I4)
   5   I = I + 1
       READ (5, 101) MATH(I), IENGL(I)
 101   FORMAT (I3, I3)
       IDIFF(I) = MATH(I) - IENGL(I)
       IF (IDIFF(I)) 1, 2, 2
   1   IDIFF(I) = -IDIFF(I)
```

378

7.—*continued*

```
     2  IF (IDIFF(I) - 20) 3, 4, 4
     4  ICOUNT = ICOUNT + 1
        IDIFF(I) = 1
        IF (I - N) 5, 6, 6
     3  IDIFF(I) = 0
        IF (I - N) 5, 6, 6
     6  Next statement
```

9.
```
        DIMENSION A(10, 10), B(10, 10), C(10, 10)
        J = 1
     3  I = 1
     1  C(I, J) = A(I, J) + B(I, J)
        I = I + 1
        IF (I - 10) 1, 1, 2
     2  J = J + 1
        IF (J - 10) 3, 3, 4
     4  Next statement
```

11.
```
        DIMENSION SCORE (1000)
        A = 0
        I = 0
     1  I = I + 1
        IF (SCORE(I) - 90.) 3, 2, 2
     2  A = A + 1.0
     3  IF (I - 1000) 1, 4, 4
     4  Next statement
```

EXERCISES 5B

1. a.
```
        N = 0
        WTAVG = 0
        HTAVG = 0
        SCAVG = 0
C READ IN DATA.  ON LAST CARD IS 00000 FOR ID TO STOP
     3  N = N + 1
        READ (5, 100) ID, HT, WT, IAVAIL, SCORE, HAIR, SPORTS
     1  FORMAT (I5, F2.0, F3.0, I1, F2.0, F1.0, F1.0)
        IF (I5) 2, 99, 2
     2  WTAVG = WTAVG + WT
        HTAVG = HTAVG + HT
        SCAVG = SCORE + SCAVG
        GO TO 3
    99  XN = N - 1
        WTAVG = WTAVG/XN
        HTAVG = HTAVG/XN
        SCAVG = SCAVG/XN
```

379

1. a.—*continued*

```
        WRITE (6, 200) N, WTAVG, HTAVG, SCAVG
200     FORMAT (10X, I4, F3.0, iX, F3.0, 1X, F3.0)
        Next statement
```

b.
```
        N = 0
        NUMB = 0
10      READ (5, 100) ID, HT, WT, IAVAIL, SCORE, HAIR, SPORTS
100     FORMAT (I5, F2.0, F3.0, I1, F2.0, F1.0, F1.0)
        IF (ID) 1, 99, 1
1       IF (HT - 69.0) 2, 3, 3
2       IF (WT - 110.) 3, 3, 4
4       IF (WT - 160.) 5, 3, 3
5       IF (SCORE - 70.) 3, 3, 6
6       IF (SPORTS - 1.0) 3, 7, 3
7       NUMB = NUMB + 1
3       N = N + 1
        GO TO 10
99      WRITE (6, 200) N, NUMB
200     FORMAT (10X, 4HN = , I2, 5X, 7HNUMB = , I2)
```

3.
```
50      FORMAT (F10.2, F10.2, F10.2)
        READ (5, 50) X, Y, Z
        IF (X - 9999.) 1, 70, 70
1       P = .01 * X * X + .001 * Y ** 3 + .05 * Z * Z
        IF (P - 100.) 2, 2, 3
3       P = 100
2       WRITE (6, 60) X, Y, Z, P
60      FORMAT (10X, 4HX = , F10.2, 5X, 4HY = , F10.2, 5X,
        14HZ = , F10.2, 5X, 4HP = , F10.2)
70      STOP
        END
```

5.

```
C   THE FOLLOWING IS AN INCOMPLETE SOLUTION
            DIMENSION ITEAM(6), W(100), XL(100), PCT(6), GB(6)
            I = 1
2       READ (1, 1) ITEAM(I), W(I), XL(I)
1       FORMAT (I1, F3.0, F3.0)
            I = I + 1
            IF (I - 6) 2, 2, 3
3       I = 1
4       PCT(I) = W(I)/(W(I) + XL(I))
            I = I + 1
            IF (I - 6) 4, 4, 5
C NOW SORT TEAMS ACCORDING TO PCT.
5       I = 1
6       J = I + 1
```

```
              12   IF (PCT(I) - PCT(I + 1)) 10, 10, 11
              10   TEMP = PCT(I)
                   PCT(I) = PCT(J)
                   PCT(J) = TEMP
              11   J = J + 1
                   IF (J - 6) 12, 12, 13
              13   I = I + 1
                   IF (I - (N - 1)) 6, 6, 14
              14   I = 1
C NOW DO SAME FOR ITEAM, W AND XL
C ASSUME THIS IS DONE, DETERMINE GAMES BEHIND
                   I = 1
                   J = 2
              30   GB(I) = ((W(I) - XL(I)) - (W(J) - XL(J)))/2.0
                   J = J + 1
                   IF (J - 6) 30, 30, 31
              31   WRITE (6, 200)
             200   FORMAT (10X, 4NTEAM, 5X, 4NWINS, 4X, 6HLOSSES,
                   14X, 4NPCT., 4X, 13H GAMES BEHIND, //)
                   WRITE (6, 201) TEAM(1), W(1), XL(1), PCT(1)
             201   FORMAT (12X, I1, 7X, F3.0, 6X, F3.0, 4X, F0.3,
                   18X, F6.1)
                   I = 2
              50   WRITE (6, 201) TEAM(I), W(I), LX(I), PCT(I), BG(I)
                   IF (I - 6) 50, 50, 51
              51   STOP
                   END
```

EXERCISES 6A

1. a. V   b. DO 3 K6 = IS, J, 2   c. V   d. V
   e. DIMENSION X(10), Y(3), Z(100)   f. V
   g. V (not a DO statement)   h. V
   i. DO 3 MA = 1, N4A2, 2   j. DO 17 IFEW = 1, N
   k. V (statement executes only one time)
   l. DO 10 I × 2 = N, M
   m. V (statement executes only one time)
   n. V

3. 9

5.
```
C ASSUME ALL STATEMENTS FROM EXERCISE 4 ARE DONE
        XN = N
        ZX = 0.
        ZY = 0.
        DO 209 I = 1, N
        ZX = (X(I) - XBAR) ** 2 + ZX
    209 ZY = (Y(I) - YBAR) ** 2 + ZY
```

5.—*continued*

```
            VARX = ZX/XN
            VARY = ZY/XN
            SIGX = (VARX) ** .5
            SIGY = (VARY) ** .5
            Next statement
```

7.

```
            IAMT = 0
      C ON LAST DATA CARD ID IS 0
            DO 2 I = 1, 1000
            READ (5, 100) ID, ISEX, IHT, IWT, ICLASS, IATH
            IF(ID) 1, 1, 10
      100   FORMAT (I5, I1, I2, I3, I1, I1)
       10   IF (ISEX - 1) 2, 3, 2
        3   IF (IHT - 60) 2, 2, 4
        4   IF (IWT - 180) 2, 2, 5
        5   IF (ICLASS - 1) 6, 2, 6
        6   IF (IATH - 7) 2, 7, 7
        7   IAMT = IAMT + 1
            WRITE (6, 500) ID
      500   FORMAT (10X, I5)
        2   CONTINUE
        1   WRITE (6, 501) IAMT
      501   FORMAT (//, 10X, 16HAMT OF ATHLETES , I5)
            STOP
            END
```

9.

```
      C ASSUME CHECKS ARE IN PROPER ORDER, I.E.
      C THEY HAVE BEEN SORTED OUT FOR EACH PERSON
      C READ IN DATA
            READ (5, 100) NUMDEP, NUMCKH, BAL
      100   FORMAT (I3, I3, F8.2)
            DO 110 I = 1, NUMDEP
            IF (IDEP - 99999) 10, 11, 10
       10   READ (5, 101) NDEP, IDEP, DEP
      101   FORMAT (I3, I5, F8.2)
            IF (I - 1) 1, 1, 2
        1   WRITE (6, 102) IDEP
      102   FORMAT (1H1, 10X, 22H CHECKING ACCOUNT FOR , I5)
        2   BAL = BAL + DEP
      110   WRITE (6, 103) NDEP, DEP, BAL
      103   FORMAT (5X, 13H DEPOSIT NO. , I3, 6H AMT. ,
            19H BALANCE = , F8.2)
            DO 20 I = 1, NUMCHK
            READ (5, 104) IDEP, NCHK, AMT
```

9.—*continued*

```
104   FORMAT (I5, I4, F8.2)
      BAL = BAL - AMT
 20   WRITE (6, 105) NCHK, AMT, BAL
105   FORMAT (5X, 10HCHECK NO. , I4, 5H AMT., F8.2,
      19HBALANCE = , F8.2)
      GO TO 10
 11   STOP
      END
```

EXERCISES 6B

```
1.        READ (95, 200) N
     200  FORMAT (I3)
          SUM1 = 0
          SUM2 = 0
          SUM3 = 0
          DO 100 I = 1, N
          X = I
          SUM1 = SUM1 + X
          SUM2 = SUM2 + X * X
     100  SUM3 = SUM3 + X ** 2
          WRITE (6, 300) SUM1, SUM2, SUM3
     300  FORMAT (10X, 6HSUM1 =, F10.2, 6HSUM2 =, F10.2,
          16HSUM3 =, F10.2)
          STOP
          END
```

3.   (a)   (b)

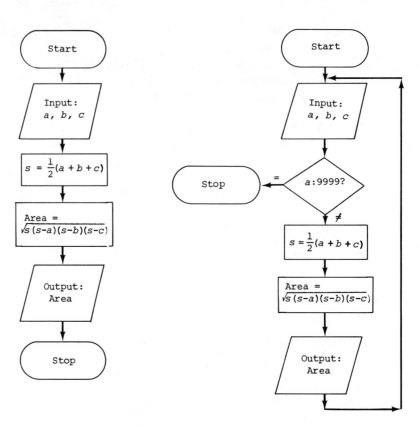

5.   READ (5, 50) M
        50 FORMAT (I2)
            A = 364.0
            P = 1.0
            DO 60 I = 2, M
        60 P = P * A/365.0
            P = 1.0 - P
            WRITE (6, 200) M, P
       200 FORMAT (10X, 5H FOR , I2, 15H PROBABILITY IS, F6.4)
            STOP
            END

384

```
7.  C SET UP ARRAY TO STORE DATA FOR SENIORS
            DIMENSION  IDEN(1000), ICOLL(1000), GGPA(1000)
    C ASSUME NO MORE THAN 1000 STUDENTS TOTAL
    C AFTER LAST DATA CARD A ZERO IS PUNCHED FOR IDEN
            ICOUNT = 0
        3   READ (5, 100) IDEN, COLL, GPA, CLASS
      100   FORMAT (I5, F1.0, F5.2, F1.0)
            IF (IDEN) 1, 2, 1
        1   IF (CLASS - 4) 3, 4, 4
        4   ICOUNT = ICOUNT + 1
            IIDEN(ICOUNT) = IDEN
            ICOLL(ICOUNT) = COLL
            GGPA(ICOUNT) = GPA
            GO TO 3
        2   INDEX = ICOUNT - 1
            DO 10 I = 1, INDEX
            JJ = I + 1
            DO 11 J = JJ, ICOUNT
            IF(GGPA(I) - GGPA(J)) 11, 11, 13
       13   T = GGPACI
            GGPA(I) = GGPA(J)
            GGPA(J) = T
    C SO THE SAME FOR ICOLL AND IIDEN
       11   CONTINUE
       10   CONTINUE
            WRITE (6, 150)
      150   FORMAT (1H1, ////, 10X, 7HSTUDENT, 10X, 7HCOLLEGE, 10X,
           13HGPA, //)
            DO 20 I = 1, INDEX
       20   WRITE (6, 200) IIDEN(I), ICOLL(I), GGPA(I)
      200   FORMAT (12X, I5, 14X, I1, 10X, F5.2)
            STOP
            END
```

EXERCISES 7A

```
1.  a. V      b. V      c.  V      d. V      e.  V
    f. V      g.  V
    h.  DIMENSION X(4)
        N = 4
        READ (1, 11) (X(I), I = 1, 2)
     11 FORMAT (10F4.2)

    i.  DIMENSION X(20), Y(20)
      7 FORMAT (F8.2)
        DO 12 J = 1, 20, 2
     12 READ (1, 7) X(J)
        DO 5 J = 1, 20, 2
      5 Y(J) = X(J) * X(J)
```

385

```
3.        DIMENSION X(1000)
          READ (1, 1) N
    1     FORMAT (I10)
          READ (1, 2) (X(I), I = 1, N)
    2     FORMAT (F10.2)
          INDEX = N - 1
          DO 3 I = 1, INDEX
          JJ = I + 1
          DO 4 J = JJ, N
          IF (X(I) - X(J)) 4, 4, 5
    5     TEMP = X(I)
          X(I) = X(J)
          X(J) = TEMP
    4     CONTINUE
    3     CONTINUE
          Next statement


5.  a.        WRITE (2, 100) X, Y
        100   FORMAT (1H1, ///////////, 2F20.8)


    b.        WRITE (2, 101) X, Y
        101   FORMAT (//////, 20X, 9HX - VALUE, 10X, 9HY - VALUE,
              1//, 10X, 2F20.4)


    c.        WRITE (2, 100) (X(I), Y(I), I = 1, 20)
        100   FORMAT (1H1, 54X, 9HX - ARRAY, 10X, 9HY - ARRAY, /,
              1(44X, 2F20.4))


    d.        READ (5, 99) (Z(I), I = 1, 800)
         99   FORMAT (8F10.3)


    e.        N = 0
         10   N = N + 1
              READ (5, 20) Z(N)
         20   FORMAT (E20.4)
              IF (Z(N) - .999E + 3) 10, 1, 10
          1   N = N - 1


    f.        WRITE (6, 1)
          1   FORMAT (1H1, ///, 20X, 1HI, 30X, 9HX - VALUE, /)
              DO 1000 INDEX = 1, N
       1000   WRITE (6, 2) INDEX, X(INDEX)
          2   FORMAT (19X, I3, 3X, F30.4)


7.  C ASSUME NO MORE THAN 1000 DATA CARDS
              DO 600 I = 1, 1000
              READ (3, 3) N, A1, D
          3   FORMAT (I5, 2F10.4)
              IF (N) 1001, 1001, 1
          1   XN = N
```

```
          SN = XN/2. * (2. * A1 + (XN - 1.) * D)
  600  WRITE (4, 4) N, A1, D, SN
    4  FORMAT (10X, I5, 3F10.4)
 1001  STOP
       END
```

EXERCISES 7B

1.
```
       X = 4.1
       XL = X + 6. * X/(X * X - 16.) ** .5
    3  X = X + .1
       XNEWXL = X + 6. * X/(X * X - 16.) ** .5
       IF (XNEWXL - XL) 2, 2, 1
    1  XL = XNEWXL
    2  IF(X - 6.) 3, 3, 4
    4  WRITE (6, 100)
  100  FORMAT (1H1, ////, 10X, 21H LADDER PROBLEM FIND ,
       135HLONGEST LENGTH TO FIT AROUND CORNER,
       2//, 16X, 1HX, /, 16X, 1HX, 12X, 10(2H. ), /,
       316X, 1Hx, 12X, 1H., /, 16X, 1HX, 12X, 1H., 6X, 6H6 FEET,
       4/, 16X, 1HX, 12X, 1H., 3X, 7(2H. ), /, 16X, 1HX, 12X,
       51H., 1X, 1H4, 1X, 1H., /, 16X, 1HX, 12X, 5H. FT ., /,
       616X, 1HX, 12X, 5H.  ., /, 16X, 1HX, 12X, 5H.  ., /,
       716X, 1HX, 12X, 5H.  ., /, 10X, 13HLADDER LENGTH,
       88X, 13HCORNER SKETCH)
       WRITE (6, 101) XL
  101  FORMAT (//, 15X, 18H MAXIMUM LENGTH IS, F6.2)
```

3.
```
       READ (5, 200) A, B
  200  FORMAT (2F10.4)
       AA = A + .1
       XL = AA + B * AA/(AA * AA - A * A) ** .5
       AA = AA + .1
       XLNEW = AA + B * AA/(AA * AA - A * A) ** .5
```
Rest of statements similar to those in Exercise 1, above.

5.
```
       DIMENSION IX(20)
       N1 = 0
       N2 = 0
       N3 = 0
       N4 = 0
       N5 = 0
       INDEX = 0
   10  READ (1, 1000) IENGL, MATH
 1000  FORMAT (20X, 2I3)
       INDEX = INDEX + 1
```

5.—*continued*

```
       IF (MATH) 20, 20, 1
   1   IF (MATH - 90) 30, 31, 31
  31   N1 = N1 + 1
       GO TO 10
  30   IF(MATH - 80) 32, 33, 33
  33   N2 = N2 + 1
       GO TO 10
  32   IF (MATH - 70) 34, 35, 35
  35   N3 = N3 + 1
       GO TO 10
  34   IF (MATH - 60) 36, 37, 37
  37   N4 = N4 + 1
       GO TO 10
  36   N5 = N5 + 1
       GO TO 10
  20   INDEX = INDEX - 1
       WRITE (2, 1001) INDEX
1001   FORMAT (1H1, //, 30X, 14HBAR GRAPH FOR , I4, 1X,
       18HSTUDENTS, ///, 25X, 22H GRADES IN MATHEMATICS, //)
       WRITE (2, 1002)
1002   FORMAT (15X, 15(2H. ))
       DO 21 I = 1, INDEX
  21   IX(I) = 1
       IF (NS) 22, 22, 23
  23   WRITE (2, 999) (IX(I), I = 1, N1)
 999   FORMAT (15X, 1H., 20(1X, I1))
       WRITE (2, 999) (IX(I), I = 1, N1)
       WRITE (2, 998)
 998   FORMAT (9X, 5H50-60, 1X, 1H., 20(1X, I1))
       WRITE (2, 999) (IX(I), I = 1, N1)
       GO TO 24
  22   WRITE (2, 999) (I = 1, 4)
 997   FORMAT (15X, 1H.)
  24   (for other intervals do similar statements)
       .
       .
       .
       STOP
       END
```

EXERCISES 8A

1. a.   X = Z - F(1.0, Y(1), 2.0)   b.   ZERO(A,C,S,W) = A - C * D/4.0
    c.   V   d. V   e.   V   f. V
    g.   N = 6 must come after the function statement   h. V
    i.   101 FORMAT (1H1, 20X, 5(2F20.4))

```
3.          FUNCTION AVG(X, N)
            DIMENSION X(1)
   C        NOTE.  THE ABOVE IS EQUIVALENT TO X(N)
            XN = N
            SUM = 0.0
            DO 10 I = 1, N
       10   SUM = SUM + X(I)
            AVG = SUM/XN
            RETURN
            END


5.          SUBROUTINE NUMB(I)
   C        ASSUME 132 SPACES AVAILABLE ON PRINTER
            IF (I - 1) 1, 2, 1
        2   WRITE (6, 100)
      100   FORMAT (1H1, 27(I), 52X, 14(2H* ),/, 52X, 1HX,
            126X, 1H*, /, 8(52X), 1HX, 11X, 2H**, 13X, 1H*, /),
            252X, 1HX, 26X, 1H*, /, 52X, 14(2H* ))
            RETURN
        1   Test for 2 and then 3 and write similar statements
```

EXERCISES 8B

```
1.          DIMENSION F(41)
            Fl(X) = X * X + 3. * X - 2.
            F2(X) = X ** 4 - X
            X = -.5
            DO 10 I = 1, 21
            X = X + .5
       10   F(I) = Fl(X) + F2(X)
                 .
                 .
                 .
```

```
3.    SUBROUTINE STD(A, N)          5.    FUNCTION ISUM(N)
      DIMENSION A(N)                      IF (N) 1, 1, 2
      SUM = 0.0                      1    ISUM = 1
      SUMSQ = 0.0                         RETURN
      DO 1 I = 1, N                  2    ISUB1 = 1
      SUM = SUM + A(I)                    K = 1
   1  SUMSQ = SUMSQ + A(I) ** 2      5    ISUB1 = K * ISUB1 + (-1) ** K
      AN = N                              K = K + 1
      AVG = SUM/AN                        IF (K - N) 5, 5, 6
      STDSQ = SQRT(STDSQ)           6    ISUB = ISUB1
      RETURN                              RETURN
      END                                 END
```

```
7.  C ASSUME CALLING STATEMENT IS CALL ONE (N, X)
            SUBROUTINE ONE (M, Y)
            COMMON A, B, C, D
            DIMENSION A(M, M), B(M, M), C(M, M), D(M, M)
            DO 1000 I = 1, M
            DO 1000 J = 1, M
      1000  B(M, M) = Y * A(M, M)
            RETURN
            END


    C ASSUME CALLING STATEMENT IS CALL TWO (N)
            SUBROUTINE TWO (M, Y)
            COMMON A, B, C, D
            DIMENSION A(M, M), B(M, M), C(M, M), D(M, M)
            DO 2000 I = 1, M
            DO 2000 J = 1, M
      2000  C(I, J) = A(J, I)
            RETURN
            END


    C ASSUME CALLING STATEMENT IS CALL THREE (N)
            SUBROUTINE THREE (M)
            COMMON A, B, C, D
            DIMENSION A(M, M), B(M, M), C(M, M), D(M, M)
            DO 3000 I = 1, M
            DO 3000 J = 1, M
            D(I, J) = 0.0
            DO 4000 K = 1, M
      4000  D(I, J) = D(I, J) + A(I, K) * A(K, J)
      3000  CONTINUE
            RETURN
            END
```

EXERCISES 9

1.	.TRUE.	3.	.FALSE.	5.	.FALSE.
7.	.FALSE.	9.	.FALSE.	11.	.TRUE.
13.	.FALSE.	15.	.TRUE.		

17.

P	Q	P .OR Q	.NOT. (P .OR. Q)
T	T	T	F
T	F	T	F
F	T	T	F
F	F	F	T

19.

P	Q	R	Q .AND. R	P .OR. Q .AND. R
T	T	T	T	T
T	T	F	F	T
T	F	T	F	T
T	F	F	F	T
F	T	T	T	T
F	T	F	F	F
F	F	T	F	F
F	F	F	F	F

21. For Q .FALSE., P either .FALSE. or .TRUE.
    For Q .TRUE., P .TRUE.
23. For P and Q .TRUE.
25. P .TRUE.
27. .TRUE   29. .TRUE.   31. .FALSE.
33. A = B = C (One of many solutions)
35. A = 3, B = 2, C = 1 (One of many solutions)
37. IF (A .NE. 1.0 .OR. B .NE. 2.5) GO TO 10
    GO TO 20
39. IF (A .NE. B .OR. B .LE. 10.0) GO TO 50
    GO TO 60
41. IF (A .GT. B .AND. C .GE. B .OR. A .LE. B .AND. B .LE. C)
    1GO TO 20

43.

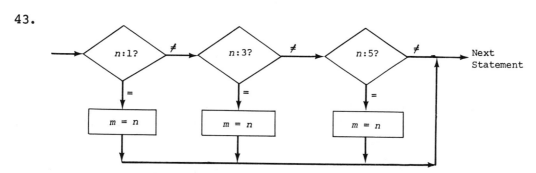

45.

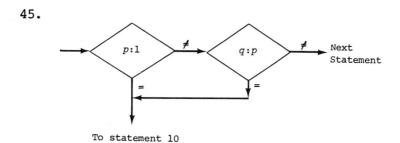

To statement 10

391

```
47.        LOGICAL A, B, C, D
           DMIN = 100000.
           NPBEST = 0
           MBEST = 0
           DO 500 NP = 1, 160
           DO 500 M = 1, 80
           A = NP + 2 * M .LE. 160
           IF (.NOT. A) GO TO 500
           B = NP + M .GE. 70
           IF (.NOT. B) GO TO 500
           C = M .GT. NP
           IF (.NOT. C) GO TO 500
           D = NP .GE. 20
           IF (.NOT. D) GO TO 500
           COST = 2.* FLOAT(NP) + 1.15 * FLOAT(M)
           IF (COST .GE. CMIN) GO TO 500
           CMIN = COST
           NPBEST = NP
           MBEST = M
500        CONTINUE
           WRITE (6, 400) CMIN, NPBEST, MBEST
400        FORMAT (1H1, 10(/), 20X, 12HMINIMUM COST, F10.2, 3X,
          113HNO. POTATOES , I4, 14HAMT. MACARONI , I4)
           STOP
           END
```

EXERCISES 10

```
1.         DIMENSION NAME(25), STREET(25), TWNST(25)
    1      READ (5, 100) (NAME(I), STREET(I), TWNST(I), I = 1, 25), IZIP
  100      FORMAT (25A1, 25A1, 25A1, I5)
           IF (IZIP .EQ. 99999) STOP
           IF (IZIP .LT. 60000 .OR. IZIP .GE. 70000) GO TO 1
           WRITE (6, 101) (NAME(I), STREET(I), TWNST(I), I = 1, 25), IZIP
  101      FORMAT (//, 10X, 25A1, /, 10X, 25A1, /, 10X, 25A1, 2X, I5)
           GO TO 1
           END


3.         DIMENSION STDNAM(25), ANSW(25), CODE(25)
    2      READ (5, 10) (CODE(I), I = 1, 25)
   10      FORMAT (25I1)
           READ (5, 20) (STDNAM(I), ANSW(I), I = 1, 25)
   20      FORMAT (25A1, 25I1)
C          TEST TO SEE IF DONE
           IF (ANSW(1) .GE. 3) STOP
           IRIGHT = 0
           IWRONG = 0
           DO 1 I = 1, 25
           IF (ANSW(I) .EQ. CODE(I)) IRIGHT = IRIGHT + 1
```

3.—*continued*

```
          IF (ANSW(I) .EQ. CODE(I)) GO TO 1
          IF (ANSW(I) .EQ. 0) GO TO 1
          IWRONG = IWRONG + 1
      1   CONTINUE
          ISCORE = IRIGHT * 4 - IWRONG * 5
          IF (ISCORE .LT. 0) ISCORE = 0
          WRITE (6, 30) (STDNAM(I), I = 1, 25), ISCORE
     30   FORMAT (//, 10X, 25A1, 5X, 8HGRADE = , I3)
          GO TO 2
          END
```

5.

```
          DIMENSION LETTER(3)
    300   READ (5, 200) (LETTER(I), I = 1, 3), NUMB, ITEST
    200   FORMAT (3A1, I3, 73X, I1)
          IF (ITEST .EQ. 9) STOP
          IF (ITEST .EQ. 0) GO TO 300
          WRITE (6, 400) (LETTER(I), I = 1, 3), NUMB
    400   FORMAT (//, 10X, 3A1, I3)
          END
```

7. a.

```
          C ASSUME WORD SIZE SIX CHARACTERS
          C ASSUME NO ZERO DIGITS
                DIMENSION XNUMB(9)
                DATA BLANK/6H      /
                DATA XNUMB/6HONE   /, 6HTWO   /, 6HTHREE   /,
               16HFOUR   /, 6HFIVE   /, 6HSIX   /, 6HSEVEN   /,
               26HEIGHT  /, 6HNINE   /
                READ (1, 1) N1, N2, N3
      1   FORMAT (3I1)
                HUNDRD = XNUMB(N1)
                IF (N2 .EQ. 0 .AND. N3 .EQ. 0) GO TO 100
                IF (N2 .EQ. 0 .AND. N3 .NE. 0) TENS = BLANK
                IF (N2 .EQ. 0 .AND. N3 .NE. 0) DIGIT = XNUMB(N3)
                IF (N2 .EQ. 0 .AND. N3 .NE. 0) GO TO 101
                IF (N2 .EQ. 1 .AND. N3 .EQ. 0) TENS = 3HTEN
                IF (N2 .EQ. 1 .AND. N3 .EQ. 1) TENS = 6HELEVEN
                IF (N2 .EQ. 1 .AND. N3 .EQ. 2) TENS = 6HTWELVE
                IF (N2 .EQ. 1 .AND. N3 .EQ. 3) TENS = 6HTHIRTN
                   .
                   .
                   .
                Etc. for up to N3 .EQ. 9
                   .
                   .
                   .
                IF (N2 .EQ. 1) DIGIT = BLANK
                IF (N2 .EQ. 1) GO TO 102
                IF (N2 .EQ. 2) TENS = 6HTWENTY
                IF (N2 .EQ. 3) TENS = 6HTHIRTY
                   .
                   .
                   .
```

393

7. a.—*continued*

```
        Etc. for up to N2 .EQ. 9
        .
        .
        .
        DIGIT = XNUMB(N3)
101  WRITE (2, 2) HUNDRD, TENS, DIGIT
  2  FORMAT (1H1, 20(/), 10X, A6, 12HHUNDRED AND ,
     1A6, 2X, A6)
     STOP
100  WRITE (2, 3) HUNDRD
  3  FORMAT (1H1, 20(/), 10X, A6, 7HHUNDRED)
     STOP
     END
```

b.
```
   C PARTIAL SOLUTION
   C ASSUME ALL WAGES ARE OF FORM ABC.DE
         READ (1, 1) (EMPL(I), I = 1, 29), WAGE
      1  FORMAT (29A1, 1X, F7.2)
         IF (WAGE .EQ. 0) STOP
   C ABOVE STOPS PROGRAM
         NX = INT(WAGE)
         N1 = NX/100
         N2 = (INT(WAGE) = N1 * 100)/10
         N3 = ((INT(WAGE) - N1 * 100) - N2 * 10)
         CENTS = (WAGE - FLOAT(NX)) * 100.
         .
         .
         .
         (Now do same as in Part a.)
```

EXERCISES 11

1. a. Invalid   b. Valid   c. Invalid   d. Valid
   e. Invalid   f. Invalid   g. Valid   h. Invalid
   i. Invalid   j. Valid

3.
```
C ONE WAY
      DOUBLE PRECISION FUNCTION ROOT(Z)
      DOUBLE PRECISION Z
      ROOT = Z ** .5
      RETURN
      END

C ALTERNATE WAY.  THIS IS NEWTON'S METHOD
      DOUBLE PRECISION FUNCTION ROOT(Z)
      DOUBLE PRECISION EPS, ROOT1
      EPS = 1.0D - 12
      ROOT = 1.0D0
```

3.—*continued*

```
   20   ROOT1 = .5 * (ROOT + Z/ROOT)
        IF (DABS(ROOT1 - ROOT)/ROOT .LE. EPS) GO TO 10
        ROOT = ROOT1
        GO TO 20
   10   ROOT = ROOT1
        RETURN
        END
```

5. a. (4.0, 6.0)   b. (1.0, −1.0)   c. (−4.0, 0)
    d. (−1.0, 0.0)   e. (0.0, −1.0)

7.
```
        SUBROUTINE POLY(A, Z, N)
        COMPLEX A, Z, POLY
        DIMENSION A(N)
        KK = N - 1
        POLY = A(N)
        IF (KK .EQ. 0) RETURN
        POLY = POLY * Z + A(KK)
        KK = KK - 1
        IF (KK .GE. 1) GO TO 20
        RETURN
        END
```

9.
```
   COMPLEX FUNCTION POLE(Z)
   COMPLEX Z
   X = REAL(Z)
   Y = AIMAG(Z)
   R = SQRT(X ** 2 + Y ** 2)
   XZERO = 3.14159/2.0
   IF (X .EQ. 0) POLE(Z) = (R, XZERO)
   IF (X .EQ. 0) RETURN
   THETA = ATAN2(Y, X)
   POLE(Z) = (R, THETA)
   RETURN
   END
```

INDEX

Euclidean Algorithm 75 (GCD)